GETTING
MOTIVATED
BY
ERNEST
DICHTER

**The Secret Behind
Individual Motivations
by the Man Who Was
Not Afraid to Ask "Why?"**

GETTING
MOTIVATED
BY
ERNEST
DICHTER

The Secret Behind
Individual Motivations
by the Man Who Was
Not Afraid to Ask "Why?"

ERNEST DICHTER

PERGAMON PRESS
New York/Oxford/Toronto/Sydney/Frankfurt/Paris

5-2-91

Pergamon Press Offices:

U.S.A. Pergamon Press Inc., Maxwell House, Fairview Park,
Elmsford, New York 10523, U.S.A.

U.K. Pergamon Press Ltd., Headington Hill Hall,
Oxford OX3, OBW, England

CANADA Pergamon of Canada, Ltd., 150 Consumers Road,
Willowdale, Ontario M2J, 1P9, Canada

AUSTRALIA Pergamon Press (Aust) Pty. Ltd., P O Box 544,
Potts Point, NSW 2011, Australia

FRANCE Pergamon Press SARL, 24 rue des Ecoles,
75240 Paris, Cedex 05, France

FEDERAL REPUBLIC Pergamon Press GmbH, 6242 Kronberg/Taunus,
OF GERMANY Pferdstrasse 1, West Germany

Library of Congress Cataloging in Publication Data

Dichter, Ernest, 1907-
   Getting Motivated.

   1. Motivation research (Marketing) I. Title.
HF5415.3.D49 1979   658.8'34   78-21168
ISBN 0-08-023687-1

Printed in the United States of America

Dedicated to my wife, Hedy,
whose biography this is as much as it is mine.

Contents

Introduction

Maybe one should write an autobiography every ten years as a sort of life accounting. Many of the developments in our lives have their origins in very early experiences and result in completely unexpected developments. Which ones triggered or served as a brake for events twenty or thirty years later?

Charlotte Buhler, my psychology teacher, studied many lives and found that a pattern could be detected and could even result in a built-in predestination of the length of one's life. Using her distinctions of childhood, adolescence, maturity (the longest period), decline, and senility, I would like to think that I am still maturing and even growing, and may not have reached full and enduring maturity. I have completed my four-score-and-ten, but physical age seems to be less important than life insurance statistics would indicate. I have always felt that getting there is most, if not all, the fun. I am still getting there and don't know whether I shall ever arrive or will like it when I get there.

In writing my story I have tried to arrange my recollections in such a way that they hang together as psychological chain reactions rather than in a systematic and chronological fashion. I was given lots of advice in this venture: "Be sure to have sex in your recitals." "Throw big names around." "Most people," I was told, "are interested in all the famous people who at one point or another influenced you, or were influenced by you." "Be frank," was further advice; and the best one was probably "Don't take yourself too seriously." I have listened carefully and decided to write my own book rather than one which would most please potential reviewers.

A man's life can serve as a lesson in living. A life is not unlike a laboratory experiment. The curious, amusing, ridiculous, shattering, and nerve-tickling stimuli are provided by four dimensional factors—it may be your position within your family; whether you were born rich, poor, or in-between; what historical events affected your life; and probably what kinds of genes you were born with. I hope that I have not always been only a passive guinea pig of all these influences in my living laboratory, comparable to a caged animal. Undoubtedly, I learned to push certain triggers to avoid pain and to secure pleasure, just as the monkeys learn, but I hope that I have also acted on a higher level, at least part of the time, and that I have influenced others. I recently received the nicest reward from a former assistant: "I should have paid you instead of the other way around. I learned a lot from you. Now as a professor of sociology, I now pass it on to my students."

As I recount remorsefully and, occasionally with some glee, the many mistakes I made, I consider them to be cash dividends. I hope I shall avoid the same mistakes, but I am sure I shall make some new ones. Perhaps these examples will serve as insights and "aha" experiences for others.

An autobiography is like an autopsy except that the corpse is still breathing. I always hesitate to talk about myself in the past tense. It is part of my life philosophy to consider myself and my life immortal. My physician told me that his problems would be sharply reduced if I and others of his patients believed in our own mortality. Maybe so. For me, life is a cruise ship, a mail boat, or a tramp steamer which stops at varying ports, each offering new excitement. Its final destination? Who wants to know.

All I have to do is open a newspaper, listen to the radio, or have other people tell me their stories to find new tasks for the continuation of what I have been doing for the major part of my life: trying to understand human motivations. Hardly a day or week goes by that I am not asked, professionally or at least as a supposed expert, why people behave the way they do, why older women like younger men, why films like "Star Wars" and other galactic westerns attract so many people. Within the course of a week, I can be asked how to motivate young people to become Boy Scouts and how to convince women that it isn't enough to merely wash their hair with shampoo—in order to really get rid of their immoral dirt, their sins, they have to use hair conditioners that penetrate the scalp more deeply than any kind of absolution. Many of these assignments can be considered unimportant and frivolous. But there are many others which are dignified enough to become subjects for doctoral theses.

We teach history classes in most schools but, up till now, very little has been done to help children to concern themselves with the future. This is a topic I worked on not too long ago, resulting in a book on futurology. *Why Is The United Nations Not More Effective?* is another assignment of which I can be proud. How does one get more voters to participate in elections in those few democracies which still exist, and not leave the selection of their leaders to a minority? When and how shall we start influencing and motivating children, perhaps through the help of toys, to abandon or never to learn their prejudices? We are using much too little time in our schools to help children develop insight into their own behavior and to find their way among the crossroads of life which are marked with completely entangled road signs. A standard expression used frequently by teenagers is that they are trying to "find themselves." Maybe this is more than a fad and has a deeper meaning.

Perhaps my friend was being more profound than he intended when he observed me in my search for the meaning of life and asked, "how do you know there is a meaning?" Maybe this is where I derived my philosophy that it is the striving, the searching, which is the goal of life. The solution to the riddle is that there is no solution.

How did I get started in motivational research, a nice guy like myself? Maybe because in Vienna, where I grew up, there were relatively few people with red hair. I was an outcast, and on top of that I was not a particularly good athlete. I played soccer; I went to gym classes; but I was also studious. We often hear that the secret of success is to like oneself. Well, I never did. I was always dissatisfied with myself. I wish I hadn't been forced to wear second-hand clothes until the age of sixteen or eighteen. I wish I had not had red hair. I wish I had been a Walter Mitty whose dreams had been successfully translated into reality. I can give you a long wish list, but I doubt very much that having self confidence is any more the key to later success than starting to have doubts in yourself. Because of these doubts I became critical of myself, and I watched continuously to see whether people around me would discover this insecurity. Self observation leads inevitably to an increased skill in observing other people.

1 A Dish of Lentils

Tracing back my life, I would have been glad to sell my rights as the oldest and first-born for an even less tasty dish than lentils. My brother Fritz is two-and-a-half-years younger than I; Oscar lagged ten years behind. In many ways, he was almost my son. When Tom, our son, was born, I used to frequently make the mistake of calling him Oscar. It must have meant something. I never had a father whom I could look up to, so I had to become one myself.

This had a very clear influence on my professional activity. As a consultant of many large companies and as a motivational researcher, I was expected to have ready answers and solutions to problems. I was not inclined to tell my clients that I too would like to find someone, sometime, who would help me solve *my* problems. In other words, and this was confirmed through recent studies, the situation within one's own family, whether one is the first-born or not, apparently has considerable influence on one's profession and total attitude towards life.

Being the first-born entitled me to the special love and concern of my mother. She expected much more from me than from the little ones. I was husband, lover and son at the same time. When I left for Paris, the first time as a student in protest against my father's urging to make a living, she wrote me long letters which had the ring of bemoaning a lost loved one. I had to reassure her that I was fully intent upon coming back. When I was less than shining in my attempt to make it on my own, she kept sending me money secretly until her feeble attempts to help me could be sustained no longer.

When my father became ill and soon died, I assumed the duties of the head of the household. My brothers—Oscar was quite young—accepted this new "father" quite readily, at least as far as not being particularly worried about the family's finances. Fritz became a Dental Assistant, but did not stick it out very long. Oscar was helped by me to pass an aptitude test as a typewriter repairman, but despite this push, never became a mechanic to whom I would have entrusted even my most broken down typewriter.

As we all grew up and drifted apart, my brothers became more and more interested in leftist movements, with the result that they felt that it was demeaning to work for a capitalist system. I became the outcast. It was an ironical twist. The fact that I was involuntarily chosen to be the breadwinner made me the "capitalist." I guess to them I belong to this category even now.

We used to have violent discussions each time I came back to Vienna for a visit. Our preliminaries usually started with such remarks as, "Well, how is the revolution going" with a reply and query as to "Which one, mine or yours"?

My professional attempts in Vienna and later on in Paris had, at first, very little to do with motivational research, although they could be classified as belonging to the area of communication and advertising. I worked first in Vienna as a secretary. I had studied French via radio and had acquired a usable knowledge to type some letters. My English was of a similar origin. After a year or so as a secretary, I wrote to my uncle, who owned a small department store in Vienna, asking him to think about the possibility of my working for him. He hired me as a salesman. I was rapidly promoted to a window decorator. Since I always drew quite well my uncle agreed to send me to a school where window decorators were being trained. In this new position it became clear that I could annoy my bosses as well as surprise them. I developed new ideas. Since I was not satisfied with decorating windows in the conventional fashion, I procured plans from an American magazine for the construction of what was then called a "three tube radio." As a result I flooded the department store with music.

It is difficult to understand today, in our age of sophisticated hi-fi systems, how much my uncle and colleagues, as well as the customers, were impressed by the phenomenon of music coming out of an enormous loud-speaker. I still remember the great difficulties I had in convincing my rather miserly uncle to give me the necessary funds to construct the radio set. Everybody prophesied that this devilish miracle machine would never really work. When I finally succeeded in bringing a new atmosphere into the cold commercial display of merchandise, without too many static noises and scratchy orchestration, I became the hero of the day.

Even today I have to struggle with the difficulty of selling an idea. I am very frequently in the position of not just being able to present an innovation, but to figure out at the same time how I could motivate the clients to bring up enough courage to at least experimentally accept such a new concept. In many of my studies I am posing again and again questions that are intended to permit the detachment from customary methods and to learn to think in new ways. It is relatively simple, at least in my experience, to develop a new idea; but it is full of thorns and requires continuous acceptance of challenges and all the energy that you can muster to conquer the clumsy conservatism of the majority.

I am now occupied with the development of new thinking methods as they apply to our future. We have spent a lot of time teaching history. Little, however, have we concerned ourselves with the possibilities which the future has in store for us. We have been threatened about future shock but have not been taught how to prepare for this frightening day after tomorrow. Being forced to think and act independently has, in its proper sense, always been the role of the father, the führer and the creative master.

My brothers had come back to Vienna after an odyssey of escapes leading them to England. They were treated by the British as German prisoners of war until Fritz was sent to Australia and Oscar to Canada. Only when they both volunteered for the British Army was the fact that they were, after all, on the "right side" officially accepted. They came back to Vienna with the Four Power Occupation Forces and decided to stay there. Each subsequent visit I make now registers a mellowing of our relationship. They even became interested in my books. When I received the Golden Medal for Merit from the State of Vienna Fritz, at least, came to participate in my honors. It was a mixture of triumph and amusement for me to receive this award so many years later from a city which I still like but which, for political and racial reasons, had forced me to leave.

Our apartment in Vienna was a cold-water flat, but we were luckier than most families living in the same building. We had a toilet inside the flat while most other families had to share theirs with other tenants on the same floor. A bathroom, meaning a shower or a tub, was a luxury reserved for millionaires, or near millionaires, in my "social club." We went with our father once a week to the public douches. In an appropriate Viennese fashion using a diminutive, they were called "Tröpferlbad," literally, "droplet bath." We usually trekked to this institution on Friday afternoon. Maybe this gave me my inspiration, decades later, when doing my first motivational study for Ivory soap, to discover the importance of the Friday or Saturday night bath. During these weekly ablutions I made a few other important observations which I have used many times since in connection with shampoos and hair conditioners and soap in the shower. I not only washed away the physical dirt, but also all the moral dirt accumulated during the week. It gave me a feeling of a fresh start. This was reinforced by the fact that we usually changed our underwear and shirts after this thorough cleansing ceremony. For Americans, the fact that one changes shirts and underwear only once a week is pretty close to barbarism. But the feeling that each bath or shower represents not only a physical cleansing, but also a moral one, has not changed very much. In a study conducted in Germany not too many years ago, we found that many people still do not change their shirts more often than once a week without apparently having any kind of ill effects.

While cleansing and refreshing myself, enhanced by a change of underwear, I also experienced embarrassment. When I recently saw "Incident at Vichy" by Arthur Miller, I was reminded of my childhood. Of course, men were separated from women, but no distinction was made between boys and men and Jews and non-Jews. Circumcision was almost exclusively practiced by Jews. In "Incident at Vichy," Jews or Jewish-looking men had been arrested by the French equivalent of the Gestapo. Their identifications and passports to either freedom or concentration camp was the shape of their penis. Taking a weekly shower was an equal ordeal for me since it could and often did involve a public declaration of my ethnic ties. I tried to hide what I considered my deformity with towels and body distortions. But, too often, I had to face my gentile brethren as hostile teasers in what, to me, came close to "hell." These incidents in the "Tröpferlbad" made me understand much better the touching drama by Miller. Since all three of us were red-headed, my brothers and I were not considered by strangers to be Jewish. During the student riots staged by the Nazis at the University of Vienna, before Hitler's invasion of Austria, I was usually left alone after a searching look by my brown-shirted "colleagues."

It made me often think that if we could change people's stereotype concepts—if blacks could look white and whites darker—many of our silly and tragic conflicts might disappear. Because of my looks, I never felt revengeful vis-a-vis the Germans. I can understand how many Jews, however, have sworn never to set foot in Austria or Germany. Since I never felt strongly separated from non-Jews, it was relatively easy for me to forget.

We had a Portnoy problem in reverse in our family. My mother was quite frequently referred to by my father as the *shickse* (gentile). Although she was not really non-Jewish, at least as far as anybody knows, she came from a small village in Sudetan-Germany. She neither looked nor acted Jewish and was unfamiliar with most Jewish rituals. My father had discovered her during one of his trips as a salesman in her remote village. She and my aunt were the only Jewish girls there and a double wedding helped my grandfather rid himself of his two daughters at the same time. This division between a symbolically non-Jewish mother and a father desperately attempting to act Jewish influenced my life considerably. I decided not to force my children to choose a religion until they were old enough to really understand what they were doing and what emotional consequences their choice would have. The results? Both of them married non-Jews. Our son married a Protestant of Dutch descent, an "almost Mayflower" girl, and our daughter married a Catholic. Joel, our son-in-law, does not practice his religion and is an agnostic. In order to please his very devout mother, we agreed to a triple wedding for our daughter. First, they were married in a civil ceremony by a Jewish local judge. Then, to please Joel's mother, they were married in a Catholic church. We had to lie to the suspicious priest that she had not been married shortly before in a civil ceremony. The third marriage ceremony was a general family gathering under a huge shade tree with all the pomp and ceremony Hedy and I had never been able to afford when we got married. Our celebration had only consisted of consuming a ceremonial equivalent of a Viennese Hershey bar. I was surprised how insistent Hedy was on having all the trimmings of a bourgeois wedding from tuxedoes to chamber music, and a catered affair. After all these years, without ever having admitted it, she apparently needed to remedy one of the traumatic deprivations in her life.

Despite the constant conflicts, usually centering around the degree of her Jewishness, she was a wonderful mother. During the First World War when my father was in the Austrian Army and I learned to look upon the French, English, and later the Americans as natural enemies, she managed to save her three red-haired boys from starvation. Since I was the oldest, I was the one chosen most of the time to go on what we called "Hamster" trips. We would pack whatever few belongings we could spare, take a train, and go out into farm country to trade an heirloom, such as an inherited mirror or painting, for a few pounds of flour or fresh butter. Each expedition was an extremely dangerous affair. It was strictly forbidden to supplement the meager rationing of the starving city with such black market practices. When the train approached Vienna returning from the country, the Gendarmery would search all passengers. We children had bulging stomachs, produced by ingeniously sewn waist bands filled with flour, copying the methods used by hamsters to provide for the winter months. When you were caught, you landed in jail. It happened a few times. We suddenly were orphaned; none of the mothers—including my own—wanted to claim any of the children. Finally, all the Gendarme could do was to confiscate the bitterly fought-for food and, most likely, use it for his own family. Often enough, frisking took place before the "Hamsters" boarded a train. We became as skilled as guerillas today in hiding in trenches near the railroad tracks and jumping on the train when it had started moving. The flour was used by my mother to re-knead and re-bake the bread which was at least 60 to 70% straw and make it edible. I can still see the yellow, rough bread soaking in a dish until it would yield and merge with the bartered good flour. We also learned to steal coal from the railroad yard and to cut down trees in the park which we had to bring to the school. This was our contribution to the survival of our classroom and lessons, as well as our way of keeping our small apartment warm during the winter.

Of course, it was all immoral and even slightly criminal. What reformers too often don't understand, because they never experienced it, is that when you are confronted with questions of survival, perishing and suffering is considered in a more primeval sense, and immoral and, what is possible worse, stupid actions are taken.

Teaching psychology, getting involved in crime prevention, fighting drug addiction, should require that the "do-gooder" first go through very realistic laboratory life-situations where starving, freezing, and fear become more than an interesting vocabulary. These lessons have contributed to my understanding of many situations and motivations in studies many years later. I am afraid of having the nightmarish childhood situations repeat themselves, and at the same time, I also feel more secure, because I know I survived them once and at least have the illusion that I could do so again. I am scared when I begin to understand that being free from all convention, being aggressively against all accepted moral standards, can be fun. We were Robin Hoods, avengers or at least daring adventurers when we climbed over the fence of the Northern Railroad coal yards and could quite easily escape the apparently not so watchful, somewhat dimmed eagle-eye of the guard. We compared our loot without the slightest remorse. I can understand, thinking back, how a pilferer—a problem I have lately worked on—can be motivated much more by his or her pride of accomplishment than by shame or even greed.

Maybe it is a crazy or even amoral idea. But I feel that all those who are professionally occupied with the understanding of human motives, such as psychiatrists, psychologists, teachers, and probably very many parents, should be sent to a very modern school which does not exist at this point. In this school they would learn to understand all the horrible things which are completely outside of their sphere of experience relating to their beautiful and brave and conventional sphere. A poor substitute for such a school of living is at least to read about it or to talk with people who have been in such situations. Not only would such a three dimensional immersion in these experiences create better psychologists but, in an indirect way, we would also learn to better understand literature, historical events, and strange mores.

I have used this insight quite often when attempting to analyze new motivations. A short time ago we examined for a company the selling of clothes for very tall people. I had to understand what it means to be taller than most of the people around. I did remember one such situation when I was in Japan and had gone to a theatre where there was only standing room. I suddenly noticed that I was at least a head taller than the people around me. I suddenly felt very exposed; I put my head between my shoulders in almost instinctive fashion in order to appear smaller. At the same time, I also made the proud discovery that I was, for once, in a situation where I could look down upon everybody else. Thinking about this situation, I could understand much better the conflict of extremely tall people. The company we worked for sold these clothes via a catalog. Many of the men, and we were dealing primarily with men's clothing, preferred to buy from the catalog so they did not have to expose themselves, in the psychological sense, in a store. We gave the advice to change the presentation of the wearing apparel in the catalog. Instead of putting all the emphasis on the photographs of the clothing, we suggested that the company prove, through the choice of situations and the text used, that they really understood the psychology of tall people. The customers were pleasantly surprised by this demonstration of affinity and understanding and thus influenced to buy more readily.

Many of our studies make it necessary to understand other cultures. In South Africa (I quote this often as one of my failures), the assignment was to find out how a new type of floor wax could be sold to the white housewife. Being an American I suggested that convenience and labor-saving be used as the major appeal. Although the situation is beginning to change now, at that time maids were so cheap that promising the South African white woman that she could save time and labor was completely out of place. Something similar applies to deodorants. Although the situation is continuously changing, it is still true that there are considerable differences in the use of these products when one compares Italy, Spain, or North Africa with more northern areas such as Sweden or Germany and, especially, the United States. To retain one's body odor, at least partially, is considered by many countries, particularly those that are located in more southern regions, as normal and quite natural.

2 Rue De L'Admiral Mouchet, Paris V (EME)

That was my address in Paris in 1929 and 1930. I had studied German literature in Vienna and dreamed of becoming a literary critic. I had to support myself and contribute to my family's expenses. I was studying and working at the same time.

I knew how to draw. For several years, before I passed the examination which would permit me to enter the University, I had worked in my uncle's department store as a window decorator. I continued to apply my artistic talents on a free-lance basis, draping cloth and arranging chinaware and toys in innumerable shop windows. My mother encouraged me to try to move out of the proletarian embrace. My father resented it. He was a spectacularly unsuccessful salesman who felt that a decent Jewish boy had no right to waste his time by surrounding himself with books which obviously had no practical value. When I gave up my job as a clerk and window decorator I had betrayed him. My ordained destiny was to make a living, as most other decent young men in my age group did. The battle raged almost every day. I don't know what decided me, possibly just wanting to be independent. I had saved enough money from my nighttime jobs to take a train to Paris.

It was my first real culture shock. Vienna appeared small and provincial compared to Paris which was frightening and overwhelming in its strangeness and size. I found a "hole" beneath an attic which was unheated, had no running water, and the toilet consisted of an opening in the floor over which one squatted, a method health-faithfuls would laud today as a natural and wholesome way of helping nature. Maybe so, but it was damned uncomfortable.

I registered at the Sorbonne, selecting courses in literature, philosophy and other impractical subjects. I strolled down Boulevard St.

The young Dichter.

Michel wearing a beret. I was a Bohemian, a student, and a starving one at that.

Leon Blum headed the Popular Front Government. I went to hear him speak. I did not understand everything, but there were lots of other young people, fellow students, in the hall. I noticed two fairly good-looking girls in the crowd. One of them smiled at me. I smiled back and my first flirtation had begun. Her name was Tassja; she was from Riga. She was vivacious, with dark hair and a warm personality. Before I knew what was happening, I had acquired a mother, a protector and an ideal. Since her father had money, it was usually she who treated me to a meal. We discussed our philosophies, our purpose in life. I became part of a whole group of dreamers. None of them were Communists. Tassja's father had suffered from the Russians and was considered a Revisionist. We were all Socialists.

Tassja was studying psychology. She tried a Rorschach inkblot test with me and told me about her studies. The inevitable happened. I switched and chose, out of a burgeoning love, psychology as my object of study. As is often the case, I wanted to find solutions for my own problems and I wanted to please my girl friend at the same time.

I may have kissed her two or three times during a whole year of friendship/ courtship. I could not conceive of "dirtying" her with my erotic starvation. How wrong I was. She expected me, as I found out later, to be aggressive—and to break down a resistance which was only pretense on her part. One day, a more dashing and daring young man came along. They are now married and living in Israel, both working as psychologists.

A lifetime later, I received a letter in my hotel room in Tel Aviv, during a lecture tour there, from Dr. Pollack, Tassja's married name. When I phoned in answer to her letter, she inquired whether I was the same Ernest Dichter whom she knew in Paris. I was surprised by her masculine voice. When she came to the hotel with her husband, we exchanged cool memories, not trying to read each other's mind. Freud once said that the reason we hate or at least make fun of mothers-in-law is that we see in them a foreboding portrayal of what our creamy cheeked lovely wife might look like twenty years later. Seeing your love after twenty years has the same devastating effect. But Tassja, whatever her looks now, had unlocked the psychology door for me.

Did I marry a psychologist later on? Not being able to distinguish one tune from another, it was perfectly logical that I would marry a concert pianist. The first time I saw Hedy was on an *Ausflug*, an excursion which replaced (with and without skis but always with a rucksack) the church or other cultural forays for thousands of Viennese. The *Ausflug* (literally Outflight) was communion with nature. We took the streetcar, *die "Elektrische"* (the Electric) and explored the Vienna woods.

Hedy and her cousin were part of the group. We surveyed each other in the street car. My attention was concentrated on Lenke, her cousin, a nice looking girl. Hedy was, so it seemed to me, too unobtainable. She was too good looking and too elegant. During the hike the invisible wall between us was breached. I began to consider the still remote possibility of courting Hedy. When she accepted my invitation to go to the theater, our spiritual marriage had begun. It took quite a while longer until my persuasive techniques brought physical results. When I saw a tiny beauty spot in the neighborhood of her navel, I vaguely remember thinking that I might see it quite often. I have not looked carefully lately, but I think it is still there, decades later, since our mutual discoveries started long before our official marriage.

I still tease Hedy about her indecision. For at least a year or longer she was not quite sure whether I was the best Prince she could hope for. I promised her not riches, but excitement; no security in the customary sense, but a never-ending task of meeting challenges. Hedy never knew my father who had died one year before our marriage in 1935. In 1934 I received my doctorate in psychology from the University of Vienna.

A short time after the flirt with Tassja broke apart, I had also lost my interest in continuing my psychology studies in Paris. The general situation was not particularly good at that time and my studies suffered under it. I was completely isolated. I studied in the evening, during the weekends, very early in the morning, and during the day I worked in an office or busied myself with a variety of jobs in order to make enough money to prevent starvation.

Just when the economic collapse of Europe became more and more obvious, caused by the bankruptcy of the Austrian *Creditanstalt*, I had the very smart idea of going back to Vienna. I can still see a colleague of mine who was going in the exact opposite direction. As far as I remember, it was on the Austrian-Swiss border while I was looking out of my train that he recognized me, and since he saw that I was heading towards Vienna, he asked with a pale expression on his face, "For God's sake, don't tell me that you are going to Vienna; what are you doing?" I explained to him, as rapidly as the stay in the station permitted, that I felt that I had neglected my studies in Paris, and that I wanted to go back to Vienna in order to get ahead more rapidly at the University there.

After a year in Paris, my knowledge of French was pretty good. I registered at the University of Vienna and accepted a position for each afternoon. My task consisted of helping two boys with their studies. This kind of occupation was labeled, very arrogantly, as a "court" teacher. It was nothing more than being a private tutor. In any case, now I only had to work every afternoon; I had all mornings free for my studies. I had decided to pursue my psychology with or without Tassja. When many years later, I reproached my son for taking so long to finish his Doctor's thesis for which I only needed a few months, despite the fact that I had to work, he used to get very angry.

My main study, at least during the warm summer months, was the public park near a church where the majority of my thesis was typed on a small portable typewriter which I kept on my knees. I had received my Doctor's degree but my dependence on my wife continued. I married Hedy, moved in with my in-laws, started a psychoanalytic practice, opened up a vocational guidance center, wrote articles, lectured; but for almost a whole year I lived from what my wife earned as a piano teacher and concert pianist. I abandoned my address, Bergasse 20, which later on became known all over the world, for another address which suited a musician much better—the Johann-Straussgasse. Bergasse 20 was not well known just because I lived there, but because it happened to be exactly across the street from where Freud lived, at house number 19.

While I developed Motivational Research only in the States, I was even then, immediately before receiving my degree and shortly afterwards, interested in applying psychology in a practical manner. I had actually never been interested in an academic career, particularly not at that time because the number of unemployed was great in Vienna and not less in the academic field. I realized, therefore, that even after I had received my degree, it would take a few years before I could get employment. I was hoping to find an unoccupied niche where I might fit in. Despite all the difficulties that existed, I did discover that, at that time, there did not really exist a scientifically-based type of vocational guidance.

About the same time, I worked with Dr. Wilhelm Steckel and August Aichhorn who, many years later, saved Freud's library. Both were psychoanalysts, but of a very practical nature, interested in a more immediate application of analytic principles. Opening up a psychoanalytic practice of a similar nature was therefore a very logical idea for me.

I also started to write articles for a number of magazines, developing a sort of syndicated column in the area of popular psychology which, at that time, was a real novelty. Recently, I began collaborating on a new magazine in this country called *Vital*. My first contribution to *Vital* concerned itself with a topic, which probably has been running through all my life—money. I appropriately called this article "Money Therapy," playing on a reversal of the initials TM—transcendental meditation—captioning the piece MT instead of TM.

Trying to figure out, independent of economic crises and other difficulties, what I can do that would be different and therefore, possibly, lead to success, has been a basic approach which I have been using continuously.

Motivational Research, which I only started in the States, has its origin in the same kind of attitude. It was clear to me that to continue in an academic psychological avenue would not lead me to a desired goal. I also felt that my whole psychological study never quite concerned itself with the real skills that a good psychologist needed. Thinking these ideas through, I developed a lecture course on how to learn to observe people. I offered this course to various organizations, including one that would be comparable to the New School for Social Research in New York. They promptly accepted my idea, and I became a full-fledged lecturer. This led later on to various unpleasantnesses with my real professor, Karl Buhler. He had approached them upon having been notified that I had been selected to teach: Why had they picked a pupil of his, rather than himself, although he was the legitimate professor of psychology and the dean of the psychology department! The answer which he received had an almost American ring to it: "Because Mr. Dichter had the idea first and not you, Professor." I have used this training, which I had to develop myself in order to be able to teach it, in many forms during my motivational activities. Today, of course, we have the help of video tapes which we use quite extensively. I have also applied it in utilizing psychodrama, originally developed by Dr. Moreno, a psychiatrist also from Vienna. Its main purpose consists of asking subjects to play people around them, products, or services. We recently used it in order to find answers on how to get more people interested in the use of public libraries where we asked people to *be* such a library. Most of them explained that a library was like a spinster, middle-aged, or older and rather passive. From such an intuitive understanding, we can often derive many practical ideas, in this case, the necessity of possibly even changing the term "library" to one of "coping center," helping people to adjust themselves to the rapidly changing aspects of modern life.

I was always fascinated by new things, probably one of the reasons why I recently completed a book on futurology. My own philosophy is that something new—a new skill, a new technique that one can learn—represents one of the real aspects of wealth. A short time after I met Hedy I started, despite my supposed lack of musical talent, to take piano lessons. I was tutored by Dr. Leonhard Deutsch, an individualist psychologist, who had developed an entirely new method. What attracted me about it was that I could compete with my new love, and also that, here again, was something entirely different, a new approach, that no one else had thought about before. Instead of playing scales, and learning notes, he asked you to hum a melody, and then find it on the piano, or any other instrument that you were interested in. We would call it today, in modern education, a Gestalt approach. In any case, it had a lot to do with the Adlerian philosophy of encouragement. After relatively few minutes, you could actually play a melody, your melody, on the piano. Only after you had learned such a total melody would you gradually proceed to discover that it was really composed of individual notes. I surprised Hedy with my hidden musical talents. I didn't tell her for quite a while about my lessons. I only mentioned surreptitiously that psychology could also be used when studying music. After about three months I was ready to perform. I played for her a few very simple Mozart sonatas. Hedy was delighted. Unfortunately, this was as far as I ever went, and many years later I started taking lessons on the cello but without much success.

Hedy became interested in the new technique and continued using it in her teaching. The cello still stands in our house or castle in Croton, feeling very lonely. When I tried to sell it I was told that it had a crack and had dried out. Every so often I have a dream that some brain surgeon might discover a secret spot in my learn-apparatus which he could stimulate electrically. I would then surprise, as a latterday Rubenstein, not only Hedy, but the whole world.

The dreams people have, and the roles we play in them, represent a very important source for psychological digs. Interestingly enough, I never dreamed about being particularly successful in the area of sports. Neither did I ever want to become a victorious or even a bad general. What I do dream about is that some areas of brain do exist, which, if properly stimulated, would increase my intelligence to such an extent that I could suddenly solve most all the problems of mankind. Having seen "Star Wars" and "Close Encounters," I have added to my fantasies the idea that I might be invited to accompany these cute green creatures, spend a few months on some remote star and then come back with knowledge which no one else has had up till now. I could cure cancer, solve international conflicts eliminating wars, or to put it very modestly, become a messiah who can use his talents in almost all areas.

I started a psychoanalytic practice. It took quite a while until I earned enough money to pay for our new partnership. Hedy, long before Women's Lib, was the breadwinner, but she still remained the devoted wife who would never allow me to wash the dishes, if this is a symbol of equality between the sexes.

Maybe what attracted us to each other was the fact that my insecurity was matched by her security. Even when, after a marriage of only a year and a half, I was on my way to Paris and exile, she seemed to be far from despair. It was simply the signal for a fresh start. We continuously discovered in each other new and unexpected possibilities and challenges. Maybe this is better and more rewarding than simply changing one's position when making love, so highly recommended by all experts in the joy of sex and sensuousness.

Hedy met Tassja later on in Vienna and then again in Tel Aviv. She always reacted to her as if she had shared my early romance. Lenke married someone else, who is now a top Communist in Czechoslovakia. Little does she know how close she had come to becoming the exact opposite—the wife of a scheming capitalist.

Insecurity never left me. Hedy has to remind me quite often that I am almost famous, that I don't have to say yes to everything, that I should defend myself and pound my chest in pride. I could have avoided many mistakes and wrong decisions had I learned this lesson.

During my second stay in Paris, I could act as the experienced Parisian. I showed Hedy where I had lived as a student, where I had eaten or, more often, starved. This time we descended from my previous association with an admiral (although only through the street name) to a mere captain. We lived on the Rue du Capitaine Ferber, which was on the outskirts of Paris.

We waited to have children until we knew where our Führer would force us to go. Tom was born exactly on the day Hitler invaded Russia. I am still proud that, when I visited Hedy after Tom's arrival in the hospital, I stated arrogantly, "This is it. Hitler has lost the war!" The date was June 21, 1941. Susie was born two years later. Why did we not give them fanciful names? We wanted them not only to be born in the United States, but to have unmistakeably American names. They made up for it by giving our five grandchildren the most unusual names they could think of, ranging from Jed to Risa Cybele.

When they come over on a Thanksgiving, Christmas, or birthday visit, I feel a little like Abraham watching how his flock has grown. Being the worrier and insecure person that I have always been (and probably always will be), I also am usually not far from the disturbing thought that now I have to think and provide potentially for all of them. Will I pass on my insecurity to them or make them feel protected?

Our son lately started to blame us for having indirectly promised him that life would be soft. Having discovered the opposite, he felt we had cheated him. Having become well known (at least in my field) added another burden. While I complained about my father never having had success, he seems to be equally dissatisfied with me for the opposite reason. Oh well! Is it at all possible that a father does right by his son?

With Susie, our daughter, we have fewer problems. She married a young man who teaches political science. They have two wonderful children and are apparently quite satisfied. In my relationship with my son-in-law there are fewer emotions involved. We often have more or less detached discussions about his or my work.

For a while now, Tom has been working for Herman Kahn, the Scientific Director of the Hudson Institute. Apparently they are getting along very well. Maybe, to some extent, Herman has become a substitute father for Tom. But Tom tries to comfort me by telling me that I am becoming smarter every year. When I complain that he was unwilling to take over my business, or at least work for me, he reassures me that he has learned a lot from me and, starting with his Doctor's thesis and his work with Herman, he continues to use many thought processes and concepts which he has inherited from me. "You see," he says, "if you are interested in immortality," which he accuses me of, "you have got it, even though I do not necessarily continue in your specific profession of Motivational Research."

3 How I Survived Jail with the Help of a Hungarian Salami

The University of Vienna had a department very arrogantly called *Wirtschafts Psychologisches Institut*, (Psychoeconomic Institute). In 1936, needing money, I worked for this Institute, conducting depth interviews on the milk drinking habits of the Viennese. I delivered these interviews dutifully one afternoon to these offices. The man who stood behind the door, to which I had a key, was a peculiar looking guy. He asked me whether I was connected with the Institute and what my name was. He had a tone of authority so I did not feel like telling him off. "You are under arrest," he growled. I did not protest. I was too stunned. Not until a full week later, having learned to adapt myself to jail, did I find out why I had been arrested. Lawyers? Call my wife? Tell me why? No answers to all these requests. He stonewalled it, as we would say today.

I was questioned about everything imaginable and unimaginable. Did I have a key to the office? Of course, I had opened the door with it. Did I have a desk in the office of the Institute? Yes. Was the money in it mine? Yes. What was the secret meaning of all these questionnaires about milk drinking-habits? What was the real meaning of the obvious code-word "milk"? I felt stupid. I was torn between having been caught as a clever operator, spy or exciting Viennese connection, and trying to convince the detective that I was really interested in the milk-drinking attitudes of Viennese. To a virile Austrian police officer, both explanations were almost equally suspicious and not worthy of a promising young man. "You are under arrest" was accepted by me without protest. It took a full week before I found out the real reason.

Without my knowledge, the Institute had been used during the Dollfuss & Schuschnigg Fascist rule of Austria as a secret mailing center from where information was sent to Brno, Czechoslovakia. A few of the students working in the Institute knew about these activities. I naively did not.

When I arrived at the jail, I met various of my colleagues from the Institute in the corridors. I could not talk with them, of course. I wracked my brains as to what could have happened. Hedy, my wife, told me how many hours she had spent desperately calling everybody she could think of to find out why I had not come home. Since we had only been married for a short while, she probably ruled out another woman as the cause of my disappearance. Finally somebody cleverly suggested that she call the police instead of the morgue.

At least I was alive and temporarily safe behind bars. Our telephone was tapped, of course. She met with some people secretly who were known as the underground anchormen. She finally found the explanation for the mystery. The next morning the papers were full of stories about how market research and public opinion research had been used to cleverly disguise the subversive socialist activities of the underground. The Social Democratic Party leaders and all the union leaders had either fled months before or were in jail.

I wonder whether the Eastern Block countries were, or are still, equally afraid of finding out what people are really thinking about. They do find motivational research applicable to their productivity problems and export and import questions. I was invited by several of these countries, as an American, many years later to hold seminars and to consult on commercial problems. Just recently I received a copy of a book on advertising psychology published in Hungary. I am the proud contributor of one chapter on the "Soul of Products." I have also been interviewed by *Pravda* and Czech magazines. I even have an account in Prague, where I deposited my lecture fees, since I could not take them out of the country. We finally used the money for a Czechoslovakian vacation.

Three or four days after my incarceration, I was awakened at two o'clock in the morning and brought before a high police official. It helped improve my depth interviewing technique. He asked me, for example, whether I had any knowledge about the clandestine doings. I truthfully denied it, but he did not accept such a simple denial. "Did you have money in your desk?" (a few shillings). I said "yes." "Aha, you admit then that you had contact with subversive elements in Czechoslavakia." He kept coming back, again and again, to this question and felt that by hammering away at it and attributing my admissions to one aspect of my relations with the Institute, he gradually would soften me up enough to admit more relevant facts. For the first time in my life I realized that a detective's job was similar to that of a motivational researcher. Not to accept simple explanations is part of his training. I often call myself the "Columbo" of human motivtions.

Did I get mad? Yes, but not Mad, mad. I stayed fairly "normal" in jail. Lesson: the human spirit adapts itself. I started writing. I analyzed myself. I made interesting contacts with other real political prisoners. The only real frustration was the feeling of helplessness. I wrote letter upon letter to the authorities, but received no answer. It took two weeks before Hedy was allowed to see me and, outside of seeing her and knowing that she, too, could take it quite well, she gave me a very tangible proof of her love which turned out to be a great consolation to me: a whole big, long, delicious Hungarian salami. I don't think there were any phallic insinuations involved, but who understands women? Anyway, I would have needed, rather, the female part of a salami, if one could attribute sex to a salami! We had a feast. I became a most popular inmate with my co-prisoners, and even some of the guards. When I was amnestied—what a word, I was innocent, I swear it—I left a hunk of the beautiful gift behind as a bequest to the less fortunate among my new friends. Whenever I buy Hungarian salami now, it reminds me of those, by now more funny than sad, days. I will have to wait for another jail term, though, before I will feel I can afford real Hungarian salami at today's prices.

The salami and the jail sojourn of four weeks became the turning point in my life. A few days after my arrest, my aunt, who lived in Germany at that time, sent me a clipping from the *Volkische Beobachter*, the official Nazi newspaper. "Was I the Ernest Dichter mentioned"? Yes, I was. But I was in excellent company. Among the other "subversives," I found the names of Sigmund Freud, Albert Einstein, Karl Marx, Engels and a few other unknowns.

After leaving jail I asked my professor, who was the head of the Aptitude Testing Institute of the City of Vienna, what my chances were of getting a job after my internship. Only two bright students were being selected every year and I was one of them. He tried to be "frank"—a word usually used when someone is about to tell you an unpleasant truth. "I am a Nazi. You can denounce me, but it would not help you very much. As a matter of fact, it would only get you into trouble," he said, "since most of the people in the police and the army are also Nazis. I would love to give you a job. You have developed a number of new ideas, but you are Jewish, are you not?" His advice contributed considerably to my leaving the country in early 1937.

For a long while, Hedy and I discussed the possibility or necessity of leaving. The most difficult decision was to abandon my burgeoning psychoanalytic practice; I was just beginning to apply psychology to market research problems.

The teaching and concert activities of Hedy, the pianist, were also hard to relinquish. We counted our losses, turned them into new "life dividends," and decided to start fresh. I went first, alone, to Paris to continue my studies, but also to make a living. Hedy followed me three months later.

All our friends thought we were crazy, that is, even crazier than usual. Leave everything behind? "You know that Viennese are famous for their *Gemutlich-keit*. Nothing like what happened in Germany can ever happen here," they repeated. Well, I was the pessimist who foresaw the collapse of the world, or thought he did. Was I gifted with special sight? I don't think so. I used motivational research. I interviewed a number of knowledgeable people who were aware of the inside story of what was happening. I talked to Nazis, Catholics, and politicians. One of the most interesting ones was a lawyer who acted as a spy for the still anti-Nazi government of Austria. He taught me to look beneath the surface. He pointed out the hidden Nazis among my "friends" and the people who I had thought could be trusted. Among them were the editors of a Catholic family magazine. Bit by bit, reading between the lines and "listening with the third ear," and observing people, the pieces of the puzzle started to form a rather frightening and sharply contoured outline of the future. Among the people from whom I least expected help were the Catholic editors. At that time, I wrote a regular column which concerned itself with psychological problems and questions. Already the way in which they reacted to this column showed me where their sympathies really lay. When I indicated, for example, that, when dealing with educational problems, it is necessary to teach children critical think-ing and not to use parental authority in a dictatorial fashion, they smiled.

Austria was going to be invaded by Hitler. The Allies would do nothing, a habit which had become only too well known. Where could I go? Why not Paris? I had treated a young man who had had a brain tumor removed and helped him in rediscovering the world. One approach I am proud of was to give him, as an assignment, to count all the clocks usually installed on the first floor above the watchmakers' shingles. This forced him to lift his head, a behavioral pattern which he had lost while suffering from the tumor. During the next session, he proudly told me the number of clocks that he had seen and that at least three different people had recognized him and said hello to him. This was a small step in helping him to rediscover the world. His father had a factory in Paris which made woven labels and decals. When he heard of my troubles he urged me to take a job with his company as a sales manager on a commission basis. While he loved to play benefactor, he had some hesitation when it had to be accompanied by a cash outlay. Anyway, it was the best offer I got and one I could not refuse. Hedy stayed behind. I had been a student in Paris and language was no problem. I lived in a Bohemian movie attic and was ready to start fresh.

For several weeks, there was not a single sale. I trotted from one clothing store to another, even offering to design the labels myself. Finally I was taught another lesson by my grateful boss. He cut in half all the prices in my catalogue of labels, permitting me to sell even at these prices, only top quality. "I shall be ruined if you succeed," he told me, but he knew what he was doing. Still I did not sell, although high prices and low quality were the arguments which I had used to explain away my previous failures. "You may have a Ph.D. in psychology," he said, "but I think this lesson which you are learning now may be worth more than all the money and time you had spent on your academic career." Right he was. I realized that selling was much less dependent on prices and quality than on the power of conviction and your own beliefs. The miracle happened. Almost overnight I began to sign orders.

When Hedy arrived in Paris, three months later, I had become more than a motivational researcher; I had learned how to apply it when my income depended on it. I have used, and passed on, this lesson many, many times since. It is always easier to first find a scapegoat and a plausible excuse than to really try, with a deep conviction of your eventual success.

A short while ago I was asked what one could do to get people to concern themselves more with health, to eat less, or to give up smoking. In order to convince them, the usual approach is to tell people that they are shortening their own lives. Despite this warning, relatively little success has been achieved in this fashion. In most countries, even when there are strict measures used against cigarette advertising, people keep on smoking more or less as much as before. If one thinks about it, one can discover that the mistake is a very simple but fundamental one. You are really trying to take away something from people that they obviously like. You are promising them something that you cannot guarantee: health.

One of the solutions which we have offered to a number of organizations was to make health as interesting as the seductive but dangerous pleasures. A whole series of attempts to get people to reduce have failed because they have only resulted in creating frustrations. Usually there is lack of willpower to carry through such a cure, even when you have been suffering from an infarction, diabetes, or other disease. Every film producer knows that murder and immoral topics represent a much more attractive plot than the more or less boring subject of health and healthy people. It is possible that this basic difference between the unattractiveness of normality and the topic of success of dramatic content has been convincingly proven through our mass media.

I often thought that something isn't quite right if what is pleasureful is forbidden and thereby offers more fun than the so-called moral and correct thing. One could muse about this fact and, if one believes in an overall god-like motivator, one could come to the conclusion that this dichotomy may have been intended. Sin has been portrayed for us in a pleasureful fashion, so that we can possibly acquire even more genuine pleasure by learning to conquer sin.

4 The Sales Pitch Which Saved My Life

It was April 1938, and my wife and I were in Paris. We had left Vienna, Austria, because we could smell some ill brown wind from across the German border. Your senses become sharper and more alert and give you more signals during dangerous times like these than in quieter times. And far-sighted friends nudged us. They were good Nazis, at least good as far as we were concerned. They did not want to have us on their consciences. But where to go? Paris and all Europe were as safe as a time bomb with a short fuse. Everybody thought we were crazy. It could not happen here, that is, in *gemutlich* (relaxed) Austria.

A committee for displaced scientists offered me a job in Calcutta, India, and I almost became an Indian, that is, an Indian Indian. I would have tested Indian textile workers to decide which ones would make good operators. I carried on long conversations between Paris and London with my potential Indian boss. He insisted on a meeting in Berlin to discuss details of my job. No matter how diplomatic I tried to be he simply didn't seem to understand why I found it less than pleasant to arrange for such a meeting under the by then quite overpowering shadow of Adolf Hitler.

Finally, something clicked in this Oriental's mind and he simply said, "Oh, all right, then. Let's meet in Marseille. I'm going to board my ship there and we can spend a day or two discussing all necessary details as to your salary, your duties, where you are going to live, whatever else one has to talk and think about when such a major change takes place in one's life." I could smell exotic India. (Many years later, when lecturing there, I found how far out its smell really was!) I was excited and somewhat frightened; at the same time, I translated fear into challenge. I rushed out to buy books about India and the dialects spoken in Calcutta. My potential benefactor assured me that almost everybody who counted spoke English and I would have to deal primarily with the foremen in the factory and they, too, had sufficient knowledge of this language. I learned about the caste system, dialects and sects. Fear became curiosity, an anti-stress technique I seemed to have been using throughout my life.

Before the possibility of my discovery of the Indian subcontinent, I had made the rounds of almost all possible countries to which a young couple like ourselves could emigrate, as long as it was far away from Europe. I had talked to various secretaries and employees and the whole palette of the type of bureaucrats that usually are assigned to or banished to work in a consulate. I have known quite a number of this particular type of human species in other countries. Having to work in a consulate in Paris, of course, was not quite the same as being banished to some remote outpost in Siberia or Kurdistan. I had been to see, in the course of a few weeks, the important people, that is important for us, the Cuban, Argentinian, Brazilian, Australian, Icelandic and other representative officers.

For some reason, perhaps because it seemed to be an almost unobtainable goal, I left the American consulate pretty much to the last, but I did go there. A young lady received me. This was the first contact I ever had with American officials, and I was very impressed. She did not waste much time listening to me. She commandeered me. Maybe she was just a representative of the famous typical American woman, although I did not realize it at that time. Her orders were crisp, clear and precise. "Here is the phone." "Call your wife." "Have your pictures taken and register for a visa as an immigrant." I answered with a repertoire of "buts": "but I have no money; but I don't know anybody there; but what am I going to do in America?" "Never mind," she said, "just do what I tell you. We'll figure out something afterwards." We had our photographs taken and returned the next day. She pulled out a list of various possibilities of entry into the United States. There was the obvious and most easily rejected one which required $5,000 per head at your disposal. Ten thousand dollars! That was equivalent to asking me whether I had a million dollars. All right, on to the next possibility—various types of clergymen. We even considered this possibility. Clergymen can be admitted to the U.S. with a special kind of visa. But we finally had to admit that I was not an ordained rabbi, nor a reverend of any possible church or sect, unless I wanted to create a new one. Did I have relatives in the

U.S.? Yes, I vaguely remembered my father, who had passed away long since, talking about some members of our family having come to the States around 1880. They, as far as I could remember, had the same name. "Why don't you write them?" I agreed. I wrote and even got an answer, although not a very satisfactory one. A third cousin of mine said, "Sure, I'll take care of you in case you really need it." I learned at a later visit that this was a rather weak kind of affidavit. Finally, we hit upon one category that seemed to offer possibilities: journalism. I worked at that time as a secretary to an Austrian journalist stationed in Paris. Since my French was pretty good it was my task to scan newspapers and magazines of possible interest to Austrian readers and to prepare memos for my boss. It was, to a large extent, this reading of newspapers and collections of other sources of information from different countries that influenced me, that after having fled Vienna, the next thing to do would be to get out of Europe.

In a way I did motivational research inasmuch as I did not rely on the superficial information which I gathered. I made comparisons and learned to read between the lines. I was familiar with this technique, partially, from my psychological studies and psychoanalysis. But I developed this approach, influenced by my journalist friend and boss in a decisive way.

It was clear that the louder the Western Powers (particularly England and France) insisted that they would not tolerate, under any circumstances, a *rapprochement* between Austria and Germany by the not too gentle methods of Hitler, the less one should believe them. I have found that this interpretation of governmental journalistic news, particularly when denials are involved, is equally valid today. When governmental spokesmen keep on repeating that they will very definitely not devalue the dollar or pound, you can be fairly sure that is exactly what is going to happen in the near future. The Mexican government, not too long ago, kept on stressing that the peso had retained its value for over twenty years. What happened? It was devalued by over fifty percent over one nice weekend.

Reading the various sources, and discussions with my journalist boss convinced my wife and me that we should consider as a final goal, for at least the next few years of our lives, some country outside of Europe. The most practical solution offered itself very soon. A fake contract offering me, in the name of my boss's Austrian newspaper, a yearly contract which would pay me $150 a month to act as a scientific "stringer" in the U.S. was the answer. Of course, my boss was cautious enough to make me sign a second letter addressed to him that the contract was invalid.

The young secretary working at the American Consulate then arranged a meeting with Llewelyn Thompson who at that time was Vice Consul in Paris. He received me. He looked at the supposed contract and then looked me straight in the eyes and said, "I would like you to produce a copy of the newspaper for me." "Why?" I asked. "I have a strong suspicion that fairly soon, if not already, there must be a swastika on the masthead." He was right, of course. But after some searching I did discover a Sunday edition which had not been defaced yet by the swastika. I made another appointment and showed it to Vice Consul Thompson. "Well, yes," he said, in a disappointing, hesitating voice. I was faced with a crisis. I was in a stress situation. I got mad. Whether it was the right reaction or not, I don't know, but it obviously worked. And, looking back, I probably made the best sales pitch of my whole life—at least the one that changed my life and my family's life most radically. I started lashing out at him and everything American, which was not popular, then. I criticized the American philosophy, the Statue of Liberty and the Constitution. "All you're interested in is having people come to the U.S. who have rich relatives or clergymen or some other occupation that is of immediate interest to the U.S.," I shouted. I had always loved, if that is the right word, America. Among other reasons, while I was studying in Vienna, I earned a good part of my living by tutoring American medical students. As a matter of fact, I even got through my psychoanalytic training for free by teaching my American analyst German while practicing my English.

Mr. Thompson was quite taken aback by my violence. "Calm down, young man," he said. "You are wrong in almost everything you say about the States. What is it that you think you will be able to contribute to the U.S., anyway?" It was at that point that I, probably for the first time, formulated most clearly what by now is fairly well known all over the world as motivational research. Neither the word nor the discipline existed at that time. "I am sure America is a wonderful country," I answered. "But I also know that it has just as many problems as most other countries. Many of these problems need solutions."

We have to understand the real reasons why people do things. Only when we know that can we figure out how to get them to do what, for one reason or another, we think they ought to do. Of course, there are issues and questions which are debatable, but obviously we all want fewer criminals; we want people to be happy, interested in their work, we want them to increase their productivity. Some companies want people to buy their products rather than those of their competitors. Scientists have been interested in finding out why man acts in as stupid or as clever a fashion as he does. But to use modern psychological and psychoanalytical ideas, not only to understand people better but also to motivate them was, at that time, a new idea.

My argument used with Mr. Thompson was new and surprising; that one can not simply ask people why they are doing the things they do but that one has to use depth psychology to find these things out. Many of these problems cry out for solutions. But first we have to find out the real reasons for the actions of people. Only when we know them can we develop practical methods to enforce positive actions or to influence negative ones in such a way that they are changed. In a very rapid sequence, I started thinking about a long list of problems which were typical not only of America such as criminality, productivity, strikes, vandalism. The list seemed to be almost endless. Since that time, many times I have had to develop the same theory about which I lectured the Vice Consul in Paris, probably in too agressive a fashion.

What motivated me in my own life was the fact that I felt I could contribute, even if only to a small extent, to the finding of some of the answers to the many problems with which we have to deal. What created the real difficulties was to convince my clients, whoever they were, that most of the things we do have been motivated in an unclear fashion. We are afraid to recognize that a majority of our decisions concerning trivial or important matters are governed by emotions which are not always easy to recognize. At all costs, we want to retain the illusion that we are guided by rational factors. I don't know where this fear of emotions comes from. It could very well be that they are experienced by us as strange forces which, once set in motion, we cannot control. Rational elements in our daily lives can be changed, stopped or started by irrational arguments. Emotions, however, seem to be, as Plato once described them, "like wild horses."

In almost every study which I have carried through since this all important first encounter in Paris, first in the States and then later on in Europe, and, finally, around the world, I have discovered that once one has discovered the right motivational trigger, it can be utilized to bring about the desire to react. Trying to understand human motivations can be as exciting and curiosity-satisfying as discovering the skull of early man, tens of thousands of years old, or deciphering the code for Egyptian hieroglyphics.

Motivational thinking can be learned but it does not depend solely on the reading of academic books in the field of social sciences. If I were being asked, as I have been many times, what is the best method for learning to understand motivations better, my advice would be to learn to observe. Learn to use your own senses, to mobilize them and exercise them. How many people have practiced *really* listening, *really* seeing, *really* smelling, *really* touching? Doing these things leads to the discovery of new worlds which had not been noticed before. Just as a good hunter does, one has to learn to recognize the slightest traces which might escape other people completely. One has to learn to observe the behavior of other people with these same sharp senses. It helps to take a course in criminolgy. Motivational research is, to a large extent, comparable to being a detective. Why should our schools not include in their curriculum exercises where apparently unimportant things have to be described by pupils? If they really observed with wide open senses, all they would have to do is to put down on paper what they have seen or heard, smelled or touched. Doing this not only sharpens the hunting instinct in the area of human motivations, but simultaneously helps us discover entirely new dimensions of which we were not previously aware.

If we try to make it clear to ourselves what good literature, poetry, and drama really does for us, what their pleasures are, we find it is the writer or the dramatist's skill in describing everyday occurrences in an entirely new fashion. A cloud can be described in a scientific fashion as a concentration of moist masses. Doing this leaves us uninvolved; calling the same clouds threatening, pregnant, floating, brings them to life. In one of my courses on creativity, I include an exercise which consists of asking the participants to describe simple things, things that they can see from their desk or work place, and to do this in such a way that the reader can recreate the original literary effort. I can look at my library, for example, and state that I own thousands of books and prepare a list of the titles. I can also see these books under a completely different kind of light. I discover then that some of these books seem to be tired, are leaning on their neighbors, others have fallen asleep and are taking a long nap. Aristocratic books, fat books, proud books, some of them standing alone as if they wanted nothing to do with their neighbors. I can describe my book shelves in such a way that every book takes on a unique personality. Some of them are arrogant just because they have golden lettering on their backs. There is the modest one which tries to hide. The descriptions which I have used require different lenses through which I have observed. Doing this takes a little more effort but it provides more pleasure to the observer as well as to the reader.

When I was in Dublin, Ireland, I was invited to visit the Mayor. I had the decided conviction that someone had simply handed him a piece of paper with my name and my occupation on it. Maybe there were also a few suggestions to help him carry on an interesting conversation with me for a few minutes. In reality, he had very little knowledge about what I was doing and who I really was. I tried to utilize my hunting tools. I projected myself into his situation and started the conversation by guessing how he must feel at having to see between twenty and thirty people in a day without being quite sure who these people really were. He looked at me, somewhat startled, then chimed in, matching my nonchalant approach, and corrected me. "No, sometimes there are as many as fifty people in a day." He then recognized the admission as a mistake and slipped over into an apology. "Yes, it's true, but I am really interested in the different occupations and types of people whom I meet in this fashion. Maybe both of us have similar occupations." I had succeeded in cheering him out of his lethargy. Maybe I was one of the few who did not talk to him the way one talks to a mayor, whatever that may be, but expressed my understanding and sympathy for his job.

To get back to my discussion with the Vice-Consul in Paris, I tried to demonstrate my understanding for the unusual situation. Apparently I used the right approach. This attempt to project yourself into the other person, although sometimes difficult, is not only important when we are dealing with a potentially life-saving situation, as was the case in Paris, but in every situation where we are trying to sell ourselves, our product, or to establish contact. It is surprising how rarely even the super-salesman makes use of this method. He is so intent upon pushing his merchandise and on demonstrating and dramatizing its superiority that, too often, he does not concern himself with the psychology of the person whom he is trying to sell.

A simple formula which I use as often as possible is to ask myself what it really is that my client, the buyer of my services, really wants to acquire. In most cases, it is much more than simply my services. Often he wants to shift the responsibility of a decision to someone else. He may be confused, too close to his own operation to find a way out of his dilemma. He is caught in a misery of choice, not knowing what marketing decision to take, what image to project, he may simply stand still and not move at all.

Mr. Thompson, the person I had to sell, was also not quite sure he was doing the right thing to really help a young, completely unknown person by bringing him to America. What must have gone on in his mind was: "Suppose I am making a mistake." Somewhere, somehow, since he was still a government employee despite his high title, he might have had unpleasantness because of his decision. On the other hand, and it was exactly this which I used as my motivation, if he had made the right decision, he could always be proud of it. He could point to how good a sense he had had, and that he had not only done something for his country, but that he had also done something important for himself.

In later studies, I was involved in trying to find out why people give to charities and to other well meaning and purposeful organizations. I found that the mistake which was being made in many cases was exactly the same one which the poor salesman makes. They dramatize the disease, the starving children, the flood, and all the other reasons why it is so important to give money. While it is true that we are all interested in these things and that we really want to help, we are all much more interested, without being aware of it or admitting it too easily, in what we are going to get out of making such a charitable contribution. We have found that a major key is the feeling that we are better than we had thought, thus we have improved our self image. At least temporarily we have changed our personality. We have discovered that we can play the good guy just as easily as we can the miser and that it is fun to be able to help other people. We compare it to playing God.

"What can you contribute to all of this?" asked Llewelyn Thompson, the

Vice-Consul. "I have been trained," was my answer, "to draw people out, to find out what really makes them tick. They may say they bought a product because it was more economical to do so. In reality, they may have bought it because it appealed to their snobbism. If I were to ask you, Mr. Vice-Consul, why you married your wife, you would probably give me an intelligent-sounding answer. Maybe you never asked yourself the question. Few of us ever do. You will tell me that you married your wife because you loved her or she cooked well, because she had money, or because she is good looking. But the truth may have been that she flattered you more than other girlfriends did. Maybe she lived closer by. It was more convenient to date her. It could have been a number of reasons, none of them as high-sounding and beautiful as the ones you would have given me as your answer. Psychologists call these superficial answers, rationalizations."

At this point, Mr. Thompson started to smile. The ice had been broken. I proceeded as best I could to explain the importance of using a depth approach which penetrates through the superficial outer layers of human behavior into understanding of the real motivations. With quite a lot of gall, I tried to explain to him that if our statesmen understood human motivation better, maybe we would not have had the problem with Hitler. People might have been intelligent enough to understand why they voted for him or at least followed him. It was their fear, their childish hope for easy solutions. That's why it worked.

I had had luck and had apparently found the right motivation. In many other cases, later on in my professional career, I have used a similar tactic in more or less risky situations. Actually it is a very old sales technique to find out what kinds of advantages the buyer could derive from his actions and to try not only to use superficial arguments but to consider the buyer as a partner. Often this results in his trying to develop additional sales arguments himself. In my situation, too, Mr. Thompson tried to develop my ideas further and to sell me on what he now understood I could possibly do in the States, on how many areas the depth psychology I had just been describing to him could be of value.

It was probably typical of America, at least at that time, that he felt that my visa would not only be of value to me but, maybe in the not too distant future, help his country too.

"Do you know that America is a revolutionary country and builds on new ideas?" How American this idea is becomes clear when one recalls the late President Kennedy developing almost the same formulation in one of his speeches in 1963.

Later on, I developed a method which I call "upside down thinking," meaning that one should ask oneself if the problem could not be approached in an entirely different fashion by standing on your head.

Somehow, somewhere, something clicked in Llewelyn Thompson's mind. "I get it. Um-hum. Ah-ha . . .'' he said. (I used this reaction later on to explain part of the approach of selling and communication, calling it the 'Aha Experience'.) He started to understand, possibly recognizing certain things within himself. "I'll tell you what I'm going to do," he said. "I will do something very unusual. I will send a telegram to Washington and I will sign an affidavit of support for you personally." As I was about to jump up with joy for being such a good psychologist after all, he pushed me back down on the chair. "I shall try," he said, "but there is no guarantee that this will work."

I was in London a few weeks later, again trying to make a decision about India, when I received a telegram from my wife in Paris: "Come back—a wire just arrived from the American consulate." I returned and saw Mr. Thompson who held out a dossier to me on which was written a big "O.K." I can still see it now, but very honestly I can't remember what color it was, nor did I care; but I knew what "O.K." meant. "Well, we did it," he said. It was interesting for me, as an example of correct communication, that this time he did not speak about himself alone or about me, but incorporated himself into the success by using the term "we."

We went through all the formalities without any difficulty. We had gotten our visas as immigrants to the U.S. Had I used the proper motivation? Had I sold Mr. Thompson? I guess so. Had I formulated the next decades of my life in this one hour meeting? Retrospectively, I must say—YES. Having been pushed into deep frustration which smart psychologists know is very often translated into anger, I had learned a very vital technique, a technique which changed or even saved my life. Needless to say, I did not accept the job in India. Rather than an Indian, I became an American.

We had our visas. Our relatives had in the meantime written another letter. We had asked them for money for the voyage—impossible. Fortunately, an organization helped us. We got two tickets on the De Grasse (a French boat which was later sunk by torpedoes during the war). By that time it was September, 1938.

We didn't have much to pack, since our stay in Paris, although it lasted for over a year, had been planned right from the beginning as a kind of in between stop. Not very long ago we were again in Paris and re-lived those last hours with sad memories. The few months that I was in Paris without Hedy I received a lot of help from relatives who had emigrated from Berlin long before us. We tried in vain to convince our cousin and his wife that, while they had escaped their destiny in Germany, they still would not be safe in Europe. We advised them to get out, no matter where, even it were Argentina, where my cousin had had a job offer. "I'm tired of running," he said. He later perished in a concentration camp. His wife survived by being hidden by a Catholic priest in the south of France. Her son served in Algeria in the French army. He married a German, gentile girl.

The girl's background is such that she could very well have been involved in the death of his father. He had enough freedom from prejudice to learn to forget Hitler's racial mania and to see a human being.

After our eight-day crossing, three surprises awaited us in New York. Throughout the trip we were worried that the war might break out at any moment and that our ship might be torpedoed. Most of us kept quite calm and simply refused to think about such possibilities. We had escaped and nothing else mattered. First of all, we arrived in the middle of one of the most devastating hurricanes, so typical, as I found out later on, for this season in America. The second surprise was that news had just been announced that peace in our time had been established in Munich by Neville Chamberlain, thanks to a magnanimous dictator. We had to undergo quite a vigorous examination by immigration officials who made you feel that indeed you had arrived in the promised land, but only if you were a perfect specimen in every respect would you be allowed to land and to settle. Suddenly, a man about 50 years old approached me and patted me on the shoulder. As I whirled around, he shook my hand, kissed me on both cheeks and said, "You must be a Dichter." We never quite determined how he knew. He said, "Well, there was something in your face, in your mannerism, and the way you walked that made me risk a kiss on your cheek." We then got our third, and most pleasant, surprise; a whole gang of Dichters were waiting to greet us! They had been notified by a charitable organization which was set up to take care of newcomers.

Possibly an unpleasant discovery for my American family, after their first pleasure, although they would never admit it, was that we did not arrive the way they expected refugees to arrive. We wore no kerchiefs, no rags, but well-fitting Parisian clothes. Adding to the insult was the discovery that we both spoke English pretty well. They did not know that we had only one hundred dollars between us, but we neither looked nor behaved like pity-inviting, poor new arrivals. Worse, we knew all the landmarks in Manhattan and could, with the help of a map previously studied, advise our "Uncle" Charles, as we called him (though he was our second or third cousin), on how best to get back to Stamford, Connecticut, from the pier. We spent a few days with them, awed by their clapboard house which, to us Europeans, was equivalent to a private villa that only some of the wealthiest people in Austria could afford. Uncle Charlie was a general medical practitioner, doing all right but far from being wealthy, well loved by the whole community.

5 I Was Just Lucky, I Guess

Hardly a week passes that somebody doesn't ask me how I got into motivational research. Searching for motives is the profession of every author, politician, in fact of almost all people. So how about me? The way they put it very often tempts me to answer with an old joke: when the call girl was asked the same question, she answered, "I was just lucky, I guess," a sort of defense against the bourgeois assumption that "such a nice girl" should not carry on so and even enjoy such immoral activity.

Here we were, practically no money, welcomed by nice American relatives who really didn't know quite what to do with us. Obviously, even in 1938, we could not live very long on a hundred dollars, which was our total fortune.

I note motives sitting in front of the TV or reading a novel. We are all interpreting much more openly than ever before. Motive-hunting has become a popular sport. Curiosity is probably one of my major motivations for the continuation of my activities. "What is the relationship between modern man and technology?" "How can we get Japanese consumers to buy more of their own products and export less?" Our office in Tokyo concentrates on this question.

Another problem was to find out how builders could be convinced to use ready-made forms for concrete. Not too long ago, I was supposed to conduct a study on the psychology of eating habits of dogs. This was, by the way, one of the few cases where I had to go beyond the motivations of humans. I had to study dogs and the relationships between dogs and their owners. I have collected a list of over 7000 such questions.

Nineteen thirty-eight and no money. I landed a job with a market research organization. I'd looked them up in the phone book and was hired. What was my first assignment? The very same one that had landed me in jail in Vienna: analyzing milk drinking habits, this time of Americans. My first salary was thirty dollars a week. I didn't know whether it was much or little. It was the first American money that I had earned. Hedy, through the help of Rabbi de Sola Pool, to whom Mrs. Loeb introduced us, started giving concerts in various synagogues and signed up her first piano students. The first crisis was over.

Several weeks later, my boss, who loved to speak French with me (at that time I was more fluent in French than in English), raised my salary to fifty dollars a week. This small research organization had assembled a number of refugee scientists whom they could hire at a relatively low rate. Among the people who worked there were many who later became quite well known. They had contacts with Professor Paul Lazarsfeld who has since died but who had moved to the States two or three years before this period. Another employee of this company was Dr. Hans Zeisel who, later on with Dr. Herzog (both of them Viennese), was employed by McCann Erikson, a large advertising agency.

We moved to our own apartment in a neighborhood which became known as The Fourth Reich because of the large number of Central European refugees who settled there. Later on it became the center of a new social immigration, that of blacks and Puerto Ricans. I still remember how much I was impressed by our doorman in a uniform, the fact that there was an elevator, and the lobby, at least, was quite elegant. Our apartment itself was small but clean, not much of a view, but it was our first real American home. Just as in Paris, we surrounded ourselves with crates which we decorated to resemble very modern furniture.

It did not take very long before our second crisis started. My boss called me in and informed me that he could not pay my salary and asked if I would be willing to work at half the rate for a while until he had recovered? I agreed. It was a very ingenious employer-employee relationship approach. I had started with thirty, had my salary almost doubled, and ended up making twenty-five dollars, five dollars less than when I started.

Was I under stress? Yes. I have learned on previous occasions, and it has helped me a great deal, to combine worry (and I am a worrier) with action. This will partly explain how I got into motivational research.

After having worked for a few weeks with Market Analysts, Inc. (that was the name of the company I was with) I had come to realize even more that what they were doing could not be called scientific or reliable. They developed questionnaires, similar to ones that are still being used today, which simply ask people: "Why do you or don't you drink milk?" As I had struggled with this problem for a long time, trying to figure out how one can ask a person why he or she does something without running the risk of receiving rationalizations as answers, I started a battle with my employer. He appreciated my French, but he did not appreciate this attack on the establishment.

"You refugees and greenhorns are all alike. You barely master the language and off you go, trying to change things."

"I thought this was particularly appreciated in this country," was my angry reply. "Do things differently and build a better mouse-trap." I don't remember his answer, but I know he didn't understand.

This battle has never ceased. Again and again I find such superficial questionnaires; often I use them in my seminars, to explain to my students how difficult it is to convince people that answers to direct questions are grossly misleading. Recently I lost an assignment because the company simply could not understand this kind of reasoning. It was an organization which competed with the official Post Office. They were interested in convincing companies to use them for rapid deliveries since they had their own fleet of planes. It was expensive to use them, but the service was much faster and more reliable. Anyhow, I lost the job. The research organization which had developed a normal questionnaire, which was supposed to be used among employees asking them directly why they preferred one form of delivery to another, won out.

My way to approach a problem is to first develop hypotheses in relation to the motivations which influenced people who used such non-postal services. My first suspicion was that these employees have, in most instances, a routine job. The possibility of a new way of transporting their mail appeared to them as a dangerous change in their routine. This meant that the company should have removed this fear of change and newness. I developed the further hypothesis that there are people and companies interested in impressing the recipient of the mail with the great rapidity of the transportation. I felt that many of these ideas were very good and intelligent, but apparently they were too much for my potential client.

My first boss was apparently equally frightened by my new ideas. I decided, therefore, to act. I asked around as to what companies had difficulties. Somebody pointed out that *Esquire* Magazine was not doing too well. I picked six companies, *Esquire* among them, an advertising agency, and a few others, and wrote them a very simple letter. I still have it in my files.

"I am a young psychologist from Vienna and I have some interesting new ideas which can help you be more successful, effective, sell more and communicate better with your potential clients."

My faith in America was restored. I received four replies. Not bad as a return for a mail-order approach. I went to see the people at *Esquire*. I was introduced to Rudolph von Stiepock. A peculiar name, I thought, sounds German. Sure enough, a few minutes after we shook hands, he switched into German, having recognized my accent, and welcomed me as a fellow countryman.

I got my first assignment: Why do men read *Esquire*? At that time, *Esquire* resembled much more today's *Playboy* or *Penthouse*. How was I going to find out? Well, I explained my idea of research. I would go out and talk at great length to a number of men, but I would not ask them why they did or did not read *Esquire*. I would simply let them tell me their associations, their experiences, their ideas and thoughts while talking and thumbing through the magazine.

What was the great discovery I made? Something that everybody knew but nobody dared put down on paper. The major attraction of *Esquire* was the photographs of naked girls. Not as naked as today's Playmates, but enough for 1939.

I presented my findings during a meeting where twenty-five salesmen of advertising space were eagerly waiting for the message from the Viennese messiah. The sales manager was not satisfied. "You have not finished all your research, Doc, have you? Are you absolutely sure of your findings?" I was. I could not understand why they did not want to accept the simple truth. I discovered it was not the facts themselves—which they had, of course, guessed—which bothered them. They simply did not know what to do with these facts. How could one sell additional advertising space with such a story, even if it was scientifically validated? I realized it was really up to me to help them utilize my findings, over and above just giving them facts. I developed the following rationale: Especially when men look at pictures of nudes, they are visually oriented. Their pupils are opened more widely, they are more attentive to visual stimuli.

"Well," said Mr. Weintraub, the sales manager, "what are we going to do with that?"

"Clear," I answered. "Once you are visually oriented, you also pay more attention to advertisements. It pays to advertise in *Esquire* because you are dealing with readers whose eyes are wider open than when they read other publications. They are visually oriented."

I was sent back to do additional interviews to demonstrate that this relationship indeed existed. We did not use any physiological instruments, but by letting people talk and comment on what they were doing while they were reading *Esquire*, we could show that the ads, too, as long as they fitted into the total personality of the publication, aroused increased visual interest.

The word "image" was developed by me around that time. I was searching for a translation of the German word, *Gestalt*, which means configuration, totality, the melody. The melody consists of more than the individual notes. The way they are arranged and put together creates different melodies, a different *Gestalt*. Nudes increased visual awareness which carried over to the total "image" of *Esquire* and made the ads more effective. Mr. Weintraub suddenly understood. "Terrific," he said. This approach was used for quite a while by *Esquire* as a sales tool.

But the real story begins with Mr. von Stiepock. The assignment he gave me could have turned into a disaster for both of us. He was impressed with the way I salvaged the situation. We met several times. He had an idea which turned out to be a turning point in my life. He and I were to go to Detroit and approach the Chrysler Corporation which had considerable problems at that time with the newly launched Plymouth car.

Before I could go to Detroit, I wanted to fulfill another of my assignments as a result of the four responses to my letters. It was for Ivory soap and the Compton Advertising Agency. I explained to the account executive who received me that, instead of asking people why they used or did not use a particular brand of soap, I was going to analyze the role that soap plays in the American culture. I'm not sure whether he quite understood what I was trying to tell him, but it impressed him enough so that he agreed to pay me two dollars per depth interview. I conducted about a hundred such interviews. I obtained permission from the YMCA to talk to young men and women, not about Ivory soap, but about their bathing habits. Among many other things, I found that the Saturday night bath was still a very important ritual. I'm sure that all the people I interviewed took one, if not two baths every day. The young girls told me, very innocently, that before they went out on a date, they bathed in a particularly careful fashion. When I was curious, they said, "well, you never can tell . . .". I found out that such things as lathering oneself completely and then letting the shower water gradually take off the lather from one's body, was not only pleasant, but had some very peculiar undertones of undressing and erotic pleasure. It was a discovery of one's own body. One of the few occasions when the puritanical American was allowed to caress himself or herself was while applying soap. My knowledge of mythology came in handy. The result was an advertising campaign: "Be Smart and Get a Fresh Start with Ivory Soap." Nothing very earthshaking, but it was based on the recognition that when you take a bath, you "wash your troubles away." You cleanse yourself not only physically, but also psychologically. It was the old story of the ritual bath, the person who feels that he has sinned soaps himself in hot water to get rid of all his psychological dirt and guilt feelings. In the musical, *South Pacific*, there is a song, "I'm Gonna Wash That Man Right Out of My Hair." It is one of many examples of the deeper meaning of a bath or a shampoo.

My next two hundred dollars came from a demand by the account executive to write a report translating all these mysterious depth interviews into practical ideas. I did this to his satisfaction and, in fact, my ideas were used for several years.

Now I was ready to join Rudy von Stiepock on our trip to Detroit, having these two first successes—the *Esquire* and Ivory soap studies—in our sales bags. We didn't talk much about how we were going to split any profits since we weren't sure there was going to be anything that we could split. We drove all night in Rudy's car (I never had owned one), and promptly had an accident. Nothing much happened, although we were delayed. When we finally arrived in Detroit, at Rudy's suggestion we registered in a fairly expensive hotel, charged to me. Rudy had some contacts at Chrysler and this was the reason we had come. The president of the DeSota Division agreed to see us. He listened, was not particularly impressed, but interested enough to suggest we call on the Plymouth Division, which, as he put it, had real problems.

We went to see Mr. Eddins. He, too, listened but he was genuinely interested. I was to study the role of the car in the American culture. He showed me a study that they had done, where they had asked people why they bought the same make of car that they had owned before. The figure at that time was about 64 per cent—I still remember it. I also remembered a course in logic at the University of Vienna and became suspicious because the answer Chrysler had received to their question was, "I bought the car because I was satisfied with the one I owned before." This was perfectly logical, and a perfectly good answer. The trouble was that it was too logical. It was a rationalization, and it was, furthermore, what I had learned to recognize in my course of logic as "tautology" or, putting it more simply, circular evidence.

For years, psychiatry and many other sciences have suffered from the same kind of scientific disease. Why is somebody afraid of narrow places? "Because he suffers from claustrophobia," they answered. Clear enough? How do you know that he suffers from claustrophobia? Because he is afraid of narrow places . . . and round and round she goes. All you're doing is placing a label on a phenomenon and it does not get explained.

Mr. Eddins was able to understand when I used this parallel and applied it to his research. "We wasted our money then." "I guess so," was my answer. "In addition you can't really use that finding," I pointed out to him, "since the Plymouth car has just come on the market. You can't tell people they will be satisfied by reminding them of the Plymouth they had owned before since there was no previous Plymouth car!"

In a subsequent meeting a few hours later, we were joined by Baron von

Munchhausen—his real name. He was Rudy's contact at Chrysler. (In a way, the whole development of events was almost like the fabled Munchhausen, a character in German literature known for his 'fantastic' stories.) This was 1939. Many Americans don't realize that Detroit housed quite a number of Nazi sympathizers then. The fact that I was Jewish didn't bother them. As a matter of fact, it probably came in very handy.

Mr. Eddins asked both these gentlemen whether they would mind waiting outside while he continued to talk with me. They were a bit puzzled, but they left. Mr. Eddins then turned to me and asked, "How did you get hold of these two creatures?" I wasn't quite sure what he meant by that, but it became clear quite quickly. The "creatures" were quite well known to the Chrysler Corporation. They owed them money and had tried to sell them other things before. Upon my assurance that I had only met one of them an hour ago and the other one a short time before, Mr. Eddins believed me. He told me that he was going to take care of these two gentlemen. I would have to pay them part of my fee, should I get the job, but I should not have anything further to do with them.

Next day the advertising agency was invited to join our discussions. I made my presentation and was given the job. The fee was $3,000. But there was a mini-disaster—a strike—and the study was delayed. In the anticipation of this assignment, I had quit my job so I was temporarily unemployed. A few weeks later, however, I was asked to meet with Mr. Getchell, the head of the New York advertising agency with the same name. I had to sell him. Apparently I must have, because I started working on the new assignment.

I interviewed about a hundred motorists and made a few interesting discoveries. Some of them have become classics. The in-depth interviews revealed that men would not admit that women influenced their car-buying habits, but they surely did. The result was to place ads in women's magazines for the first time in car history. I also found that two percent of car sales consisted of convertibles. Again, quite logically, Chrysler Corporation decided to spend part

The alluring convertible.

The Plymouth ad after the study.

of its advertising budget on pushing convertibles. My approach to my work and to many aspects of my life has always been to ask "is it really so?" "Could it not be different?" I became suspicious of this low figure. I suggested an experiment that would place a convertible in one showroom, a sedan in another, and count the number of people who would step into one showroom or the other. What I discovered was that at least six or seven times as many people walked into the showroom where the convertible was exhibited. The conclusion was obvious— the convertible had much more power of attraction than just the two percent. The new ads, based on my research, now showed the convertible prominently. I also found that very young men bought convertibles frequently, and more often before marriage than afterwards. There was another peak of the purchase of convertibles, which at first I could not understand. This occurred when a man had passed 45 or 50. The explanation was found in the symbolic significance of a convertible. It represents youth—the wind blows through your hair, you feel much closer to the road and the landscape. Many men have a secret wish for a mistress. This wish becomes stronger as they get older. Buying a convertible represented the realization of this wish, without the expense and the guilt feeling of having a live mistress.

Of course, most bought the sedan: the "wife," comfortable and safe. The convertible, the "mistress," youthful, was the dreamer. It was psychologically desirable and effective, therefore, to use a convertible as the sales attraction, the "bait." The sales ratio of sedans to convertibles stayed the same. Today, due to air-conditioned cars, the convertible has been replaced by the sports car.

This story was published in many magazines and newspapers all over the world. It still happens quite often. Not too long ago the Austrian Consul General, meeting our son, reminded him of this true anecdote. The fact that a journalist picks up such an example is in itself proof that the interpretation is correct. The representative of the mass media has the feeling that this comparison is a correct one, because he discovers within it his own similar forms of wishful thinking. In many instances we can recognize ourselves in such stories. We laugh about it; but we are really laughing about ourselves.

The convertibles are not as popular as before. We find the same tendency as far as sports cars are concerned. This desire for rejuvenation is a very basic motivation. Many years later I discovered a similar form of wish in connection with men's clothing. I dubbed our whole public relations campaign, which was developed by me for Dupont, the "Peacock Revolution," about which I shall talk later on. We had found that many men dressed in a rather drab fashion, but needed only a little encouragement to discover color and lively patterns. Men, particularly at a later age, are more easily influenced in this direction. This hunger for color expressed itself also in the almost complete disappearance of the white shirt for a period.

Discovering a manifestation of human motivation in one area often permits the application of the same understanding and insight in quite a number of other areas. When faced with the necessity to defend myself against the peculiar kind of accusation that in order to practice motivational research, one really has to be especially gifted—"Not everyone can learn this kind of thinking and creativity" —my answer is that one can learn thought patterns and how to apply them in many different ways.

6 How I Almost Lost My Viennese Accent

Before finishing my Plymouth survey, the advertising agency which handled the account, J. Stirling Getchell, made me an offer. This time my job was to analyze every conceivable product and the motivations for buying or not buying it.

J. Stirling, or, as we called him, "Getch," had discovered psychology. He asked me to tear out all the pages of books dealing with human motivations and clip them together and put them on his desk. A strange request. I tried desperately to explain to him that motivations are much more like a clockwork, an engine. They could not be lined up in a disjointed fashion. You would have all the parts but would have lost the whole, the interrelationship. Maslow and other psychologists have attempted to establish hierarchies of human needs. They are partially correct but what they often overlook is, indeed, the interdependence of our needs and their mutual influence upon each other.

No sooner had I started working for Getch than my name appeared in public, in a small newsletter called *Tide*. Playing upon my Austrian background, the headline read, "Herr Doktor Dichter" and it continued to tell about my work for the Chrysler Corporation and the first discovery.

The power of publicity became obvious to me when my picture and a two column article appeared in *Time* Magazine. The caption read, "Viennese

Psychologist Discovers Gold Mine for Chrysler Corporation." I soon received numerous offers from other advertising agencies who wanted to participate in this new bonanza. Getch called me into his office and gave me excellent advice: "You're on your way to becoming well known, if not famous. This is one of the most dangerous things that can happen to a young man. Don't let it go to your head." He raised my salary to $150 a week which was quite remarkable in 1940 for a man 33 years old. We rented a house in Forest Hills with an option to buy, which we exercised fairly soon.

When the Plymouth study was half finished, Getch and I, along with a few other people from the agency, went to Detroit to present our progress report. The agency received a million and a half dollars in additional advertising contracts, and I a bonus of $600 with which I bought my first car. What I consider to be real "chutzpah" now is that I had almost finished the study on the motivations of car buying without having owned a car in all my life. But then, a physician doesn't have to have all the diseases in order to be able to understand them or cure them. While I was making my presentation in Detroit, in one of those silly combinations of pride and negligence, I realized I had laced my shoes too tightly and I didn't dare to interrupt my presentation to loosen them. Within an hour after the presentation, my foot started swelling; it spread to my leg, and by the time I got back to N.Y., I had developed a full case of phlebitis. By coincidence, my boss also developed phlebitis. At that time, penicillin had just been discovered. I was treated by Dr. Dudley White, the same physician who treated President Eisenhower. My boss paid the bill. I was in bed for about eight weeks with instructions not to move. As I remember, the physician told me that if I did move it would be about as dangerous as standing on one leg on top of the Empire State Building. This was certainly a very colorful way of putting it. I survived the phlebitis attack, though I had one or two more bouts several years later. Getch wasn't so lucky. He died when the disease hit him a second time.

While working for the agency I developed a small staff. We organized our interviewing techniques in a more disciplined fashion. I was given a secretary for whom I did not have very much work in the beginning. She kept sharpening my pencils. I was not quite Americanized enough, although she was good looking and young, to express my interest in her in a more direct fashion.

One day she told me about her brother-in-law, Dr. Henry Lee Smith. He taught phonetics at Columbia University. When she introduced me to him, he asked whether I would like to lose my Viennese accent. We debated whether this was really desirable for a psychologist starting out. We finally agreed that he would at least give me power to eliminate it whenever I wanted to and reproduce it again when it seemed to be opportune. The best way to describe what he did with me is to compare it to the kind of job that Prof. Higgins did with Liza in *My Fair Lady*. He recorded my voice, gave me cards on which he noted the typical mistakes that German-speaking people make in pronunciation and intonation—pronouncing the "l" in a flat way, not rolling the "r's" all the way in the back of your throat, but using the tip of your tongue too often in order to produce the correct sound. And, of course, not to forget the devil of the English language, the "th." After experimenting and working with him for about two months, I indeed had almost lost my Viennese accent. During these travails, we debated what kind of American accent I should have. (We agreed that it should be an American one.) Dr. Smith's specialty, which he demonstrated on radio programs, was to be able to discover the local origin of the person—whether he came from Boston or Texas—sometimes in an almost frightening fashion. He could even tell whether this person came from South Boston or from North Boston by their accent. We agreed that I would have an all-American accent. That way people would not be able to quite locate my origin, but would not be suspicious of my foreign background.

During the three years or so that I remained with the advertising agency, I worked on a wide variety of problems. One of them concerned the psychology of smoking. Considering myself an anthropologist, I decided to use film clippings. Getch gave me a couple of hundred dollars and I went out and became a roving photographic reporter. I still have the film. I went to Rockefeller Plaza and photographed people in a candid camera fashion while they were watching the ice skating and smoking at the same time. Some people warmed their hands on the cigarette which they held in an inverted fashion. Another type smoked and chewed gum at the same time. Some Western Union boys whom I caught in the act were lighting each other's cigarettes in a secretive fashion while goofing off and standing behind the corner.

Observing human behavior in this fashion became a hobby and a scientific discovery trip for me. Why did people smoke? Obviously not just because of the addiction to nicotine, but for many other reasons, too. Tightening your lips around a cigarette gives you a feeling of security. It was like battening down the hatches when getting ready for battle. Therefore, cigarette smoking was a way of combatting stress. You were forced to breathe more or less regularly when inhaling and take a deep breath; thus, despite the now known dangerous effects of smoking, the immediate advantage of it was to help people relax because of the more rhythmic breathing habit that smoking produced. Smoking, of course, is oral satisfaction, Among the more outrageous kinds of conclusions that I drew is that holding a cigarette in your mouth is comparable to sucking at the nipples of a gigantic world breast and deriving from it the same type of satisfaction and tranquilizing effect that the baby does when being nursed.

Going on a motivational safari forces you to look for explanations in an uninhibited fashion. Suppose you had landed on an unknown island and discovered a primitive tribe and you filmed their habit of putting dried and cut up plants into a wrapper which they then lit up and placed between their lips, breathing the smoke from this burning, pencil-like rod at regular intervals. You might further put down in your notes that the town enjoyed blowing out the smoke—that they were not as much interested in carrying out this activity when they could not see the smoke—that the way in which they finally extinguished and crushed this plant rod was quite revealing as far as the personality of the individual was concerned. Some did it in a very gentle and deliberate fashion, others almost in an irate crushing, aggressive way. Such an analysis would certainly make a very acceptable erudite anthropological report. When you are writing a similar report about the motivations of smoking in our modern world you become suspect.

When studying the use of soap, I again used the film technique and discovered that while the advertisers stressed cleanliness, the consumers quite obviously, particularly when children and not too inhibited yet, enjoyed dirt at least as much as cleanliness. What is the basis of this statement? Watch children when they dry their hands. They look expectantly at the towel. When they discover dirty marks on the towel, they are, in an only mildly concealed form, elated. They produced an imprint! When we wash our hands after having done some particularly dirty garden work or cleaning our cars, we grownups, if we can only be honest about it, do enjoy the dirt rolling off our hands. Have you ever watched people wading in mud? When we blow our noses and feel unobserved we quite often look at the results of our effort in the handkerchief. The same thing happens in the bathroom.

I kept on collecting observations and insight into human motivations, slowly building up a library. It served the agency for the development of many successful advertising campaigns. The fact that it could be put to this use was, however, almost incidental to me, and still is.

One of the last studies I did while I was under Getchell concerned radio commercials. What was their role? By looking upon them, in a broader context, as a form of intermission, I arrived at new understandings. I went back to drama. Do we want, if we have seen violent action in the first act, another type of violent action continued during the intermission period, or would we prefer a period of calmness in order to be ready for the murders which happen, not only in Shakespearean dramas, in the second act? By looking at the commercial, not just as a sales effort, but in the total framework, I became aware of such factors as mood, something that I call "rhythmic complementation"—the relationship between the rhythm of the preceding and succeeding programs. These studies on commercials were published in a book by Paul Lazarsfeld, who was my statistics teacher in Vienna and had come to the States about a year before me. One of his articles on the art of asking "Why?" had greatly influenced me. He used to refer to me as one of his two star pupils. The other one was his wife, Dr. Herta

Herzog, who for many years worked in motivational research and market research for McCann-Erickson. In his article, Dr. Lazarsfeld explained that when you are asking "Why?" the word can be interpreted in several ways. What was it about the product or situation that influenced you? What were the channels through which you heard about the product (radio, newspapers, word-of-mouth)? What was it within yourself that motivated you? What needs did you have to buy, or to act, or to vote in a particular fashion? The little word "why" can be misunderstood in at least three different fashions. As I found out later on in many of my studies, there are many other aspects of misunderstanding. I had to add quite a bit to this approach from the recognition that not only are there possible logical misunderstandings, but also psychological ones stemming from our subconscious.

This study on radio commercials brought me to the attention of Dr. Frank Stanton who was at that time Research Director of CBS. Being himself a psychologist, he appreciated my somewhat unorthodox approach to the function and effectiveness of radio commercials. More than that, he told me that whenever I needed a job I should simply call on him—he would have one ready for me. A few months after Getch's death, this is indeed what happened. Frank Stanton kept his promise, and I was put on as a program psychologist by CBS and stayed there throughout the war years, expanding my motivational hunt first through the analysis of the reasons why twenty million American women listened to soap operas day after day.

Another one of my confrontations developed very soon after I had concluded the first part of my research. The purely statistical approach was utilized by a group of people working as consultants for CBS, such as Dr. Robert Merton, Dr. Lazarsfeld, and Carl Rogers. Their approach and mine represented two fundamentally different ones. They took a group of approximately one thousand regular listeners to soap operas and a group of non-listeners and analyzed in every conceivable detail the supposed differences between these two groups. Their study revealed practically none. My approach was to interview, with the approval of Frank Stanton, nearly two hundred soap opera listeners. I was interested in finding out why these two hundred women listened and what they really got out of it. My conclusion was that they learned lessons in living. I also utilized content analysis. I tried to understand what the basic pattern of a typical soap opera was. Almost every one of them had what I called a "female führer"—Joyce Jordan, M.D., Ma Perkins, and similar dominant female figures—who acted as advisors in these sketches. They were surrounded by a host of weak, undecided characters who, from installment to installment, got themselves into various, sometimes sexual, sometimes marital, but hardly ever economic, problems. The listeners identified themselves with these weak characters and in a vicarious way received the same advice that Ma Perkins would dish out to her dramatic subjects in need of help. The only thing wrong with this approach was that the lessons were usually wrong. If a blonde interfered with a marriage, she was knocked off in one form or another and the couple lived happily ever after until the next crisis occurred.

What was even more dangerous was my attempt to see a parallel between this approach and fascism. There, too, we are dealing with a caudillo, a führer, a duce, a strong leader who is the father of his people and pretends to be able to solve all their problems. They can relax. They don't have to do any worrying themselves. He is going to take care of it. The only difference was that in these soap operas, long before women's lib, this role was being performed by a woman. Fascism is not just a political phenomenon. It is primarily a psychological one. It is much more comfortable to be able to rely on someone else for the solutions to one's problems than trying to solve them oneself. These were the results and was I in hot water! Frank called me and gave me a psychological cold shower. "I may agree with you," he said, "that the soap operas are potentially dangerous, but do you realize that our salaries are being paid from the income from the sponsors (most of them soap companies—thus the name soap operas)?"

I interviewed Milton Berle, trying to analyze various types of comedy, and attempting to understand that a comedian very often acts as a psychotherapist. He can make jokes about marriage, we can laugh about them and find release for our own anxieties and hostilities. My work became more and more interesting.

When the war broke out I volunteered, not being particularly fond of Germany. With my knowledge of German, it was relatively easy for me to analyze Hitler's speeches and, what is more important, to develop counter-propaganda. I analyzed, while at CBS, the problems of returning veterans and war widows, and helped in the search for new radio and TV programs, which had just come into their own. I even went as far as taking a course in order to become a fledgling TV producer. I failed miserably. I could never keep the sequence of commands straight such as, "Take camera one, take camera two," so I finally decided this was not for me. I stuck, instead, to the analysis of TV programs and the development of new ones.

I was not a very good employee. CBS, a very large organization, could not keep me fully occupied. I had started to become better and better known. I continually received invitations to talk and quite frequently these talks involved controversies with the defenders of the realm of conventional statistical market research. Later on, they would be dubbed as "nose counters" while I represented the qualitative approach—going into depth, using small samples instead of large, representative samples. I became more and more convinced that understanding and knowing why two or three hundred people did what they did was much more revealing than asking one thousand or two thousand people often misunderstood and misinterpreted questions and then tabulating the answers as if they were the infallible truth. The worship of percentages had been held up to me as a typical American affliction by Lazarsfeld. He predicted I would never be successful with any of my new-fangled ideas. They were too European. Luckily, he was wrong. The famous anthropologist, Dr. Margaret Mead, whom I had met very early after my arrival in this country, had made it clear to me that what I was really interested in and actually was practicing was what she would call cultural anthropology. "I have been studying the natives in New Guinea and Samoa and you have become fascinated with the natives of New York. We use comparable methods to the ones that you have discovered in your work."

Through publicity and seminars and lectures, I received various assignments outside of my job. Since I wasn't a very faithful employee, and not particularly busy, I carried through a number of these assignments while being paid by CBS. I was a fast worker and thus always had extra time on my hands after having finished the assignments resulting from my job. One day, I had asked for a meeting with Dr. Stanton; I wanted a raise, although I was doing quite well by now. When I came to his office, he had a number of studies lying on his desk. He had obviously read them shortly before. When I pointed to them, he said, "Yes. By the way, this is the sort of research we ought to be doing here. It's fascinating! It's really a whole new approach." Since I recognized them as my own which I had done partly on the outside, partly on CBS's time, I felt a little embarrassed, but finally my pride took over and I asked Frank to open the studies again and look at the inside page. He did. "You wrote those studies!" he exclaimed. I complained bitterly that I had to do them on the outside because my boss, Mr. Churchill, at CBS, did not understand or did not want to understand my more psychological approach in research. Nothing that could not be adorned with a percentage was real to him.

A few months later we had another meeting, Frank and I. Again, it concerned the raise and my unhappiness with my job in not being able to carry through the kind of research that really interested me. My hunt for motivations had widened. Stanton suggested that I was a typical entrepreneur and no matter what he might do I would probably never be quite happy being an employee. "Have you ever thought of starting out on your own?" he asked me. I had, but I had been afraid of it. He then proposed a very neat solution. "I will give you a contract for a year as our consultant. That will tide you over."

He had confronted me with the necessity of making a vital decision. Where was I going to find an office, a secretary, clients? By forcing me to face my fears, he helped me to overcome them. I quit, did consultant work for not quite a year for CBS and, sooner than I thought, I was on my own—trying to be different, establishing myself and my Institute for Research for Mass Motivation. I used brown stationery and brown ink. When I received my first contract for Columbia

Records, the person who gave me the assignment told me that he was impressed by my unusual stationery and the total brownness of my approach. My first office (I can't even remember the address now) was a back room without windows located in somebody else's office. Within three or four months, I could afford a real office. My first secretary helped me overcome hesitations by showing her belief in me. She offered to work for nothing until I could pay her ("But then you have to pay me a good salary!"). She was ready to take this risk. After a while, I dropped the word "Mass" because it sounded too much like the People's Republic and some people felt or misunderstood that what I was doing was in some mysterious way politically subversive.

Looking back at these first few years of my successes, mastering and overcoming the possible handicap of a Viennese or Austrian accent was only a minor achievement. It convinced me again that many more things than we normally assume depend on motivations and less on basic ability. If Kissinger really wanted to get rid of his German accent, or Kurt Waldheim his Austrian one, they could do so. An interesting part of this motivational lesson is that the unlearning and learning of new habits and attitudes should start as early as possible.

7 Insecurity—The Key to Success

Mr. Updegraff, a good friend of mine for many years, re-discovered me after reading an article in the *Harvard Business Review* in which I stated that an advertising agency is in reality a psychological laboratory. He was consultant at that time for Lever Brothers. He proceeded forthwith, as many others have done since, to analyze me. "Ernest," he said, "don't ever lose your insecurity. It is the secret of your success. Because you yourself are insecure, you can understand other people and discover what makes them tick."

Thinking back, this insecurity probably dates back not just to my poverty as a child which played an important role but, as seen from today's higher tower of retrospection, a silly one—my red hair. In Europe, where I grew up, I was usually the only one, not only in my class but within the whole school, who had red hair. Had I grown up in Scotland, I would have been just an average boy. This way I stood out—but in a negative way. I could only compensate by becoming "outstanding' in a positive way. I had to be different, or make an asset of the fact that I already was different. I had the fear, which turned out to be quite erroneous, that no girl would ever look at me. At the age of 9 or 10, I dyed my hair. When it grew back red underneath, I must have been quite a sight. After a few months of probably being one of the first child customers of hair dye, I gave up.

Theodor Reik wrote a book on *How One Becomes a Psychologist*. He analyzed that by thinking that you are different, you start to observe other people to find out if they notice that you are different. Trying to analyze their reactions for traces of approval or disapproval, we learn to observe other people. It is an ingenious, although never proven, theory explaining how some people do become involved in psychology. It certainly applied to me since I felt my red hair made me different.

Most scientific research starts with creativity. You observe a phenomenon; suddenly something strikes you as being significant. One of my early motivational studies was conducted for a manufacturer of pipe tobacco. Having become a "people watcher," I made a habit for a week or two of watching all pipe smokers—the way they opened their pouch, stuffed their pipe, lit it, puffed at it. Almost every one of them then did and still does smell his tobacco first. Does pipe tobacco, then, serve as a form of masculine perfume? Do men really prefer, in most cases, aromatic tobacco? Our subsequent study proved this to be the point. For quite a while the company ran a successful campaign built on this discovery of the motivation of pipe smokers. Our study also showed that most men, while liking this disguised perfume, were embarrassed to admit this too feminine attitude. The ad which I recommended said, "obviously masculine aromatic tobacco." Men were thus given the "permission" to use tobacco they really liked without having to be embarrassed about its good smell. Of course, at the present time, there has been a complete reversal . . . men are exuberant purchasers of good-smelling after-shave lotions and colognes.

Once we discover such an interesting type of repeated behavior (as in the pipe smoker), we proceed through lengthy interviews resembling a form of mini-psychoanalysis, to interview anywhere from a hundred to three hundred people selected from various groups—depending on the problem— in order to prove or disprove our original hypothesis. To a large extent, what I am doing is cultural anthropology—observing the very often peculiar and hilarious customs of human beings. Why do women paint their lips? their nails? put various types of metals into their ear lobes? Why do men wear colored pieces of cloth around their neck without any obvious practical function? Why do people inevitably ask, when buying a casket, whether it really locks tight? The reasons for the thousand and one peculiarities of human behavior are often fascinating, ridiculous, or depressing. My red hair led to insecurity and, through some rocky detours, to my skills in becoming a psychological sleuth and Sherlock Holmes.

It has always been a riddle to me why academic departments of anthropology have not concerned themselves with the habits and customs of the savages of Berlin, Frankfurt, Paris, New York and Chicago and, instead, have financed costly expeditions to Papua. It is still fascinating to me to discover that it is almost impossible to sell a Twentieth Century man, with all his sophistication, an electric shaver that does not weigh enough. In formulating an hypothesis, first by creatively looking around, by pursuing all possible avenues with the searchlight of investigation, a relationship was found between the caveman's heavy stone weapon or a tool and the electric shaver. Heaviness has, for a long time, been associated with strength and solidity. Large companies making aluminum tanks had great difficulty convincing a very sober, well-trained engineer that DUR aluminum was just as strong as cast iron or steel. His caveman mentality prevented him from accepting this engineering fact.

Is there one over-riding motivation that I could name, I was asked. Maslow and others have set up whole hierarchies of human needs and motivations. In my opinion, the most important one is the desire for security. Once we're born, we want to return to the womb. We want to be protected. We want to avoid pain and suffering as much as possible. We accumulate money, power, titles, almost all forms of incantations against the gnawing and grinning devil of self doubt. Yet, just as my own insecurity has helped me, it is one of the most maligned motivations.

When I become enmeshed in intricate philosophical discussions with idealistic friends who work for or dream of creating the perfect world, I too get excited but, more and more often for the past few decades of my life, I have come to realize that the so-called paradise that we have been driven out of and would like to get back into, most likely would be indistinguishable from hell. We have been living, nurtured by many religious organizations, with a gigantic illusion. Political leaders, philosophical systems, advertising have projected this glittering Fata Morgana in front of us—as the carrot of our life. Once you have paid up your mortgage, put your kids through school, accumulated enough money—then, the promise is permitted to blossom according to this illusion.

What is the reality? The real definition of happiness is what I call constructive discontent. Getting there is all, not just half, the fun. Stress and insecurity and whatever its labels may be, are the most beneficial movers and springs of our life: Trying to reach a goal but having the goal itself recede is the real mystery of happiness. As parents, we try to make our children feel as protected and secure as possible. Instead we should continuously try to teach them to adapt themselves to new circumstances. Even in everyday school life, children should occupy different seats at different weeks of the year. They would avoid knowing only those sitting to the left and right of them, and possibly the ones in front and in back of them. What we need is more rotation of our daily patterns. Whenever our children are exposed to the concepts under various disguises of the high plateaus of achievement, where one can rest, we as parents should counteract these notions and convince them that there are always mountains behind the mountains.

Of course, a feeling of love and protection is all important. In my life it came as a form of dynamic security or insecurity, teaching me the necessity of continuously having to adapt myself. Every so often I go "slumming," living on frankfurters or reusing and repairing objects which should be thrown away. It reassures me. If needed, I could still do without.

Does motivational research have to concern itself with security and insecurity? Indeed it does.

A furniture company was convinced that American women wanted permanent and solid, heavy, everlasting commodes, dressers and beds. Having a German name, they tried to make the most of this combination of stereotypes. They offered secure, and almost handcrafted pieces reeking of solidity. Our study discovered among other seven year itches, a furniture itch. Women wanted to be able to change and rearrange their furniture at least every seven years. Maybe it was a substitute for changing the marital partner. Recognizing this true motivation, the company successfully followed our advice and now features light, modern mobile furniture.

Everybody has his "red hair." Instead of trying to dye it we should realize that this difference is an asset. I discovered it in a slow process of biographical retrospection.

If astronauts ever discovered a planet where everything was perfect, people did not have to grow up but were born fully grown, never got sick and simply disintegrated after eighty or ninety years, it may at first seem as if they had discovered the planet '*Perfectia!*' Perfect security without the pains and trials of normal human life would be as close to hell as we can picture it.

You can cover up your insecurity by shouting "I am the greatest!" à la Muhammed Ali or you can accept it as a trigger, a wound-up spring which provides you with the elan, the meaning of your life. Dr. Victor Frankl talks in his books about logotherapy, an action-oriented cure. "Human existence exists in action rather than reflection," he writes.

The voltage needed for such action is insecurity whether it stems from red hair or from any other inequality, imagined or real.

8 Have You Tried Making Love Under Water?

We were doing a study on swimming pools. Why do some people use them and how can we motivate others to do so? Our respondents told us that the day they had installed the pool a new life had started for them. Neighbors discovered them. They stayed at home much more. A press conference was arranged to announce the findings of the study. The company we worked for was the Esther Williams Pool Company. Miss Williams, the former movie star, took me aside and complained that we had not emphasized one of the most important motivations: making love under water. According to her, this was one of the most delightful experiences. I was somewhat shocked and pleasantly surprised by her frankness. My personal feeling was that a lot depended, of course, on your aqueous partner. Since Esther was still quite young and I, too, she would have done very nicely. I admired her natural and uninhibited approach to human motivations.

My encounters with people who were either famous then or became so later on usually were of a similar nature. I don't mean involving discussions of a sexual nature, but discussions which revealed uncomplicated and open people. I met Sonny and Cher while waiting in the wings for an appearance on a Johnny Carson show. I was being interviewed on a study I had conducted for DuPont on the psychology of socks, which we dubbed "soxology."

On similar occasions, I met Pat Boone, Sammy Davis, Jr., Shelley Winters, and Gig Young. Most surprising to me was that despite their frequent appearances on the stage, most of them were unexpectedly nervous, pacing up and down before they were called out. I was proud that my nervousness seemed to be at least better hidden. It became clear to me how important publicity is when numerous people called me afterwards, telling me they had seen me on TV. What I had actually said was much less important to them than the fact that I was eligible for admission to the shrine of the electronic church.

On the David Frost show (I had met him first in London), I demonstrated psychodrama, a technique which we use more and more in order to analyze people's feelings about a particular product. He asked me what some of my more interesting motivational studies in the past few weeks had been. We put on a little show using a volunteer from the audience, a young lady who was asked to portray a typewriter. She promptly stretched out on the floor, both arms extended as if she were about to be crucified. As it turned out, she was really expecting to be typed on. At least that was her way of putting it. Her arms were the rollers of the typewriter. I was only repeating on stage what had already been found in our study: a typewriter was, for many people, a feminine product. Making the keyboard more receptive, more concave, was one of our recommendations. The study also revealed that most typists would have wanted the keyboard, in general, to be adaptable to individual needs: the keys should have a surface which could be adjusted to fit the size of your fingers. We even questioned whether the keyboard and the mechanism of a typewriter could not be separated and controlled electronically. Some of these ideas are being translated into new product ideas and concepts, the modern word processing machines, by the sponsoring typewriter company.

I was flattered, yet somewhat annoyed when, after my second appearance on TV, I was asked to join the actors' union, AFTRA. My protest that I was not an actor did not help. Maybe I did not want to protest too much either. Were I to be a real actor, I would at least qualify as a comedian on the stage. I love it when my audience, who come to hear me deliver a lecture, laughs. I have long given up reading a script. I have been told that I can make quick contact with my audience and that I have a sense of humor. I do and I don't. In my everyday life, I am rather pessimistic and introverted. I don't mind being by myself for hours. That is why, even though a psychologist, I have a feeling of embarrassment when people are classified, with or without tests, into various types. It would be more correct to evaluate them according to their ability to play various roles. Some people have only a limited repertoire and keep on repeating the same role; others can change roles without even having to change costumes.

When I was a child I was extremely shy. I did not even address my own parents directly. It was more familiar for me to say, "Did Mother bring me anything?" than to say, "Did you . . . ?" (not that she very often brought me anything, whichever phrase I used). When people came for a visit I would hide. Sometimes when I stand in front of 300 or even 1000 people, I feel schizophrenic. I cannot believe it is really me having the nerve to do my verbal acrobatics. Once in a while when this happens, I develop neurotic symptoms: I can't breathe or swallow properly. I have noticed that Eric Sevareid sometimes showed the same symptoms when delivering his usually very incisive political analyses.

I have always admired my cousins who, even at the ages of five or six, were held up as examples to me. They were without any inhibitions. They could sing in public or perform at birthday parties. When I was called on to do likewise, it was almost as if I had been condemned to die in front of a firing squad. My cousins, my brothers, my mother and I, often spent our summers together. We rented a small room from a farmer. It was during one of these summer vacations, when we boys had been left alone, that I was introduced to an immature form of intrafamily homosexuality. My more precocious cousin Max invited me to play with and to savor his little penis. Most likely, I permitted him or even invited him to reciprocate. I admired him for having all this worldly knowledge. He also gave me my first lesson in masturbation.

Alfred Adler, whose lectures I attended in Vienna, made the point that we often over-compensate for our weaknesses. It could be that my shyness led me first to admire extroverted and nervy people and, later on, subconsciously permitted me to play the role of a famous person. At least that is how I feel. Whether I meet Teddy Kollek, the Viennese mayor of Jerusalem, or spend a weekend with former Governor Munoz Marin of Puerto Rico, I hardly ever feel that we are on the same level.

A second or third cousin (we have never been able to determine the exact relationship, only that we are indeed related) is Misha Dichter, the well-known young pianist. He told me that several times he had been asked if he was related to the "other" famous Dichter. We compared notes about who was more proudly embarrassed about the other.

Whenever I am introduced before giving a lecture or a seminar, I am not quite sure they are really talking about me when a variety of adjectives are pasted onto my name. Which reminds me—and I am sorry that it is one of the most dramatic details of my encounter with Munoz Marin—how we relieved ourselves in his garden after several martinis where we had discussed his political moves to win the election, he started his performance with: "To the Queen!" Of course I like it if, at a party, someone asks with awe, "Are you THE Dr. Dichter?" or if I am told that Marshall Mc Luhan knows me or that Toffler (although somewhat negatively) quotes me in his book on *Future Shock*. Many times I have been slapped on the shoulder with a chummy remark such as, "How are your guilt feelings, Doc?" when I don't have the slightest hint as to who this person is or how he came to know about me.

If you grow up as poor as I, it is difficult to find models that you can hold before yourself. In my eyes my father was a failure, although a nice enough man. I hardly ever had an intellectual discussion with him. He did not serve me as an ideal which I could look up to, starry-eyed. Nor did I ever have the chance to tear him down; he was never high enough up for that.

What I do remember about my father are little details. For example, he took me on a sales trip when I was about 7 or 8 years old. He was a travelling salesman, who often went into the Austrian provinces selling various sewing accessories like buttons, threads, and also, occasionally, some textiles. He owned a horse and a wagon (at least I think so); maybe he just rented them. This was just as interesting for me as it is today for young people if their father has an elegant car. It gave me a little bit of a feeling of superiority. Our grandson, Sasha, when approaching 11, already knew how to drive a car, although not legally allowed to do so, and was proud when his father permitted him to drive occasionally. I was allowed to shout at my father's horses (there were two of them) and use a whip.

On the other hand, I cannot remember ever having had a real, intellectual discussion with my father. Quite the contrary, he was opposed to my studies and even to the phenomenon of books themselves. He always felt that books were a luxury that poor people could ill afford. We were extremely poor. Since he could never provide sufficiently for us, we occasionally had to starve. Therefore, my father could never serve as an ideal for me. It soon became clear to me that he had been a failure in a number of respects, not only in his inability to care for his family, but also as far as his intellectual qualities were concerned. In a way I loved him, and I am sure he loved me too. In a way, it is comical and/or tragic that now the relationship between me and my son, (or our son, as my wife reminds me), is far from perfect, although it seems to be continuously improving. He took a terribly long time to get his doctor's degree in anthropology. He interrupted his studies to join the Peace Corps and later became a carpenter. The main problem, which we have discussed many times, is that, according to him, I am too high up on a pedestal. He keeps telling me how he has suffered, ever since he went to high school, when his teachers used to make remarks about me. This would usually start with, as he tells it to me: "Isn't your father..." upon which he, quite annoyed, replied, "Yes he is, but that doesn't mean that I have to be as good and as successful as he is. I am who I am." His complaint was that I burdened him with my success almost as much as my father put a burden on me because of his lack of success.

My ideal, if one can call it that, was my rich uncle. He owned a department store in Vienna where I worked for a few years. I was told, when I was beginning to show the first stirrings of potential innovativeness and was a fledgeling success, that I took after my uncle. He had been to the United States and came back with new merchandising approaches and ideas of self service. None of his children (they were different cousins than the ones I told tales about before) were successful. It could be that, secretly, he adopted me as his rightful son, although he never went as far as expressing this thought verbally or financially. He gave me a job when I asked for one and encouraged me to try out new ideas in his store.

Installing a loud-speaker and building what we proudly called a heterodyne three tube radio set, which I constructed from plans found in an old American magazine, was largely due to our shared enthusiasm for new (then considered crazy) ideas. I also developed turntables for the department store's window upon which merchandise was displayed. My uncle sent me to a school for window decorators which helped me a great deal later on to earn a living while I continued my studies. Shortly after I finished this course, I became an assistant to the "Chief Decorator." I still remember that my uncle's department store in the Brunnengasse had 48 windows. Every month, at least one of the windows had to be redecorated.

For a few months I tried to convince my uncle to give me the job of the obviously much older chief decorator. This type of ambitiousness is apparently part of my built-in drive. I could notice it and others probably could too during my employment at CBS. I was never satisfied just to carry through the assignments which were given to me, although I think I satisfied my employers. I was a peculiar type. Today I would be called an over-achiever. On the one hand, the bosses like this overambitiousness; on the other hand, it created difficulties for them. More than once they told me to keep my pants on, to just do the job, and to be patient.

In this department store, which was called Department Store Dichter and which still exists, I learned quite a bit about selling. I did not just decorate windows but also substituted as a salesman, especially during holidays like Christmas and Easter. I still remember a few of my very useful mishaps. In one case, a lady came in with a handbag which she wanted to exchange. Thinking she had purchased her handbag elsewhere, I pointed out that the lock really didn't close properly and that the seams weren't perfectly finished. While I looked for other things to find fault with, she interrupted me to say, "Hey, just a moment, young man. You are getting yourself into more and more difficulty and I am sympathizing with you because I don't know how you are going to get out of it. The fact is that I bought this very handbag in this store where you are working." Well, I don't know what I did. Obviously I got red and apologized. She took pity on me and explained that I should be more careful next time. Since I had apparently not had too much experience, she would not tell anyone else. I exchanged the handbag as rapidly as possible in order to get out of the unpleasant situation.

I had, however, learned a very valuable lesson which I have used many times since. It is quite common, particularly today in American advertising, to criticize the product of a competitor. I wonder how many advertisers ought to be reminded of my experience with the handbag. Our studies show that a negative approach often leaves a negative feeling about the product you are trying to push.

I also worked in the cosmetics division selling various types of toilet water and perfumes. In order to demonstrate the superiority of our products, I would open a bottle, smell it myself, and then turn it over to my customer. The head of the cosmetics department observed me one time and gave me a bawling out which I never forgot. Here was another lesson which I have applied since. When a salesman tells you, "I, myself, wear this kind of suit," you might answer "Well, it may be all right for you, but I still would not wear a suit like that." Using oneself as an example, or an ideal, while working as a salesman may backfire.

My father had finally calmed down. I was earning money and, as a good Jewish boy should, brought the money home. I was also earning additional money, a sign of my insecurity, acting as helper half the night for the chief decorator. We often stayed up until three or four o'clock in the morning working on the displays. In this fashion, I collected a whole list of clients who were, at first, the chief decorator's clients but who gradually started to have more confidence in me.

I worked for almost four years in my uncle's department store, from my fifteenth to my nineteenth year. After about two years, I became more and more impatient, and it became clear to me that I would not get very far as a sales person. I started taking courses which allowed me to go through the curriculum which I had interrupted, and which was required in order to eventually pass my final exams which would entitle me then to enter a university.

My uncle most likely never realized that some of my female companions and teachers were partners and objects of my sexual training course and were also provided and paid for by him. In any case, our exploits took place on company time. I remember a dark haired, somewhat cross-eyed girl of about 16 or 17. I was about the same age then. She permitted me various ten finger exercises into the various forbidden terrains in and on her body. Since all this exploration had to be carried out somewhat hurriedly, standing up behind rows of kitchen utensils and sundry china ware, glasses, and, around Christmas time, behind dolls and electric trains waiting to be given a place in the visible shelves at the front of the store, we had to be very inventive. "How to make love in a stock room" might be an appropriate title. It might even become a best-seller in today's sex literature. I am making a note of it in any case. Since I was younger then, I found it more rewarding than Esther Williams' suggestion of making love under water.

We watch our grandchildren while at the beach or dressing and undressing, playing with their equipment without embarrassment, boys and girls alike. I wonder whether they have more fun or less. No one scolds them except for a cleverly disguised glance between my wife and me.

I always felt that the figleaf in Paradise enhanced Adam's desire and represented a devilish precedent for hidden persuasion and inducement to seduction. It was probably not so much the downfall of mankind as the beginning of the enjoyment of sin. I wonder whether the churches and their life-long servants have ever expressed their gratitude for the beginning, the discovery, and the continuation of sin. Where would they be without it? Unemployed and miserable. No one to threaten with Hell. Heaven would be terribly over-populated.

9 Vacation From Myself

During a return visit to my native Vienna, we were watching a performance of the world-famous Spanish Riding Academy. Everything was going according to schedule. Suddenly one of the riders slid off his horse and lay sprawled out on the ground without any kind of movement. Helpers rushed to him and carried him out. As the public learned later, he had suffered a stroke and died almost instantaneously. There was a hushed silence among the many hundreds of spectators. Later, many of us met at a banquet and discussed not only the death of the rider, but our own lives. Why were we rushing? Why did we not slow down and enjoy ourselves more? We realized that sooner or later we might suffer a fate similar to the man from the riding academy.

Many years ago, I read a book entitled *Vacation From Yourself*. It was written by a German author, Kellerman, and as far as I know has never been translated into English. The book is at least fifty years old, yet it describes in a wonderful way what we are slowly beginning to rediscover now—a sort of "stress clinic." A psychiatrist meets a wealthy American (in German novels Americans always were wealthy), and tells him about his ideas. Most people try to play a role, as if on a stage, which they have chosen themselves. They are wasting an awful lot of their energy and time trying to act out this role. They hardly ever take time out to separate the "real" from their "fake" selves.

In 1948, our family moved from Larchmont, New York (our children were already born; Tom in 1941 and Susie in 1943) to a farm we bought not far from New York City. I wanted lots of space and, if possible, to play the gentleman farmer. We now owned not only an old farmhouse, but also a combination chicken coop and cow barn and 20 acres. For quite a few years I had been advising advertising agencies. I decided that it was now time for me to "find myself"—a new thought at that time. I remembered the book I had read many years before and planned an experiment based on that author's advice.

The cow barn could be converted into three apartments. So with this in mind, I put an ad in the New York Times which said, "Vacation from yourself. Eat with us, drink with us, sleep with us, spend a stimulating summer on a psychologist/writer's farm." We received over four hundred replies in the course of the next few days. By Sunday morning enough people had come so that not only the three apartments which I had planned were rented, but also an empty hillside! One of the potential summer guests would not be shaken off when told there was only room for three apartments. "Anybody who can write an ad like that can also learn how to build a summer bungalow. I want you to build one for me over there on that hill." We did. We hired a German carpenter who lived in one of the unfinished sections of the cow barn to construct the apartments and the bungalow. We had four families spending the summer with us. The fact that we got so many takers had puzzled me, but the explanation was really a simple one. I had hit upon a very widespread human need: the vacation from yourself.

We had a wonderful summer. I did not follow all the sequences indicated in the original book but, with some modifications, I tried a number of interesting anti-stress techniques. According to the original scenario, every visitor to this fictional German or Swiss farm was stripped of his identity. He could select from

LIVE WITH US

And other thinking · modern people. on our 20-acre farm-estate; our 8 new warm and cozy cottages are modern furnished; low rentals; ice skating on our own pond, skiing, music, fireplace chats, horseback riding, beautiful fall, winter and spring, also all year. Walk to station, stores; one hour commuting. Dr. Dichter, Montrose, N Y. Peekskill 7-1625; TR 4-1192.

Ad run in New York Times.

colorful clothes, but these clothes would not indicate nor permit guests a social standing. Everyone was on a first-name basis. The resident psychiatrist or psychologist would invite each registrant to spend 24 hours all by himself, and to write down (I did it with a tape recorder) what he really wanted to get out of life, what he had done right and what he had done wrong in his opinion up till now.

What the original author described, and I rediscovered, was that there were some people whose unhappiness was based on never being able to see the results of their work, or having to wait very long for it. To this category belong many intellectuals, writers, producers, and scientists. Artists would see immediately the result, if not the success of their work. The therapy which I tried was very simple. Those who were frustrated by the too-long-delayed realization and demonstration of the success of their activities were assigned such tasks as cutting a lawn, pitching hay, chopping down a tree. The others were given a task like planting things, where they had to wait for the harvest to see results.

My wife and I ran this stress clinic for about six or seven years. With each new season new people came, recommended by the participants from the previous years. We still have many friends from this period. Many well-known people, at least now well known, came to visit and spend some time with us: Leonard Bernstein, Jules Dassin, and many others. We had concerts, discussions, and an unusual children's camp where a lot of emphasis was put on discovery and return to nature.

Our farm, however, should not only be inhabited by humans; we also wanted animals. Since I was afraid of a cow, I bought a goat. It was a she-goat, but despite all my attempts, no milk. I complained to the farmer from whom I had bought the goat. He explained that you can't fool Mother Nature, that even a goat has to be bred in order to produce milk. He then asked me what I really wanted. I told him that my dream was to live off the fat of the land, a dream many people have today, as a way of escaping the rat race and stress of modern living. After a thorough psychological analysis of my motivations, the farmer sold me a cow. The condition which I insisted upon was that with the price of the cow would go a training program on how to milk and take care of the cow. He agreed. He inquired about my profession. I explained to him that I was a psychologist. He ascertained that I knew enough about the biology and the anatomy of the cow to know approximately where the milk came from. His advice was to lock the barn door, get a pail, sit down underneath the cow on the left side, and to start squeezing the udder. I have never found out why one has to sit at the left side of a cow, but I obeyed and with some trepidation started my gentle massage of the cow's four couplets. When the pail was half full, something seemed to irritate the cow and she stepped into my beautiful, clean, white pail of milk with her dirty hoof. I didn't know what to do. I stopped—like a mother in the first week of confrontation with her first baby—ran to the phone, and called my rural adviser, the farmer. He told me, "You have two alternatives. You can either take the milk and cook it, or throw it out, clean the pail and start all over again. In any case," he said, "you are well on your way to becoming a dairy farmer." He gave me a few hints, such as how to judge ahead of time whether the cow would make any unexpected movements, or even worse, let her other natural urges take their normal relief. (In case you are interested, he advised me to use my arm while milking, as a kind of seismograph, sensing ahead of time what the cow might do.) After a day or two, I became more adept. I even taught my family how to milk.

We indeed began to live off the land, or at least the cow. The milk was much too fat, however, and our American-born-and-raised children insultingly refused to drink it. They wanted to have "their" milk, "real" milk, the milk that is bought in the store, not this heavy, almost yellow and thick milk which came from a somewhat dirty animal. Fortunately, we soon had quite a number of neighbors as our customers. The cow had been tested, and the milk was incredibly delicious although not pasteurized. We also learned to make butter and cheese.

After a few months, a new cycle started and the cow had to be bred again. We found a bull. The payment for service was $15. If it did not "take" (as it was called), the farmer would bring back the bull a second time for half the price. It did not seem a bad way to make a living for the bull—or rather for the owner of the bull. Our cow had a calf, we raised it, and now had two cows which gave us twice the amount of milk as before. Eventually we ended up with four cows and a few bull calves in between which we slaughtered. We were drowning in milk! What could be done with all that milk? Chickens could be fed milk. The result: we ended up with 2000 chickens! We then had not only 30 to 40 gallons of milk a day, but hundreds of eggs too. We even added pigs, horses and bees. Our human colony of "vacation from yourself" families increased also. We had 17 families coming back year after year.

Then disaster struck. A hurricane ripped off part of the roof of the chicken coops. The chickens got wet, and caught some fancy disease. Half the chickens died. I tried to diagnose scientifically what was wrong with them, but finally had to call for help and to send some of the sick and already dead chickens to the Agricultural Research Station. About two weeks later (by that time more and more chickens had gone to their heaven), I received a diagnosis with the "helpful" remark that there was no cure for this disease. We tried to recover as much as we could. After some inquiry the answer was obvious: we had to kill the rest of the chickens and try to sell them to restaurants in New York City. This is exactly what we did. For about three days we had a bloodbath. Psychologically, this was interesting for me. Once again, Freud was proven right: we all have a killer instinct and killing is very close to sexual excitement. To my shock and surprise, I discovered that after I had gotten the knack of chopping off the heads of the chickens, I had an erection. Sex and death are indeed related. Ever since this chicken episode I try to avoid, as much as possible, eating chicken in a New York restaurant. I know very well that the disease that my chickens had wasn't contagious, I was reassured of that by the Health Inspector. Also, what I had done was quite legitimate, as long as the chickens were still bleeding they were okay for human consumption.

How did the vacation from myself end? Quite uneventfully. My enthusiasm, not only for eating chicken but also for raising them, began to wane. We were successful with our egg farm, particularly when I hit upon the idea of selling fertilized eggs. (You need a rooster, whose enviable job it is to take care of about a dozen chickens, to crow and to consume enormous amounts of feed.) The fertilized eggs can then be used by hatcheries. The going rate was one dollar a dozen, twice as much as for regular eggs. In addition to our milk customers, we also had an egg route which Hedy took care of.

After the chickens died, I put my creative activity to good use. We altered the summer dwellings into year-round apartments by "winterizing" them. All we had to do to make it successful, was to give them fancy names. One of them was called The Hunting Lodge. It had a gallery, accessible through staircases leading to what remained of the second floor after we had taken off half the ceiling of our double-decker chicken coop. The Swiss Chalet was the new name for our cow barn. Both these places are still rented.

Oh yes, the cows. The motivational research business had grown quite rapidly and when I came back from one of my trips to California, Hedy simply had had enough. She had sold the cows. As so often in the past, she had more courage than I. I probably would never have been able to be so decisive. I never admitted it, but I was quite glad that I no longer had to milk the cows.

All in all, the vacation from myself bungalow colony was quite successful. We ran it during the period when our children were growing up; we did not have to send them to camp since we had our own camp. We acquired a number of skills and our son is still proud of the fact that he knows how to milk. He used this knowledge during his stay in a kibbutz in Israel.

I too, have made use of this experience on our "vacation from yourself" colony. Since then I have carried through many studies dealing with dairy products and the psychology of farmers. I have a much better understanding of the vagaries and ironies of economic relationships. For example, when our chickens were laying eggs very well, inevitably feed prices would go up and egg prices would go down.

Still, I have not lost my longing for farming. In fact, I am beginning to discuss the possibility of a new career. One of the possibilities I always seriously consider is at least a vegetable farm, or perhaps an increase in the size of my greenhouse. I have a whole collection of literature on this subject and have found that my early interest in our little colony has again become popular among young people. Movements such as those exemplified by the *Whole Earth Catalogue* and the increase of interest in organic foods was something I had anticipated at least 25 years ago.

10 Why Not Live in a Castle?

An interesting test, used to reveal the whole purpose of a person's life, is to ask what he would like printed on his tombstone. Two words—"Why not?"—are the ones I would choose.

For several years after I had started working on my own, I commuted to New York City like everybody else who had an office there. Some time in 1952, I decided to start working at home on Fridays and then on Mondays. About a year later, despite the protests of my wife, I asked myself, "Why Not?" Why could I not give up my office in the city and move up into the country? I looked around to find something suitable. A real estate broker finally told me about a huge 26-room stone mansion on top of a mountain in Croton-on-Hudson. I showed it to my wife. She was appalled. "All we need to do," she said, "is put a moat around it and have an armored knight watch the entrance." It was built in 1912 in the English Tudor or French Breton style. I never quite found out which description fits best. It had about 11 bathrooms and a 65-foot-long living room. The building was three stories high and contained an honest-to-goodness pipe organ. I secretly made a ridiculously low offer, a figure that today would barely buy a shack. This was on a Friday afternoon. Monday morning the broker called and told me the bad news: the owners had accepted my offer. By adding up the

The Castle.

rent I had to pay in New York City, I figured out that within a year to a year-and-a-half I would have gotten the purchase price back by saving the rent money. I bought the building. We had about six employees. I gave up my office in the city and we moved in. We all felt lost in this stone mansion, which we jokingly referred to as our "castle on the Hudson."

I don't want to write a story comparable to *The Egg and I* or *Mr. Blandings Builds his Dreamhouse*, but we did have similar experiences. Within a few weeks, we had to fix the well. The electric wiring was faulty and the plumbing had everything wrong that could be wrong. Anyway, we made our own repairs. Most importantly, having all these empty rooms became a peculiar challenge. I had to fill them somehow, preferably with employees—employees who would be busy. This meant hustling as many jobs as possible. Eventually, I had 65 employees. At that point, even as big as the castle was, it had become too small. We decided we did not need eleven bathrooms. Some of them were sizable enough to be turned into offices, which we did. The "why not?" question had paid off.

Clients came to see me and they did not mind at all that I did not have offices in New York City. As several of them told me, the setting was unique enough so that they would remember it. Even if I had the most elegant offices in what at that time was probably the ultimate in status, Rockefeller Center, they would probably confuse it with 79 other offices. The castle on the Hudson was unique enough that it would be permanently remembered by them.

Looking out the window in my office I can see mountain ranges, the Hudson River and occasionally, during the winter time, I can see a family of deer. We have made a habit of feeding the deer salt hay and leaving them apples which drop off our trees but are not good enough for our consumption. This is a sort of thank you note for them and an invitation for them to continue visiting us. They apparently have understood the message and have returned again and again.

In the last decades, the idea of having an office outside the city has increased considerably. In a way, I have put our little village of Croton on the map practically all over the world. Not far from our location is the Hudson Institute, whose scientific director is the world famous Hermann Kahn, a good friend of mine. A few years ago I bought the Institute, that is, the real estate there, as an investment. In addition there are a number of famous authors living in Croton, such as John Cheever.

In order to preserve my view of the Hudson, I had to cut down a few trees. Almost everyone who comes here for the first time admires the unusual location and my innovative spirit to have located my office out here. A peculiar form of European chauvinism is often expressed by many of our foreign visitors who say, "You've established yourself a piece of Europe right here, haven't you?" When I point out to them that this is more likely a typical American concept they usually feel let down.

Of course I had asked "why not?" before when I left Austria, long before anybody thought of any danger. I left Europe in time. There have been many such "why nots?" in my life, and I have used them very effectively in approaching management and marketing and advertising problems.

In a campaign in Germany advertising sanitary napkins I suggested, probably for the first time, that a man become the main topic. He would ask questions about women's attitudes towards menstruation; the manufacturer would explain to him the reasons. Later on, I called this approach the over-the-shoulder advertising. Of course the ad was read not only by men, but probably primarily by women. For the first time, the manufacturer did the explaining for her, which she herself most likely was too embarrassed to do. The manufacturer of sanitary napkins became her ombudsman.

Another "why not?" episode that I was very proud of concerns my indoor swimming pool. We returned from a trip to the Caribbean, having been fleeced, not being able to get flight reservations, and coming back dead tired from what was supposed to be a wonderful vacation. I analyzed what I had enjoyed most during my trip. It was the possibility of swimming every day. I looked around

Indoor pool.

our house, and decided that there was no reason to protect a car by a solid garage. I moved the car out, and inquired from various pool manufacturers whether or not they would be willing to install a swimming pool where the car had been living a very peaceful and protected life. I could not find a single pool manufacturer who would respond positively to my question, "Why Not?" I finally decided to do it myself. I hired a bulldozer and dug a hole. I got a plan from the Portland Cement Association, and, together with a mason, we built the indoor pool. It has been working beautifully almost two decades.

I have to mention that one of my additional "why nots?" was to ask myself, after having moved my office out of the city, whether I could not make life even more comfortable by not traveling back and forth even between the property which we owned within a few miles of our castle, and move right in to the castle. This too worked out very well. We added a number of rooms by opening up the house to the south side. For some mysterious reason, all the nice views had been overlooked and were blocked by heavy walls.

In order to be able to cut openings into the three-foot-thick fieldstone wall I bought an electric hammer, which I learned to use. I found that a very important lesson in overcoming stress is to use your own creativity. The trite objection is that not everybody is creative. This is only partially true. By asking the question, "Why not?" frequently enough and in situations where apparently it has no particular application, I have found that it is possible to come up with unusual approaches. I suggested once that bathtubs should be large enough to permit bathing for two. I was laughed at. One of the biggest problems in practicing a "Why Not?" philosophy is to develop a thick skin. Many of my ideas have created only a giggle at first. Now, a number of companies have started making such bathtubs. Whether there is an erotic implication involved or not is really unimportant. It is an interesting new approach. The Romans, by the way, already knew about it. In a study on toilet paper, we found that a wet toilet paper has some very obvious advantages. The Wet One is a new brand on the market, which was developed on the same principle as Wash 'n Dri towelettes. This discovery was made by simply asking whether men and women use toilet paper in the same way. In many respects, they do, but in other respects, they don't.

As I became more successful and as more of my "Why not?" products were successfully brought out on the market, I learned to ask this question more and more frequently. I wrote a book which is called *Why Not?* and concerns itself with modern management principles. Why not build an organization in such a way that no hierarchy is the perfect type? I suggested that it become much more intuitive and flexible than organizations are today. For example, when the grocery clerk discovers that his sales are slowing down, he should not wait until his supervisor, the sales manager, calls him on the carpet. Instead, he should take the initiative and call up the sales manager and report his difficulties. The clerk's argument against this approach, and it is a very logical one, is that the sales manager is, after all, a better trained person, he makes more money than the grocery clerk, so he asks him to explain and to help him redress the sagging sales curve. My approach makes it impossible for the sales manager to simply pass the buck. Of course he, in turn, has the possibility of going to the next level and asking for help there. In other words, instead of having the president of the company go through each level of responsibility, putting the whole burden on the lowest-rank, and usually also the lowest-paid, employee of the enterprise, the process is reversed. It is usually referred to as management from the bottom up. It is the result of asking, "Why could it not be done differently?"

Because of this type of question, I am rather optimistic as far as the future of mankind is concerned. There are, of course, many books which warn us that we are going to starve to death because of over-population, that our environment is going to become completely polluted, and that we are going to run out of energy. The actual facts point to an entirely different development. The world of tomorrow is really going to be ours. That is the title of another book of mine. I was influenced to write it in order to combat the pessimistic thinking which seems to be so prevalent. I tried to suggest in this new book that we have to learn to think differently when we contemplate the 1980s or even the year

2000. There are so many new sources of energy that we are only gradually beginning to suspect.

When I read that the Polaroid Corporation makes it possible with their new cameras to focus electronically by a type of radar arrangement which measures the distance between the object and the camera and translates it through an electronic chip, then I begin to be convinced that many other possibilities will open up. We are going to use agriculture AQA which is going to complement agriculture. The more data I collected for this book, the more I became convinced that we are at the beginning of the real conquest of the world as far as modern transportation, nutrition, cities, and energy are concerned.

I have found that creativity is one of the methods which we often forget when we talk about combating stress. It is easy to say that creativity is something that you are born with, but this is only partially true. Challenged by this kind of assumption, I developed a course for the American Management Association designed for the purpose of helping people to learn to think in a more creative fashion. It contains about a dozen principles, the most important one being to learn how to pose very simple, primitive and often stupid questions.

I have learned to develop my own creativity through courses in logic and epistemology which I took at the University of Vienna. I was very much influenced by my philosophy teacher, Professor Moritz Schlick. Students were encouraged to participate in week-long seminars for the purpose of learning how to pose questions. I use this method in many of my motivational studies. Many people are perplexed when they are asked "What are you really doing?" or "What is the purpose of your product?"

One of the biggest problems in learning to be creative is to stop being afraid of ridicule. You have to develop a thick skin. In one of the studies carried through by our Zurich office, under the direction of Dr. Doebeli, we analyzed the possibility of establishing an automatic device which will spray your behind and then dry it with hot air. The whole contraption is called "Closomat." Funny? Yes, but actually quite hygienic and quite pleasant.

Asking "Why not?" or applying methods of creativity can also be fruitful where management questions are concerned. In another book entitled *The Naked Manager*, I challenged the established views concerning the hierarchical set-up existing in most organizations. I also suggested that rather than believing in and defending management by objectives, one should consider that in today's world, the objectives are continuously changing. In other words, part of the training of a modern manager should be to go to Las Vegas and learn how to gamble and to adapt himself so he can become much more flexible.

In another series of booklets entitled *The Human Factor*, I took up, bit by bit, each one of the customary management roles, and tried to go beyond them. We state quite glibly that every good manager should learn how to delegate, but we do not ask ourselves often enough why such delegation does not always work. One of the reasons I have found is that the person who delegates is often afraid that the person to whom he assigns the job may do it better than himself.

We also have not accepted that a bad mood or depressed feeling can be more contagious than a cold. And yet we consider it perfectly normal when an employee calls in and announces he is staying home because of his cold, but we are taken aback if he does so because he declares he is in a bad mood.

Many of our economic and energy problems could be solved with greater creativity. President Carter has asked us to consider the energy crisis like the Civil War. Had he instead presented it as a creative challenge, the possibility of applying "Yankee ingenuity," he might have had more luck. Instead of asking people to drive a smaller car, much less emphasis should have been put on the size of the car than on the idea that the

Elevator chair.

smaller car is a much more flexible, more adaptive and a more modern kind of car than the dinosaur. We have to accept that the average American, and citizens of other countries too, want to express their power through what one also calls the "mechanical bride," but there is not only brute muscular power, there is also the power of a dancer, a sprinter.

I wanted to get from one floor to another in my building, and I didn't want to spend the money on a spiral staircase, nor did I want to lose the space required to install regular steps. Why not install an electric hoist, the type used to life engines out of cars? I got one from an automotive company in Chicago. I attached a monkey chair to it. Not only I, but our grandchildren as well, have a lot of fun with it. It can take a weight of over 2,000 pounds. Even after a heavy meal we hardly ever reach this limit.

Instead of a blackboard in my office, I covered the doors with white plastic sheets. I can write resolutions and tasks on them. They stare into my face until I have taken care of them, and erased them with a wet sponge. Since, like everybody else, I always lose things, I decided to make a general reminder filing system, entitled, 'Where, Who and What,' and this is where I have listed all the locations and possible spots where things could have been filed or misfiled. It does not work perfectly yet, but we're getting there.

The "Why not?" philosophy can be applied to almost anything. Max Eastman, in a book called *The Enjoyment of Laughter*, put down on the very first page all the things he claimed that you could possibly learn from reading his book. At the end of the first page, he invited you to read three more pages, and then swore that now indeed you would know everything that you could possibly find of interest in his book. Of course he had no objection if you kept on reading the remainder of the book, covering a couple of hundred pages. This is the kind of "why not?" approach which I like. I have copied it in some of my books. It is not quite applicable to this one.

Recently someone quite correctly suggested that $15 million is being spent every year in New York City alone in selling tokens. With an increased subway fare, the riders could simply be admonished, as they already have been in connection with buses, to have the exact fare ready and to drop the fare into the turnstile. After all, it is possible; even most of the bridges and thruway toll stations do it. Why couldn't it be applied to the subway system?

It took many years before someone decided that setting a weight limit for airlines in the jet age was more than ridiculous. When I traced back the origin of the limitations I discovered that they dated back to the Pony Express days. The airline officials in charge of making regulations simply took the figure 44 pounds (and 66 for first class) and made it their guiding rule. For the last few years, at least in domestic travel, these limitations have simply been abandoned. Someone found that it cost a lot more money to collect and write overweight tickets than the income from them amounted to.

One of the first things we do when we are called in by a particular industry to discover new approaches is to ask systematically fundamental, often stupid-sounding questions, more or less involving the "Why not?" approach. Instead of getting a measly amount for your old refrigerator when you trade it in, why not, if you are living in a one-family house, keep it around, in the basement or on the second floor, possibly even in your bedroom? You may feel like a martini. Without having to run down and then come back with it and risk its being too late for whatever you had in mind, you can mix your martini right on the field of action.

As far as offices are concerned, I have suggested that in order to provide the employee or executive with exercises, a square be cut into the floor and a miniature trampoline be installed in this opening, on which you can jump up and down. Of course it is ridiculous, but it works. The executive may just do so because he is enraged or because of his fat. Many clients seem to be partially disappointed after we have finished a motivational research study, because many of the answers are simple. They are common sense applications. "Why didn't we think of it before?"

A practice accepted by almost all banks, at least in the United States, is one where overdraft can be avoided by a simple device that you apply for a loan at the time that you open your checking account. Provided your credit is good, you automatically have $300-500 or even $1,000 more in your checking account to draw on in case of emergency. Of course, once that loan has been exhausted, then the bank must get tough. But it was a way of combining more sales for the loan department and avoiding a negative feeling when receiving a letter from the bank advising you of an overdraft. A hospital supply company complained to us about their problem of deliveries. They were being informed too late by the purchasing agent of the need for cotton bandages, and whatever other material the hospital needed. We suggested that they establish a depot in the hospital and replenish it at their own convenience. Nobody before had dared to question the normal process of running out of supplies, ordering them, and having them delivered; usually either too late or in a rush.

11 Don't Flush!

Our castle is admired a great deal by our visitors. Twenty-six rooms! We are proud of it and give guided tours at the slightest provocation. But our castle has also been a continuous school of life for us. When we bought it for next to nothing, it was much too big. A few years later, it was filled with 65 people on our staff and it was too small. I had not been intelligent enough to anticipate changes in our business and in our life. Recently, I was interviewed by a reporter who wanted to know how intelligent people could fall for obviously fraudulent schemes of land purchases in Arizona or Florida. One of the explanations I gave him was that we all suffer from the myth of continuity. I, myself, invested in a real estate syndicate. It did very well and kept increasing in value. The stock split several times until the inevitable happened. Over a very short period it slid from 30 to 1¼. I had been reassured by the steady progress of the company. I was being scientific; after all, I judged its soundness by previous performance. What I had not calculated on was that things might suddenly change. Just as my physician told me, he would be able to manage his patients a lot better if he could convince them of their mortality.

The castle has not ceased to challenge us continuously. For about a year or so we had no water problem. A pond and a well next to it with an imposing

1200 foot water-line provided us with all the liquidity we needed. The well dried out. We drilled a new one. That worked for a while until trouble developed all over again. The water supply became more precious to us than champagne. "Don't flush!" became the standard greeting with which we welcomed most of our guests. We became the first conservationists. We deepened the well. Wonderful—we watched the gauge on our watertank with delight; then again it went down to a trickle. Several thousand dollars went down the well hole. My philosophy is not to let major or minor disasters get me down. I also think I have a scientific mind, so I applied it to the well problem. There was a mysterious gushing sound in one of the walls of the basement. It could be just the spot where the 70 year old pipe comes from the well into the house. "No sense breaking up the wall," I was told by the experts. "Get a new pipeline directly from the well at a much shorter route than the old line into the basement and into the watertank." "But why not look for the leak in the old line in the meantime?" I asked. "You can't fix such a leak." Well, I won. We found the leak next to a joint and it was repaired in no time. We may still have to put a new line in next spring. In the meantime, our gauge pleasantly surprises us almost every day by indicating gallons and gallons of water supply. We celebrated with a bottle of champagne. Now we can flush whenever the urge arises.

I call my way of dealing with stress the 'organic way.' Maybe it is just the common variety of change between manic and depressive behavior. I have spent many hours in taking things apart which did not work and, more frequently than the experts predicted, put them together successfully. I am not awestruck by experts. When you have learned to read and to use a few simple tools, you are on your way, if not to becoming a licensed plumber or electrician, at least to being able to compete, in many instances, with them. I take free lessons from tradesmen. I watch how they handle tools, what little tricks they use, and then do it myself the next time.

Creativity is another very important aspect of overcoming water, financial and emotional problems. I call it upside-down thinking. For quite a while, I had pains in my left side. A school friend of mine, a radiologist, told me he saw cysts on my left kidney. I traced my pains back to my spine by studying amateur anatomy. The orthopedic surgeon confirmed my self-diagnosis. What has always puzzled me is how many people, including myself, accept the opinion of so-called authorities. The main reason is, possibly, that it permits us to give up our own responsibility and to play the role of children. If I were to make a tally of how much the acceptance of wrong advice, just because it was pronounced in an emphatic and convincing way, has cost me, it would probably add up to a sizable sum. My advisors represent a good-sized regiment. They are stock brokers, bankers, lawyers, physicians, and assorted friends. If I could rewrite my life story or help others to avoid mistakes by studying mine, my most important lesson would be to learn to look at facts rather than simply believing what we are told. One of the techniques I apply is to challenge a salesman or the proponent of a cause and to watch his reactions. Exposed to stress and the need to defend himself, you frequently will find cracks in his arguments and contradictions in his assertions.

When you have to make up your mind between two or more possibilities, it often helps to use what researchers call the Delphi method. Have the person, whether a physician or any other authoritative advisor, repeat his story a few days later. If it remains the same, the facts presented may be correct. More often than not, changes occur in the citation of proofs.

Before I decided to come to the United States instead of going to India, I conducted what I thought was scientific research. I interviewed twenty or more people who had been to the States and asked them about their impressions. Almost all of them gave me negative reports. It took me a while to figure out what had been wrong in my search for the objective facts. All of these people lived in Paris. They had returned from the States. The reason? Most of them could not make it, either because they could not adapt themselves or did not have enough stamina. I had permitted a faulty factor to creep into my analysis.

I was offered a trip to Japan as part of a study on why people would or should prefer a Japanese airline—Japan Airline. I eagerly accepted. One of the questions was whether Americans might not be afraid of taking a plane possibly piloted by a former Kamikaze pilot. Of course they would, or so I thought. Having learned, however, to be more cautious in my motivational explanations, and remembering my experience in Paris, I unearthed a simple but crucial error in my thinking. The majority of the people whom I met in the plane flying to

Seminar in Japan.

Japan were experienced travelers who loved the Orient. The Japanese pilot did not disturb them one bit. Another anthropologically and motivationally interesting fact was discovered. Japan Airline officials wanted the decor in the plane as Western as possible. This was, to them, a proof of superiority. The Western travelers, however, wanted to experience the Orient as quickly as possible while the Japanese travelers wanted to experience the American way of life equally as soon. A compromise was finally arrived at after I delivered my report. An American and a Japanese acted as co-pilots on alternating flights. The hostesses changed their flight uniforms from a Japanese kimono to Western clothing and back again, depending on the direction and distance of the plane from its origin and destination. In searching for motivations it is often necessary to lift several layers of easy assumptions and to reject the obvious explanations.

I am convinced that this contrariness has helped me in establishing my identity. It was easier to do it in this fashion than by being a golden boy. I am still being introduced, in my lectures, as controversial; and I like it. I had to study Greek in the second year of what Europeans call Gymnasium. I refused. I could not or would not understand the reason for knowing a dead language. Whenever the professor called on me to read a text or to translate a school assignment, I reiterated my original decision taken at the beginning of the school year that I would not study Greek, by utter silence. I have to mention that the student had the right to eliminate this language from his program with the approval of his teacher. My teacher, a blond, righteous German prototype to whom the classics were at least as holy as the Teutons, refused me this permission. His reason (probably correct) was that I was just being ornery. I was intelligent enough and I would regret it later on. However, I persisted and never learned Greek.

The important experience for me was that, with what I call persistence, I could win a victory. When a client confronts me with well-founded facts, my tendency is to search out a crack in his arguments. I apply the same irreverent approach to many aspects of my own life. It has gotten me into trouble but has also often helped me to have fascinating experiences or to find answers which have eluded more conformist thinkers.

I once spent a delightful weekend in Zanzibar for no particular reason except that the name had always intrigued me. I was flying to Johannesburg but, by changing planes, I could interrupt my flight in Mombasa and take a boat to Zanzibar. In the foyer or lobby of the hotel, which belonged to a Dutch woman, was a tropical-type ceiling fan and huge chairs made out of straw. My room was located on the first floor. After I had rested for a while and had unpacked, I suddenly heard a knock at my door. In came a young, very good looking Arab youth. At first I did not know what he wanted; then he offered me his love, in a more or less direct fashion. I thought all he was interested in was an apparently well-endowed traveler, but I soon discovered that what he had in mind was something else. When I told him, partially shocked and partially amused, that I had never tried anything like that and that I wasn't really interested, he shook his head and went away.

I then decided to explore Zanzibar. The doors of the houses in Zanzibar have very complex carvings. They created the impression of being in the country of a 1001 nights, much more Arabic than African. After a while of promenading,

I was approached by an older Arab gentleman, who accompanied me for a while and acted as a guide. Soon, however, the topic turned to the universal subject of sex. He asked if I might be interested in a nice girl, insisting that she was clean. I had first thought that meant she had bathed, but apparently he had meant clean from a health standpoint. Maybe he had found out that I was not interested in the male youthful beauty. This elderly man spoke very good English; he told me I could not meet this Arab girl within the city limits since this was not allowed. He never used the term prostitution. I would have to take a taxi to an abandoned house, the girl joining us on the way. In any case, he kept on stressing that I should avoid talking about money with this very nice girl. That matter would have to be straightened out with him. Of course, the whole thing was immoral by bourgeois standards but, as you know by now, I am a person who is continuously curious. To have an experimental Arab girl was something that intrigued me. I was somewhat naive as far as the dangers involved. In due course we stopped and, indeed, a heavily veiled girl got in and hid on the floor in the back of the car. After driving quite a distance, we were both unloaded and entered a fairly cold and empty room that contained only a bed. The elderly gentleman left us to our destiny.

After I had returned to my hotel, it dawned on me as a sort of flashback that I could have been robbed or killed; but, during the experience, none of these thoughts occurred to me. I remember that I was, if it is possible, more shy than the girl. I had to go through the motions that are expected of a man, so I asked her to get undressed. She did so quite slowly and then, in a dutiful fashion, lay down on the bed. Then the terrible thing happened: she started to yawn. Although I was fairly young at that time, I might have been ready to perform my paid-for duties. I was not sufficiently impressed by her now completely unveiled beauty to get into the right mood. She did not speak a word of English nor did I speak Arabic; we could not communicate. All that might not have ruined the possibilities, but the fact that she yawned was the dot on the "i" or whatever the parallel might be. The result was quite obvious; I gave up, permitted her to get dressed again, and called my guide and sponsor. We drove back into the city. On the way back the girl was dismissed into a dark side street and I returned, an experience or a disillusionment richer. At my hotel I could have felt very moral, but as a male my feelings were more disappointed. Zanzibar was not only not as full of spices and excitement as I would have believed by its name, but it was also disappointing in the affairs of other sensuous stimulation.

When, several years later, I saw an Italian film where the gruesome details of the massacre of the Arab population of Zanzibar was shown, I had the doubtful pride of being able to remember my weekend experience. A black boy had acted as my guide, explaining all the racial hatred by making me aware that almost all the tradesmen were Arabs. He told me the blacks were going to take over. "I shall be rich when I grow up," he said. He was guarding, as a sort of baby sitter, Arab children. "I am learning as much as I can from them so I can take their place later on," was his most frequent comment.

I have often felt that practicing clinical psychology, and applying it to the analysis of human motivations, depended a lot on applying principles of good detective work. Many people confuse the techniques of psychoanalysis with interpretations, symbolism, and uncovering childhood memories. A much better description is the one of practicing the skill of a psycho-detective.

When I practiced psychotherapy in Vienna for a few years after receiving my Ph.D., proudly remembering that for about twenty years I had lived exactly across the street from Sigmund Freud, I gradually learned to observe, to listen with "the third ear" as Theodor Reik called it. Trying to understand a patient (or client as they are called today) is comparable to the feeling of heightened senses which drug addicts describe as the most pleasant part of taking a "trip." You concentrate, not unlike what is done in transcendental meditation. You combine listening to a patient with listening to your own psychological seismograph. You feel a vibration when you know that you have found a meaningful clue.

You are being told by a young lady, for example, that she loses one job after another. She does not know why. She is afraid of people, she says. As an analyst, you have a ready tool and that is the one you sharpen during your training: to reverse, to stand the statements made to you on their head. Your suspicion, quite often correct, is that she is really afraid of having a steady job. She is arranging circumstances in such a way that she will be fired. Once this *Umkehrung*, this head-stand, has been achieved, you are much more capable of helping her. You then have to search for the reason behind her real fear, the fear of staying on one job for a reasonably long period of time. The parallel in her case was that she showed similar behavior patterns in her love life. She could hold on to a man no better than she could hold on to a boss. She did not want to. She wanted to have freedom of choice. It takes a while to develop this 'Alice in Wonderland' type of looking-glass and to use it in many different situations. To the untrained person, you appear to be controversial. You don't leave things alone. You try to stand them on their heads.

The field of psychology is like a country where a complex coded language is spoken. We learn in physics that an object cannot both be here and, at the same time, not be here. The phenomenon of ambivalence, however, proves that you can love someone and hate him at the same time. A person can be manic one moment or, as the German poet Goethe put it, "Himmelhochjauchzend" (shouting with heavenly joy) and, a few minutes later, be depressed or "zu Tode betrübt" (be deadly sad).

In searching out motivations, this skill of irreverence, of questioning what the so-called objective facts reveal, and shaking them up to see whether they would not fall apart or assume a different combination, as in a kaleidoscope, has succeeded in stimulating my sense of discovery.

Although I did not directly develop the idea of 'The Tiger in the Tank' for Esso (now Exxon), I laid the groundwork for the symbolism used. I can easily trace it back to the analysis of a patient who, in his dream, fought with a powerful animal. His own explanation was fear of dogs and other supposedly ferocious creatures. He fought with them the way Old Testament prophets challenged God. It was a symbolic way of fighting and loving his father. The tiger is, most assuredly, not a lovable animal. But it commands respect as most fathers do. My commercial work was thus very often closely associated with the growth of my clinical skill.

Shortly after I came to the United States, the problem arose as to what I was going to do to make a living. In Vienna I had practiced psychoanalysis. In Paris, I had tried to develop applications of my skill to commercial and related problems. I remember meeting some chap from Dubonnet, the aperitif company. When I explained that I wanted to find out why people really liked their beverage and how it could be sold better, his answer was typically French, or what we usually associate with French characteristics: "That is the way we make it and if the public does not like it, that is just too bad for them. Why don't you go to the United States? They have such an open society that they will try to follow the slightest whim of the public. I think you will be successful there." He did not know how right he was.

When I arrived here and tried to explain how ingenious my approach was, I was greeted with the prediction by almost everybody that I was completely wrong in my judgment of Americans and American businessmen. "They seem very much interested in new ideas, but that is only a myth which they have spread or permitted to grow up. All they really accept and believe are statistical and apparently solid facts. Your psychological concepts will frighten them and they will laugh at you. You better give up your expectations." "We'll see about that," said the controversial voice inside of me. I remembered having thought that Frenchmen were emotional, erratic and disorganized. I had found them very hard-headed and mathematically accurate in their life's calculations.

Looking for contradictions has helped me in many ways. Working in different countries, I found the so-called "real" Frenchmen, "real" Germans, and "real" Italians to be much less aware of the so-called characteristics than someone like myself, acting as an observer without any national basis.

Shortly after I came to the United States, I began using this irreverent questioning of the truth, no matter how well established it seemed. Everyone had told me that Americans did not really understand psychological subtleties. I, therefore, would never succeed with my idea of a complex analysis of human motivations. People simply bought products because they were better or cheaper and not because of some mysterious symbolism and deeper meaning. Voters elected a candidate, not because he had charisma, but because he really was better qualified.

Such cocksure and, to me banal, pronouncements were signals which triggered my desire for controversy. When no one thought about moving an office into the suburbs and into country surroundings, that is when I did it. When everybody was convinced that nothing could go politically wrong in Austria and that Hitler had no chance whatsoever, I left. Later on, I discarded similar assurances in the Europe of 1938, and left altogether.

Rather than modestly practicing conventional market research and perfecting my English, I started with my controversial approach of motivational research. Whenever someone told me it could not be done, that was enough to mobilize my spirit of adventure. My lifeline, if I were to draw a graphic representation, would then be a very convoluted and jagged one.

12 Thank You, Mr. Packard

Whenever somebody tries to make other people aware of my "fame" or the controversial nature of what I am doing, they sooner or later use as a memory trigger Vance Packard's *The Hidden Persuaders*. I do remember when Mr. Packard came to see me. It was in 1956 and we were lost in our castle with our staff of six. He spent a few days in our offices, studied a number of our reports, and a few months later showed me a rough manuscript. Despite my supposed knowledge of public relations, I must admit that nothing in the manuscript led me to expect the spectacular, literally world-wide attention which was created through this book. Since I am quoted on almost every other page, I became known as the chief villain—the Chief Hidden Persuader. Some of my clients who read the book told me facetiously, "We wish you were half as good as Packard makes you out to be." Others seriously suspected me of having paid Packard to write the book. My reminding them that it was an attack against me did not seem to impress them.

Indeed, very soon after the appearance of the book, I received invitations to go to India, Australia, and to some of the remotest regions of the world. I could not possibly imagine that these people would be interested in motivational research. My business started booming. I appeared on many television and radio programs, in discussions with Mr. Packard, and, since I modestly think that I am a better speaker than he is, I felt that I was up to the challenge. The argument was centered, for the most part, around the morality and immorality of what I was doing: manipulating and persuading people with mysterious means to do things that they never intended to do; to get them to vote, to buy, to act in almost an hypnotic state. What was my answer?

I tried to explain in a previous chapter what I am really doing: cultural anthropology. I concern myself with the customs and habits of the people living in this world, regardless of whether their habitat happens to be Paris, Frankfurt, Chicago, New York or Samoa. I try to take a fresh approach, and not be misled by stereotypes. In other words, to first set up creative hypotheses, as any good researcher will do, and then to use the techniques discussed previously to prove or disprove my hypotheses as to what makes these people behave in a special way. The only difference between my methods and traditional anthropology might be that the results are not gathering dust, but are being used. Governments or companies might be interested in how to reduce growth of population, how to improve the image of a country like Mexico (which I have visited often), or such ridiculous problems to us, as consumers, as how to get people to eat more frankfurters. Even that problem is not quite unimportant to the company making them.

I distinguish between 'why' motivations and 'how to' motivations. Do I have a real answer to Packard's attacks, which of course have long since died down? Yes and no. The easiest answer would be to say that I'm not concerned with the specific problems for which the motivational research techniques are being used. In other words whether the end justifies the means. I realize that this is not a satisfactory answer. I have my own philosophy as to which tasks to accept and which causes to reject. But all along, I'm more interested in perfecting the techniques of persuasion.

The Mexican government decided to develop a strip of peninsula, Cancun, and make it accessible for use as a new center to attract well-heeled tourists. They asked me to set up a center for motivational research and management techniques on this tropical island. Sometimes I am frightened by the faith people have in my ability to really influence others by clever techniques. The difficulty lies in freeing yourself first from your own reactions, to try to understand through interviewing and other techniques the motivations of people who might be quite different from yourself. For example, my own feeling about this island was not entirely positive. Although the Mexican government was attempting to control its density, there were already quite a number of huge hotels and I was afraid that sooner or later it would begin to look like Miami Beach.

How do you get people to give more blood to the Red Cross or similar institutions, to become less superstitious; to change, to abandon long-established habits? What Packard never quite understood, or didn't want to understand, was that there is no hidden persuasion involved. What I'm doing is using a more sophisticated way of education. People practicing hypnosis have been demonstrating for a long time that you cannot really, even when you use hypnosis as a means, make somebody do something that, deep down, he is opposed to. The same thing is true as far as motivating someone is concerned. All I'm really doing is freeing that person, or group of people, from fears, from false hopes. Sometimes I am able to show them how to overcome their fears and make use of them. I'm certainly not the first one.

When the Protestant Church, with great success, created not only the slogans, but also the accompanying philosophy that cleanliness is next to Godliness, they formed the foundation for the success of Lifebuoy soap (and all the scores of other products dealing with the deodorization of the human body). They put a fear into people of their own body odor. Had that not been done, no soap company, no Arid, Sure, Safeguard, or whatever else could have been successful. All I do is advise the advertisers how to make use of this already existing fear. I do plead guilty that I personally really don't believe that by reducing body odor people will be happier.

The technique which I developed, however, in bringing about the success of such a product, is exactly the same technique that has to be utilized for example in making people participate in a program of adult education. In my role as a Distinguished Professor of Nova University I was recently asked the real reason why people joined, at relatively great cost, a university extension program (University Without Walls) which permits them to get a degree, even though it might not help them in their professional career? What I discovered was that these people had a fear of stagnation, of not getting anywhere in life, of getting too old. When the program was offered, this was a relatively easier way than a formal university education to reassure oneself that one had not copped out, although quite a number of people did drop out. Those who stayed on did so with a feeling of "I made it." My help consisted of advising the University to play, if you want to use this word, on this fear.

The more I think about it, the clearer it becomes that the whole field of education, the combatting of prejudices and the reducing of fear of change, are all interrelated. Prejudiced people usually are those who have organized the world around them in a neat and orderly fashion. It may have something to do with color, with wealth (in Germany people who are well off are automatically called better, *bessere Menschen*, people). No one is aware any longer of the prejudice involved in the fact that you can be poor and also a better person and be rich and be a worse person. What we are asking a prejudiced person to do is to abandon his well-ordered world and to substitute an entirely new, and very often additional, order. We are telling him that there are no psychologically or physically black and white people, that most of us are grey. This is frightening. Appealing logically to a person to change a brand, to deodorize himself, to become educated, to abandon a prejudice, have all the same title in my book on motivational philosophy. You can do it by describing paradise and the hope of a beautiful life, the cleanliness, the discovery of truth which will come to you by being less prejudiced; or you can appeal, unfortunately usually much more successfully, to the fears of people.

Sticking for a moment to education and prejudice, some years ago I was asked to help in convincing white landlords to admit blacks as tenants. An appeal to their feeling of tolerance or moral principles was not very successful. What we discovered was that they were afraid that the real estate values of their properties would go down, but more that their whole well-organized world would collapse. A series of 10- to 20-second slogans over the radio and a number of similar approaches were apparently helpful. These slogans simply consisted of having two white people talking to each other. One with a frightened voice tells the other one, "Have you heard, blacks have moved into the apartment house very close to us?" The other person, equally excited asks, "What happened, what happened?" The first person simply answers, "Nothing." This is an attempt to motivate people by using their fear or combatting their fear. It is quite different from arguing with them logically, that sooner or later, particularly with the new laws, they would have to admit blacks, and they might as well do it now.

I've written a number of books answering Mr. Packard. I must, and want to, thank him. Not only did he help me in my success, but he reinforced my conviction that what we need is more methods of persuasion rather than fewer. While he exaggerated, and often distorted, the facts, resulting in helping to make his book a best seller, what he actually achieved was to present my approach as a threatening and fearful one. What I resent is that he did not point out its necessity and usefulness.

Imagine what would happen if we had a very effective motivational department attached to the United Nations. Many of the problems in the Middle East and South Asia and almost everywhere, which are partially being resolved by discussion but partially also by mutual threats and actual exchange of bullets, could be solved by bringing about a better understanding of the emotions, the psychological factors, the motivations involved in the two or more opposing camps. Everybody accepts the fact that machismo, pride, the desire for virility, and its demonstration to the rest of the world are, and have been, involved in many conflicts.

I am being challenged lately, not so much because of Mr. Packard's accusation which used fear to help him sell his book, but over whether or not it is really possible to change human nature. I'm not always sure, but I think the answer lies not in the ridigity of most of us, but in the lack of more sophisticated approaches. In *Motivating Human Behavior*, I tried to describe various approaches on how such changes can be brought about. The most radical approach is to put a gun in somebody's back. At the other end of the scale are methods of inspiration. Christianity and many other religions are more or less successful examples of this, although one could argue that any kind of persuasion technique which had in its wake so many wars, inquisitions, cruel pokes and still has not succeeded in reducing brutality in mankind would have to be considered ineffective. How was it possible that a Christian nation like Germany slaughtered six million people? What happened? Had they never been converted, since the cross only had to be bent into the swastika to throw them right back into barbarism? The real problem, in my opinion, lies in the fact that we have spent too much time on the illusion that it is enough to give people the ten or more commandments, to admonish them, to promise them Heaven, and threaten them with Hell. If we had spent all these thousands of years to develop techniques of how to implement the commandments, we might have been further advanced by now.

A large company once approached me with an interesting proposition. "We want to hire you, but we are going to determine, through a committee, for what goals and purposes your techniques are going to be used." Since they assured me that I would not make any less money, possibly more, than I was doing in my private work, I agreed. Within a few weeks it became clear, however, that we could not even get over the first hurdle, which was the creation of the committee. Some of the Republican members felt that the motivational techniques should be applied for the goals of the Republicans. The same thing was demanded by the Democratic members of the committee. Religious and moral questions were being discussed. We spent many hours in analyzing whether it was defensible to tell people to buy cars, since it would only increase traffic jams. We could agree easily that the committee would not work on motivating people to smoke cigarettes. Liquor raised new questions. It finally all bogged down because we could not agree what were the really essential aspects of human life. Should everybody become educated? (But where would we take the "Indians" from?) Everybody would want to have more and more. The rising level of aspirations, which is taking place by itself, proved how right these fears were.

Sometimes human habits change just because the time is right. More and more, people are interested in preserving the environment. They reject rows and rows of houses and high-rise apartments. Growth began with standards that used to be accepted but are now being questioned. Low density in building, a feeling not only of keeping populations down, but protecting areas by permitting only a restricted number of buildings, not only are being discussed but are made into laws. A whole new life style is being developed which involves a return to basics, to nature, and the more genuine values. Environmentalists have called me in to find out how they can "sell" their goals. At the same time, however, I've also been asked how exaggerated fears of growth can be mitigated.

An important part of motivational techniques consists in discovering trends at a time when they are barely noticeable. In one of his later books, Packard talks about the Status Seekers. Almost by the time he had finished his book, the role of status had changed considerably. In many of our studies we have discovered that, particularly, younger people became much more interested in expressing their individuality. Even such widely accepted motivations as deciding on a career had lost their attraction. The Dale Carnegie Institute had not noticed this change. They continued to promise in their ads to potential participants, more money, becoming better public speakers, and making a career. We pointed out that they were behind the times, that they would be better off in stating in their advertising approach that a career was not the only positive result of a diploma from a Dale Carnegie course. The new ads talk about finding oneself, even the possibility that some of the participants may not feel better, but worse, but will have developed more insight and more self-motivation.

Studying how to motivate people to get back to the inner city from which they had fled because of crime, pollution, and racial problems, we found that the division between country, suburb and city was not quite as prevalent any longer, and certainly not desired. People wanted a return to greenery, naturalness. The architects and builders, however, were and still are slow in recognizing these trends. They told us that it was an impossible task, that it was not solvable by architectural means. Our study showed that as long as the inner city looked the way it did, it could not attract people back. Here again, techniques convincing planners to listen and to note changes in trends became an important part of our approach.

13 Sex and Sales

Robert, my old schoolmate, asked me for some advice. Our sex searchlights were meeting in a knowing and mutually understanding twinkle after having surveyed possible sex objects. The last question I expected was the one which he whispered. "Do you think I am too old?" "For what?" I asked innocently. "I can't do it anymore," he said, "with my wife." I caught on. "So why don't you try a young chick?" "I tried that, too. It does not work either." I conjured up all my knowledge about impotence and how it is, in most cases, only psychological. I tried to hide my pride in my own prowess. We were about the same age—somewhat past sixty. At the same time, I was considering offering my consolation, not condolences, to his wife. Upon surveying the possibilities, I decided I could do better.

Sex, in my opinion, is not necessarily the most important thing in life, but it definitely is one of the more pleasant things. Naturally I will always stress officially that sex should be connected with love, but as a realistic man, I also know that there is something called curiosity. For many men, success in this area is necessary. At the same time, this challenge quite often represents a reason for stress. There have been some studies that pretend to prove that sexual adventures of an extra-marital nature are much more dangerous, particularly if you have had a heart attack, than if you do the very same thing with your own wife. Maybe Masters and Johnson and other researchers have permitted their moral philosophy to get the better of them, and have simply tried to rob us of extra pleasures. At the same time, I find that it is somewhat insulting, as far as wives are concerned, since sex relations with them are described as not being particularly exciting or at least less exciting than with different women.

Sex is a lot of fun, but to many men it can be a challenge and a source of stress. Masters and Johnson have reassured most people that, except in rare cases, age or other factors such as illness rarely play a role in our difficulties.

When our son was "coming of age," since we were always very open with him in these matters, he reported on his "first." His experience is at least as frequent as the one of my friend. He was far from sixty, and closer to sixteen. Thus, age has little to do with the "problem." "I sweated, I was nervous, so was she, and before I knew what had happened, it had happened." Never mind the scientific name. Hollywood, T.V., and falsified reports by his friends had built up the wrong expectations in him, although I had at least tried to warn him by telling him what had happened to me in a similar stage. I had secretly hoped he might be luckier.

We probably lie more about sex, romance, and love than about many other experiences. Were we more truthful, many problems now on our stress list would be reduced. Maybe we would have fewer divorces and fewer marital quarrels.

When we celebrated our fortieth wedding anniversary we kidded each other about how we could have stood each other all that time. We did not use the word love, but proved it, which is more difficult.

We have a half-open marriage. Hedy at least pretended that she did not mind my middle-age escapades. I did not tell her directly, but my body or its most expressive part did. One day, I could not perform. We both searched for the reason. I guessed. I had a very sexy secretary who would get next to me behind the desk and "play," while being hidden from any sudden visitors. We also developed a technique, which I highly recommend, of asking her to bend over the desk to hand me my dictations or other office material. Since she wore very low-cut blouses, a very comfortable opportunity for a "reach-in," if not for a full "love-in," was created. After a few days of these various "hors d'oeuvres," we became interested in the main dish, the consummation of which took place on top of a very uncomfortable desk in an unoccupied conference room. At the next opportunity, my body betrayed me and Hedy guessed. She pried the rest of the story out of me. Once I had confessed, and she, true to form of a modern understanding wife asked, "Did you have fun?" I exaggerated the discomfort somewhat and told all. Divorce accusations? No. She laughed. I did, too, immensely relieved. No more problems in any which way.

For a while now, the situation became reversed. At home I was okay, but it did not work any longer with the inventive secretary. Another confession was necessary. She, too, was understanding, and it worked like a charm. The love potion was a change in attitude and putting sex in its rightful place.

When our daughter could no longer be protected by chastity belts and dire warnings, I, yes, I (with the consent of my wife), wrote an article which was later published: "Father and the Single Girl." I told the story of how we gave our daughter freedom, and admonished her only to be careful and to be sure that she at least liked the young man.

The lesson, which some people may consider to be immoral, was that too many girls get married either to defy their parents or to finally have the "great experience." An unhappy marriage, I have always felt, is too high a price to pay for biological curiosity.

Did our daughter become promiscuous? No. Her only complaint was that, when she told her schoolmates about our attitude, she became the envied black sheep. Furthermore, we made her temptations much less overpowering, which was our secret hope in our approach. She married the second boy, loves him, and has two children. She still remembers the "trick" we played on her.

Many of our stresses and problems are brought about by outdated hang-ups and so-called moral concepts which are too often based on hypocrisy, fear, jealousy, protection of our own egos.

My friend's wife could help him a lot. They could both forget their age which had, most likely, little to do with his problems.

When I reached fifty, I marked it on my calendar. Somehow I expected radical changes to take place. As someone reminded me, at least two-thirds of my life had gone. At sixty, I did the same thing. Now I am looking forward to another mark, I don't know in which color, when I reach seventy-five. The discovery which I made, and which is not made known enough, is that life went on. It is a continuum.

Another one of our hang-ups is to think in terms of plateaus, of reaching a date, after which things change and get better. Seldom do we accept that they're getting radically worse. Psychologists have discovered that there are at least five phases in everybody's life: childhood, adolescence, maturity, old age, and senility or death. Mozart, like other people who died young, lived all five phases within a period of about thirty years. It is almost as if, comparable to a bio-rhythm which is often discussed today, we also have a life rhythm. People seem to sense how long they are going to live and pass through these phases in the proper rhythm.

I am more inclined to believe that, with the help of your own motivations, you can flatten out this curve and be as active and productive during your so-called old age as during your maturity. We are getting "old" much later than in previous years.

When I came back from Holland in 1919, immediately after the First World War, where I had been sent with many other thousands of starving children from Vienna, I lost a year of school. Ever since then, I felt I had to make up for it. I had gotten sick in Rotterdam with a kidney disease. The family which had temporarily adopted me unadopted me and sent me to the hospital. I stayed there for about two months, not realizing how serious my disease was. My mother could not visit me because Europe was still ravaged and she had no money. I found out only later how much she had suffered for lack of news from me.

What I remember from my Dutch stay was the two children of my family whom I must have seduced to play games

Drawing by E. Dichter, of a Dutch boy.

of show and hide. We jumped up and down in bed, we slept in the same room, practicing an infantile form of exhibitionism. Of particular interest to me was, of course, the girl, since I had no sisters. The parents discovered our nightly or morning entertainment which, to us, took the place of television or comics, and probably was a lot more fun. We could not understand what upset them so much. I was the dirty foreigner who had come to spoil the virgin-pure children with my Austrian and Viennese permissiveness, probably practiced by my parents. Their outcry about my being a dirty ten year old sounds strangely familiar now, except that I am now being called a dirty old man.

I have used, by the way, this parallel between dirt and morality several times in my consultation work on detergents and soap. My first "discovery," that soap can be used to become morally clean again, comes out of the same realization. Dirt can hide things, evil things, danger, the devil. White is clean; cleanliness is next to godliness. Angels are always white and devils black.

Could our race prejudices have something to do with this? I analyzed it years later, in a chapter I wrote for Dr. Marrow. Blacks belong to a different, secretly threatening species, maybe only because they have black skin. I always enjoyed finding such apparent, but often overlooked, relationships. Why are angels above us in heaven and devils beneath us in caves and coming out of crevices wildly screaming and hiding in a veil of sulphur and brine?

Americans, in particular, wash their sins away continuously with the help of dozens of deodorants, Lifebuoy soaps, ladies' shavers, and depilatories.

Many sexual hang-ups come from this fear of dirt. Sex is slimy. The man enters secret threatening cavities. As children, we like to wallow in mud, but are soon punished for this pleasure. Spending some time on the Dead Sea in Israel, I discovered that the bathers enjoyed covering themselves with the supposedly healing mud and floating on the water. They flung big balls of the mud at each other, rejoicing as much as the pie-thrower in a vaudeville act.

I have started a collection of illustrations of peculiar aspects of human behavior. Many of my studies derive insights from observing, listening, and asking people about these peculiarities.

I try to understand my own experiences by collecting, as any anthropologist does, case histories of other people. The explanations are often startling, or so simple that people become angry with themselves for not making their own discovery.

Many companies have assigned expensive studies to us to find out some basic "Aha" experiences. A feeling of, "Aha, that's it. Yes, he is right. That's why we do it."

I have often been accused of being a Freudian. I don't quite see why this should be an accusation rather than a compliment. In reality I am not; I am much more an eclectic. By popular opinion Freud is always associated with sex. While I am fairly open-minded about sex, I am absolutely not compulsive about seeing it in every product and in every analysis. I think it is true that the pleasure in sexual explanations is looked for by journalists and by quite a number of my clients. It has happened repeatedly that someone has complained, in a somewhat facetious fashion, that he did not find anything in the study that was particularly erotic. They say, "You are known, whenever possible, to introduce sexual explanations for human behavior." Not true. But, by the same token, I am not afraid to use it as an explanation when it fits. I do not think that all of human behavior can be described in this fashion.

It is also often difficult to distinguish between sex and expression of powers. A few days ago I was being interviewed on the subject of why people like to browse in hardware stores. Tools are an extension of one's personality. You wander around a hardware store, almost as if it were a toy shop for adults. Each new tool opens up a whole new world for us. It permits us to penetrate the undiscovered territories of the plumber's, electrician's, or carpenter's world. A special kind of drill may represent a key to a magic kingdom. As I progressed with my explanations, the reporter asked me whether there wasn't any sexual implication involved in tools. The journalist was an attractive young lady. I reminded her of the double meaning of the word "screwing." She then proceeded in a fake, scientific fashion, to ask which came first. I had to tell her that I was sorry, that I had never really found out.

As an eclectic, I search for explanations which go beyond lazy labeling of human behavior. If I pose the question, "What are neckties for?" a simple answer could be: decoration or expression of one's personality. If I go a step further and wonder whether it may also have a phallic symbolic significance, I begin to raise eyebrows. I am the dirty old man who sees sex in everything. In Germany, with the help of a creative advertising agency, we translated this shocking possibility by showing an old, very wrinkled, and limp tie (you must get the comparison) hanging on an old man. The moment, in the next scene or ad, he had put on a new tie—smooth, colorful, erect, and manly—he had shed at least ten years. We did not refer to sex. How come everybody, or almost everybody, seemed to understand the hidden meaning? Did the sales go up? Yes, quite a bit.

During this study, I had to pose the question: What is the real purpose of a tie? I could have been satisfied with the explanations that it is a decorative piece of material, that it expresses the personality of the man, and that in most instances a tie is friendly and colorful. While all these things are true, one of my hypotheses was that there must be more to it. During our study, we could see quite often that when a strange woman, let's say during a cocktail party, starts playing with a tie of a man married to another woman, his wife starts getting nervous. Were she to simply slap his shoulder or do something similar, the wife would not get nearly as excited. It then took only a few additional steps to set up the hypothesis that the tie was probably more than a decoration and was, in fact, a symbol for virility.

The 'Tiger in the Tank' was another worldwide, successful translation of sex into sales. I did not select the animal, but I did contribute to its origin. What is gasoline? Our studies always go back, whenever possible, to asking fundamental, stupid questions. Without gas, the car is dead. Since the energy crisis, we have become even more appreciative of this powerful fluid. Maybe I would recommend at this time that the advertisement use the slogan "A camel in your tank." A gas tank is mysterious and dark like a womb. It can be fertile or sterile. The hose of the gas pump resembles you-know-what. Rational? Who cares? The symbol of power, of virility, of strength, goes through the oddly shaped nozzle into the receptive womb and gives it power and strength. It worked practically around the world.

I want you to realize that I am just amazed as the infidels are. How can such a contrived mixture between sexual allegories, mysticism, and caveman symbolism result in millions of dollars of very unmysterious cash through increased sales? It is not any more puzzling and should not raise any more eyebrows than the fact that nations kill each other because they speak different languages, or one tribe comes from the mountains and the other from the valley.

My first sex experience was with a part-time maid. She must have been intrigued with my virginity. Why is so much less fuss raised and much less drama attached to it when a male is concerned? The lesson is valuable. My shock was to discover her pubic hair. I expected her to be as pure and as white as I innocently associated with a woman's body. I did not have *Playboy* to educate and prepare me. Maybe that's why I wrote an article on "Why Men Like Breasts." I wrote it first for *Playboy*. They rejected it with the remark that on second thought they did not like such a clinical analysis of their two main selling points. It has now appeared in *Cosmopolitan*. The article explains that man differs from his animal counterparts in that man's affection for the breast is basically a psychological rather than a hunger need. I have discovered that man has a basic need to fill the palm of his hand, a very sensitive area. To a man, then, embracing a woman's breast with the hand creates a feeling of mastery. A man who is anxious and insecure is apt to be attracted to women with large, opulent breasts; their largeness seems to provide him with the extra reassurance he needs.

Although nude photos of women provoke thoughts of sexual satisfaction on the surface, the article points out that "The breast promises comfort and security but, oddly, also suggests danger and risk. Psychologically speaking, reaching for a breast is comparable to symbolic mountain climbing—getting to the top, overcoming the obstacles in one's path, conquering the highest peaks."

Do you remember the Edsel? Sex was responsible for a half-billion dollar blunder. The Ford company asked us to find out what they did wrong. Three things, at least were found. All involved wrong marketing thinking. "We need a family of Ford cars covering all price ranges. We don't have a medium priced car." Presto: the Edsel. "Let us pick a Ford family name." Presto: the Edsel. Some designer who knew little about human motivations thought making a well-engineered car was enough. He castrated the car. It had a gaping hole at the front end. Our survey showed that the otherwise inhibited Americans were referring to this oval shaped opening either as a lemon or, the more outspoken ones, as a hole which needed a bit of pubic hair around it to make it more real. This was a major reason for the flop. Our suggestion, which recommended

Sexual symbolism of the Edsel.

calling it a "Jet intake," came too late. I would love to add this picture and story to my collection of "Believe or Not" exhibits about human motivations.

A manufacturer of frankfurters asked me to analyze why men and children apparently liked frankfurters more than women. Women felt guilty. It was an admission that they were lazy and did not take good care of their families. "My wife gets mad at me," one of our respondents told us, "when I munch or suck contentedly on my frankfurter. She reacts the same way when I smoke a cigar."

We had analyzed cigar smoking several years before. "They don't like the smell," many said, "particularly if the cigar has gone out." Some women, those who smoked one themselves had different, more positive, attitudes. Cigars are a secret demonstration that a man if need be, can get satisfaction, albeit oral, without the succor that often has to be bought in one way or another. "This we cannot have," is the woman's reaction. "We want to be needed; otherwise we may not be needed." Thus, they hate cigars. Their reason: a nice, intelligent-sounding one such as the aroma hangs in the room or he gets the ashes all over the rug.

Why do men have to have creased pants? It is an insult to the soft, unspoiled fabric to artificially break it and make it conform. The history is interesting. One of the princes of Wales had a suit delivered from Saville Row. It came in a box and the pants were folded to fit. When they took them out, they had a crease. He wore them to the social occasion he had wanted the suit for. Everybody admired the new fashion.

There is, as you can suspect by now, a deeper reason. The crease gives a man the feeling of poise, of neatness, and most importantly, a sort of secondary feeling of erection. Armies recognized this as soon as this fashion became accepted and insist (with the exception of the Red Army) on giving every soldier a living example of erectitude. From there to courage is only one parade step. Chest out and stomach in led, also, to a further development; the discovery of a similar function by the corset. Contrary to the common belief, the Prussian officers wore them first. Although neither the courage of a soldier nor the anatomical accents are required of a woman in the same way, girdles have had their days and were discarded for increased body freedom. They are now making a come-back. The buttocks, according to some zoologists, used to have the same sexual attraction as breasts have for humans. Only because humans adopted a position for procreation which must look absurd to a monkey, anthropologists living on the Planet of the Apes have the famous breasts take on an importance which have provided magazine publishers, movie producers, and even me with much pleasure and profits in various forms.

Naturally, we studied the real reasons why sales of girdles had dropped off. Women's lib objected to the confining nature of the old-fashioned girdle. The most important reason, however, was the disappearance of the touchable and visible "cheeks" and separation caused by a girdle.

Sears was the first to bring out a new version: the "molded girdle." Now you can feel and see again. We came to this insight through group interviews where we asked men and women to talk about this part of their anatomy. They did, and with glee. Men finally confided that the girdle felt like a brick wall. It turned them off. Since we did not want that to happen, nor make them feel inadequate because they could not get the girdle off quickly enough, a light-weight girdle, some even with Velcro (a sort of Blitz closure), and a girdle shaped to reveal all the body contours were brought on the market. Sorry to boast again. It worked. Sales went up.

Here is my dilemma. If an explanation which shocks some people is nevertheless the right one, proven through research of various types, but primarily proven because it worked, should I feel bad, blush or do battle when I ask people to step into the Twentiety Century with their thinking?

14 My Presidents: Those Who Did and Those Who Didn't Make It

If you've ever seen the movie, "The President's Psychologist," you can understand my feeling when I received a serious call from a psychologist friend of mine who asked me whether I would be willing to be of help to a person very high up in the American government. He could not tell me who it was. Was I willing to come to Washington? I would find out everything that was necessary afterwards. How could I say no? It was much too intriguing. Upon arrival in Washington we met another gentleman, and the three of us proceeded in a cab. It couldn't be the President we were to see. It wasn't. It was the Vice-President, Hubert H. Humphrey. We were kept waiting. I met various secretaries. When we were let into his office, he slapped me on the back and jovially asked "How are you, Ernie? You look wonderful." I was a little bit taken aback, not so much by the friendliness, although being still in many respects a European, I felt it was not quite the thing that I would have expected from the Vice President of the United States. What bothered me was his remark about my looks. He had never met me before. I naively asked myself how could he tell whether I looked fine, better, or worse. It did not take me long to discover that this was his general manner, the manner that he had somewhere or somehow learned behooves a politician. I was awed, curious, and slightly apprehensive. We all went out to lunch. The two gentlemen had told him that I was the Hidden Persuader Number 1, and I could be very helpful in facilitating his nomination and, eventually his Presidency.

On the way to the hotel the car was guarded by Secret Service men. We were sitting next to the Vice President and they were riding in a car behind him. When we arrived at the hotel, however, there was so little protection that there could have been a dozen people or more who could have taken a shot at the Vice President. Not only did he not seem to care, but he went out of his way to shake everybody's hand—from the bellhops on up. He knew everybody and everybody seemed to know him.

We spent over four hours in the private dining room, discussing motivations of voters and what, specifically, could be done to help him win the election or, first, the nomination. Throughout the interview and lunch I was worried about lack of secrecy. Vice President Humphrey, when he saw my anxious look, reassured me and said, "They are all very nice chaps, don't worry, just relax." We talked about images. The Vice President's major complaint was that people kidded him about talking too long. He asked me whether, if he used a stopwatch and then sent to all journalists an accurate timing of his speeches, this would help. I was somewhat taken aback. I tried very hard to explain to him that I did not agree with this approach. It would not change his image very much. Facts alone are not sufficient to change people's minds. He was better off (at least that was my advice and opinion) to joke about his talking so long, and to laugh with the journalists. He seemed to accept this advice after a while.

You may ask yourself, how can one help a politician? It is not at all what most people imagine. I had great influence, and did not want to have any, on the Vice President's platform. I served as a communicator who informed him about what were the real dreams, wishes, hopes and fears of the American people. It was up to him whether or not he would promise answers to these uncertainties. We conducted a psychological poll—psychological, because we did not just ask people what they thought about the Vice President, or whom they thought they would vote for, but instead we used somewhat less orthodox approaches. For example, when they were thinking of the various candidates, what animal came to their mind? Which one of the candidates would they be willing to go into business with? And most importantly, how did they look upon Nixon, Wallace, Humphrey and other candidates. Nixon came through as the fox. How did they look upon the candidates from a viewpoint of being related to them? Did they think of Humphrey as a father, an uncle, a son, a brother or a husband?

A couple of years before, I had done a similar study in Italy with very positive results and some disasters. We posed the same questions to the Italian voters. Our answers indicated that the Socialists and Communists were compared with lions, tigers and other ferocious animals; while the Christian Democrats, the leading party, was unfortunately too readily associated with a placid, pleasant, but not very aggressive cow or sheep. The disaster came about when this report, which was, of course, highly confidential, was stolen by a secretary and turned over to the Communists. I received a call from Rome, while sitting proudly in my office in the States, informing me that my name had made the headlines in all the Italian newspapers in a very peculiar way. "Christian Democrats hire American psychologist famous for his successes in selling soap and toothpaste to now sell their party and their candidates to the gullible Italian people." Over the phone we discussed briefly what to do. They had denied that such a study had been conducted, but my recommendation was that I come to Rome, and explain. They agreed reluctantly. When I had to change planes in Milan, I was surrounded by more than twenty journalists, and I learned to appreciate the phrase "No comment." A press conference was called in Rome, I mustered all the Italian that I had learned over the years. I had luckily discovered that Adzubai, Khruschev's son-in-law, had been hired by the Communists during the election to do something very similar to what I had done for the Christian Democrats. The papers later on reported that I used my Viennese charm, which sounded like an accusation. Of course they didn't admit that the Hidden Persuader could really persuade them, but the affair seemed to have been resolved.

The very positive aspect of this study was that, based on all the findings, we ran two major campaigns for the Christian Democrats. In one of them we showed a picture of Karl Marx, who fortunately always is shown with a beard. I guess at one time he must have been clean-shaven, but no such pictures are ever used. His photograph was made to hang on one nail. Underneath we wrote, "Il Communismo e vecchio" (Communism is old). To parallel this campaign, we showed a very buxom, young girl, showing as much of the upper part of her attractive body as the Church would permit, using the headline this time, "La D.C. a veinti anni" (the Christian Democratic party is only twenty years old). The campaign was a success. The only admittedly quite clever response on the part of the Communists was to scribble, in rather rude words underneath the picture of the twenty year old girl, ". . . and it is time that she be . . ." followed by a four-letter word, although in Italian more letters were needed. The Christian Democrats won. What I had done was to change the image of the Christian Democratic party to an aggressive, young, alert and humorous one, from the one which it had had too long, of being serious, paternalistic and behind the times. I wonder how many times particularly young people vote for socialist or communist parties because they seem to be more alert, aggressive, and simply younger.

I met at regular intervals with the late Vice President Humphrey, his staff and speech writers. He was nominated. We conducted psychological surveys at regular intervals and, at one point, it became clear that, comparable to the situation in Italy, the American voters wanted a radical change. What they were afraid of was that Humphrey would follow President Johnson's lead too much and they would simply get a President who would continue his policies. I have been told that, had the election taken place two weeks later, Vice President Humphrey might have won. Who knows? Maybe I would have ended up as a right-hand man or even in a role comparable to Henry Kissinger, not a very enviable prospect.

Well, as we all know, Vice President Humphrey lost. I sent memo after memo and placed frantic calls to his staff that all the indications of the polls were that people wanted a break with Johnson's policies. My recommendation was that Vice President Humphrey declare himself against the war in Viet Nam, and dissociate himself from Johnson's policies. I got an interesting insight into problems of loyalty and interior party politics. Humphrey told me that he did not dare show disloyalty to his boss. "I would never be able to get a job even as a school teacher," he declared. "Johnson would cut me to pieces." My insistence that he would never dare to do anything like that in public, that Humphrey would gain so much strength by being his own man, had no effect. I also recommended that he should remind the voters that you cannot judge a future President by the role he played as a Vice President.

We counted three types of voters. They still exist, and probably will always exist. There is the visceral type of voter, who wants gutsy, quick, and radical solutions. He will follow the leader who offers him this promise. The other extreme on the scale is the blue-eyed idealist, who also wants relatively radical solutions, but without any real or psychological bloodshed. He wants to salvage and cleanse the world once and for all. In between is the mature voter whom I call the realistic type. He is the one most difficult to reach because the only language that he will accept is a blood, sweat, and tears approach. Most of us, however, are more inclined to dream of a strong leader who can solve, if not all, at least most of the problems for us.

In a very recent survey, we interviewed 250 people and they told us that they have learned their lesson, that Nixon and Watergate showed them that, in the final analysis, it is the negligence and the laziness of the voter which permits the wrong man to get into office. I can only hope that this last survey, where the people we interviewed told us that what they really needed was not only a solution to economic problems, and the misery of unemployment, but a spiritual goal, represents a true majority.

It was interesting that, having gone through a period of affluence and then a recession and depression, the voters discovered that even the affluent period did not bring them real happiness. One of the major problems democracies are faced with is the lack of goals. Communists are being told what they are working for and striving for. That it happens to be a misleading goal is beside the point. Most of us need a psychological goal that we can try to reach. Maybe the Human Rights issue, as presented by President Carter, does offer such a goal. Apparently it is a very effective statement since the Russians are not too pleased with it.

I have been thinking quite a bit about some of the problems that exist in connection with Eurocommunism, particularly with young people, and what the real reasons are that Eurocommunism seems to have been making partial headway. Putting it in marketing or motivational terms, democracy really lacks a color. Communism is red. They also have a trade-mark, the hammer and sickle. Unfortunately, the average person needs symbols of this type. In addition, very few leftists or admirers of communism have experienced what it is really like to live under communism. One of the suggestions that I've made which, unfortunately, has not been accepted yet, is that in the western democracies, we institute a day of communism. Everything would be treated the same way as if you were living in Russia or any other one of the countries behind the Iron Curtain. The *New York Times* would look like the *Pravda*. It would consist of only about four pages. Its contents would be almost completely censored. Radio and television would be continuously full of propaganda, probably at least as often as our broadcasts are normally interrupted for TV commercials. There would be long queues in front of all food stores and, even though our bureaucracy is quite bad as it is, this would be ten times worse. At the same time, there would be no strikes. There would be very little, if any, discussion about the stock market, inflation, and similar economic problems. My hope would be that, experiencing such a life under communism for 24 or 48 hours would have a sobering effect.

The frightening question which also poses itself is whether quite a number of people might not discover that they would rather have such a superficially quiet form of dictatorship than the continuous discussions, fights, scandals, and corruptions which they are experiencing on a daily basis under democracy. Too often we forget that people living under an authoritarian regime are basically happier than those living in a democracy. They don't have to make decisions. Everything is being done for them.

In a recent telethon, the Democratic Party mentioned that Adlai Stevenson and Humphrey had made requests and set forth goals which made them unpopular and caused their defeat. A fairly short time afterwards, the very same goals, including those of McGovern, were adopted by the opposition party. In a way, it made me feel better since I had also worked for Adlai Stevenson.

I felt very proud of my political jobs. Not all of them were failures. The Chancellor of Austria, Bruno Kreisky, had asked me during a previous election whether I could be of help. There the problem was of convincing the rank-and-file and the party bosses of the Social Democratic party that the old-fashioned class struggle and many aspects of its psychological grammar had become outdated. I raised the question of what the young Austrian worker really wanted—a car, or a second car, two vacations a year. In other words, did he want to truly participate in capitalist enterprises? What he did not want anymore was to be an outsider. Kreisky won.

A similar task confronted me when I was called, in Paris, to come as rapidly as I could to Caracas, Venezuela. Doctor Raul Leone was running for election. His sponsors were getting worried. Immediately after my arrival in Caracas I organized a psychological poll. I studied the campaign literature which included a barefoot peasant, supposedly the symbol of Venezuela, a figure of folklore. A study showed, however, that again, young men and women wanted television sets, cars, and certainly not propaganda about barefoot folk heroes. Another problem was that the Leonist Party had black for their party color. All the other colors had been taken by the opposing parties. Still another problem was that Leone hardly ever smiled on the posters which covered almost every empty spot on highways, in the cities and in the villages. We had Leone's picture re-taken, now smiling, and the folk hero was replaced with a modern, success-oriented young Venezuelan; and, in what may seem like an insignificant or almost silly approach, we changed the black party color to resemble the shape of a target. Hundreds of thousands of little arrows were made and distributed, and the slogan was "When you vote for Leone you are right on target." Of course I'd like to think that these measures, plus the report on the problems which were really on the Venezuelan's mind, helped Leone. He was a poor speaker. It was impossible to change his rhetorical ability in such a short time. The next best thing I could think of was to make an asset out of his lack. The opposition leader was glib, overly intellectual, an excellent speaker. My candidate was simple, humble, and a man of the people. He lived through his term of office, which for quite a long time had been very unusual for a Latin American.

My general lessons from these forays into the domain of power concentration left me both proud and disillusioned. When I witnessed how Vice President Humphrey bawled out his staff because he had not gotten enough space in the newspapers, and how Doctor Leone was afraid to go into the universities for fear that he might be personally attacked, and how Kreisky, in a way for practical reasons, abandoned many of his original socialist and Marxist concepts (he could just as readily have become a politician for the opposition party), my conclusion had to be, at least for the people that I had met in the political field, that they are far from being supermen. They were vain and they had many weaknesses.

One should also consider the possibility that we are probably approaching a time where the dream of supermen in leading positions has been shattered. There are apparently no more personalities like Adenauer, Churchill, Kennedy, and others around, at least for the time being.

When Hubert Humphrey died, we tried to make a posthumous hero out of him. It is true that he was first to develop the idea of the Peace Corps, had all of his life been a supporter of liberal causes, and had concepts of a far-reaching, global nature. At the same time, having had personal contact with him for over two years, my conclusion was that he should have been called, much more appropriately, "a happy worrier" than "the happy warrior." In many of our meetings, he showed a high degree of frustration. He never liked the role of Vice President. He worried about the space he would receive in the newspaper often more than whether or not his ideas had been correct. Possibly, because President Carter, who had for a while looked like he might be, at least in the moral sense, a superman, had let many people down, they latched on to Humphrey, at least after his death.

If we really were to believe in democratic ideals, we should also learn to accept the fact that the chancellor, the president, the operative head of state, whatever his title may be, is, and should be, a representative of the people and not a strong father figure. It is psychologically understandable that we want to be led, that we are afraid of personal responsibility and freedom. Maybe this is one of the reasons why more than three quarters of the new states created in the last 10-20 years and represented in the United Nations, cannot properly be called democracies. Mrs. Ghandi tried, despite all her democratic professions, to solve the many problems of India by dictatorial means. Maybe it was a victory for all democracies that she was defeated and a return to democracy took place.

I have often dreamt of the possibility of introducing into our schools, as early as possible, educational methods which really concern themselves with democratic education. One would almost have to start in kindergarten. One course would deal with decision making. How can we expect an 18 year old to decide intelligently, during national elections, when, all through his life, he has never been confronted, except maybe in minor ways, with the need to choose between alternatives.

A further problem is that we have never been trained to control or understand our emotions. Here too, we could have a quasi-clinical-democratic education which would teach us how to distinguish between phony demonstrations by a candidate such as kissing babies, and those of a more critical nature.

Adlai Stevenson, whom I erroneously advised to smile more often and to be less intellectual, tried very hard. I have a wonderful letter in my possession in which he thanks me, and then informs me that he had discovered that he was not a good enough actor to do what I had recommended. He was right. The few times that he tried, it was a lot worse than his supposedly condescending and somewhat arrogant and brilliant way of public speaking.

One of the many causes for stress comes from billing ourselves as superstars. We run, we try, and we pursue a role which we have set for ourselves. This is okay, but every time we suffer a defeat, which is inevitable for most of us, we begin to tear down our old dream; we behave like the politicians. We should instead try to find out what our real strength is, and develop it, even if it does not coincide with the norms and stereotypes which we admire. Looking back at my own life, I am wondering whether my insecurities and inferiority feelings had much more to do with my success than my abilities. Trying to overcome these shortcomings resulted in the discovery of potentialities within myself which became very useful to me.

Too often we behave in our daily life like poor politicians. Maybe it is a hopeful sign that many of our present leaders seem to have gone in the other direction now, by stepping down voluntarily from their pedestal, and by presenting themselves in a more modest and human fashion. Carter is one of the politicians who tried to do this, in contrast to the imperial stance assumed by Nixon. The fact that Carter was attacked, and many people expressed disappointment with him, may indeed be due to a deeper feeling of disappointment in having been robbed of a king or emperor.

15 How I Discovered Today's Caveman

Cavemen are supposed to be extinct, have been for at least thousands of years, yet what keeps me fascinated in my motivational work is the discovery that while we have advanced, many of our aspects of behavior can best be explained by better understanding their psychology.

Thanks to Mr. Packard and some successes, we soon filled the castle on the Hudson with over 60 people and opened offices in eleven different countries. I continued to discover motivational curiosities which can make you either laugh or wonder. Why do women paint their fingernails? Its origin is to be found in the almost animal-like original desire to make one's extremities appear longer and to frighten the enemy by putting his expected blood on your fingernails. Of course, no woman today would think of her beautiful fingertips as an instrument of war. If anything, they have turned into an instrument of love.

While we are discussing hands, have you ever tried to tickle the palm of a good-looking girl? You take a 50-50 chance. She's either going to slap you or you might be well on your way. The palm of the hand is an erotic zone, one we normally don't think about. How did that come about? During the last months in the womb, the embryo touches the palm of his hand with his thumb. When the baby is born, one of the first reflexes is the desire to fill the palm of the hand, to reach for things, to grasp things. This is, by the way, one major difference (outside of the more or less hopefully expected better development of our brains) which distinguishes us from other animals. Even there we have competition, because some of the higher apes also can develop this grasp action.

As I have been told, some of us, particularly men, never lose this desire to fill the palm of their hands, if not with money, at least with the well-rounded breasts of their girlfriends or wives as we pointed out in a previous chapter, or by patting or grasping the female buttocks. We use this finding in helping to develop not only doorknobs that fit, tickle, and sensuously excite the palm of the hand, but also in studying levers and handles of technical and industrial instruments. They are more eagerly reached for and more skillfully handled if they take advantage of this biopsychological phenomenon.

I am often asked what keeps me going. What makes Ernest run? I think it is this desire for discovery which every good scientist has. It makes headlines if a professor discovers the remains of men somewhere in the deserts of Africa and can trace them back over a million years. But to me the discovery of the sensitivity of the palm, and particularly the translation of it into practical measures which industry can use, makes it even more interesting. Adding to my collection of curiosities of human behavior is the fact that expressions of extreme joy and extreme grief resemble each other so much. In a way, it is a proof of some of the very complex philosophical concepts by such people as the German philosopher, Hegel, who claimed that if you intensify quantity long enough and increase it enough, it eventually changes its quality. We have an everyday example of that—if you add enormous amounts of sugar or saccharine to your coffee, eventually it tastes bitter. An itch is an irritation, particularly between the toes, yet scratching it gives you an extremely pleasant feeling. The stronger the itch, the stronger the pleasure. Something that started out as pain turns into enjoyment. If you ever suffered from athlete's foot, you must know what I am talking about.

What about lipsticks? They now come in all colors, but the preferred one is still red. Its deeper meaning is that we're trying to simulate youth and permanent life. Pale blue lips are the sign of old age and even death. A famous cemetery has a whole cosmetic department where one of the major things done to corpses is not only to fix the hair, but put on makeup, and pay particular attention to dead lips. A woman choosing a lipstick might be shocked to learn that, of course, the lips are a sexual organ. In some so-called primitive tribes, not only the normally visible lips of the face are painted, but also the lips of the vagina. The relationship between the two is quite obvious. If you can't accept it, let me remind you of a joke: When someone was asked how to define lips, he came up with the answer that the kiss (and we're not talking about kissing on the cheeks) is an inquiry on the first floor to find out whether the basement is for rent. Full lips are a symbol of sensuousness, even of lust. Thin lips signify asceticism. If a girl wants to be attractive she makes her lips redder and fuller. In studying the psychology of lipsticks I found these meanings. They are partially hidden, but not too difficult to bring to the surface. What proves them to be correct is that, when they are applied in the manufacturing process and in advertising, they indeed work.

Body language plays a very important role in non-verbal communication. Have you ever wondered why we shake hands? A very simple explanation, and probably a correct one, is that while shaking hands we cannot make a fist, we cannot fight. Therefore shaking somebody else's hand is a more or less direct expression of our peaceful intentions. Analyzing the psychology of gloves, I could make good use of this fact. Shaking hands with somebody with gloves on is a more distant type of expression of friendship than taking off your gloves for the purpose of shaking hands. In a recent analysis of homosexuality and its relationship to products and advertising, we found that the average person is still repelled by seeing two males, in an ad or in reality, touching each other, hugging each other, or kissing. This is considered acceptable among Russians, Latin Americans, or maybe Frenchmen, but certainly not among clean, puritanical and normally heterosexual Americans. Yet the advertiser is discovering that the gay market may be a considerable one, and inadvertantly, through pictorial illustrations, without shocking anybody, such situations have been introduced into modern advertising. The two men touching each other by holding a pole and being involved in fishing while at the same time smoking a cigarette, sends a clear-cut message.

When we sit in a car and have feelings of aggression, we can let them out, unfortunately too easily, by just pushing the gas pedal down. In analyzing the potentially extremely dangerous outlet which a car represents for aggressive feelings, I have recommended to the Safety Council that a second pedal be provided, which you push instead of the gas pedal, which permits you to get rid of your hostilities. Car manufacturers for many years, until the energy crisis, kept on stressing power. Young people are particularly interested in the ear-shattering noise produced by souped-up racing cars and motorcycles. Speed, power, noise are all almost directly traceable to the animal within us. We still gnash our teeth when we are mad at somebody—we don't bite him anymore. Chewing gum or bubble gum are innocent remnants of such peculiar aggressive behavior.

Detergents suffered for several years from the fact that, under normal circumstances, they do not produce any suds. Even quite intelligent housewives associated the quantity of suds with the effectiveness of the washing tool, the soap or detergent. The phenomenon is explainable because the lather represents a mysterious, active, continuously bubbling and moving aspect. We still believe in many superstitions and mythical relationships. The housewife knows little about the chemical processes in removing dirt. In her mind it is the lather, the suds which produce the miracle of removing dirt. Detergent manufacturers saw themselves forced to add (and they still do, to some extent) artificial suds to their detergents since it was cheaper than educating women about how detergents really work.

What makes people buy a house? If you ask them, they will tell you it is the construction of the house, its price, its roominess; but my studies have shown that the only way one can really emotionally establish a contact with a house is through the doorknob. This is where you can touch the house. Another possibility is through the soles of your feet, if you take your shoes off. I learned the importance of this experience from watching Arab carpet salesmen in Morocco. They invariably ask you to take off your shoes in order to feel the softness and the lushness of the rug. Designing a doorknob, therefore, in such a way that it gives you a feeling of solidity can do more than taking the potential buyer into the basement to show him the copper tubing and excellent plumbing when you are trying to sell a house.

People are funny, but there is usually a deeper reason for their behavior, sometimes dating back tens of thousands of years. In one of my early studies, I was interested in finding out how people could judge the quality of a car. It was simple. They slammed the door. If it produced a heavy, deep, sonorous sound, the car must be solid. I have to admit that this bit of psychological trickery has been so successful that almost all car manufacturers have taken advantage of it.

One of my dilemmas is discovering such aspects of human behavior and then using them—not really to trick people, but to motivate them for a specific purpose. The purpose, of course, can be very ridiculous. I would be one of the first to admit that it is nothing more than a game to convince the housewife to buy one type of detergent rather than another, unless it is really radically different from a competitive one. This is rarely the case. I could use these very same insights quite frequently, however, for purposes that most of us would consider to be more legitimate.

How do you get a person to stop smoking? Working for the Cancer Society, I recommended that they recognize that to the smoker puffing at a potentially dangerous and almost ridiculous white stick does, definitely, provide pleasure. To smokers, a cigarette provides not only satisfaction, but also a feeling of security. A cigarette permits you to close your lips around an object and thus in a way to batten down your hatches. When we are frightened, we usually have two types of possible reactions: either we let our mouth and everything else inside our body (including the production of diarrhea) hang loose, or we tighten up—our mouth gets dry, we close all our openings. A cigarette permits us to do that in a socially acceptable form. Pointing all this out to the Cancer Society permits them to stop showing the person who coughed himself almost to death in a T.V. commercial, then telling him that he could add five to ten years to his life by cutting out smoking. I could succeed in making these appeals more effective. The new ones show a smoker more realistically enjoying himself. The Cancer Society promises that if he wants to cut down on his smoking he could also enjoy the fresh, clean air if he can find it, and get more pleasure out of his food. Whether you are an atomic scientist or a medical researcher or are involved in understanding human behavior, you are always confronted with a typical kind of stress and dilemma. What is the real reason why you're doing it? Even curiosity could be challenged as a motive.

Once, in Western Samoa, I had been occupied with helping the Samoans to get their independence. One of my vitamin clients who became interested in this political issue sent me there. I took my wife along, which the Samoans told me was a mistake because they more or less feel that love is something to be enjoyed, but not limited to just one woman. We spent several weeks on Samoa. One of the greatest difficulties I encountered was the misunderstanding of the missionaries of various churches, of which there are at least fifty, ranging from the Catholics to the Seventh Day Adventists, and everything in between. They felt that the natives (who, by the way, are quite intelligent and do not deserve at all the implication which we so-called civilized people usually connect with this word) had no need to become independent. The missionaries even objected to an increase in education. "They're quite happy now," was their observation. "Why open up the Pandora's box of desires and wishes which they could not easily fulfill? Leave them alone," was their advice. These groups with vested interests considered such normally very desirable goals as helping people get their independence or helping them become better educated to be equally as immoral as my work in helping a manufacturer to sell more soap.

I have always been inclined to be more pragmatic in my undertakings. Staying in an ivory tower and doing research without worrying about what purpose it served is much less dangerous. It definitely avoids getting into conflicts. In observing children while analyzing their reactions to toys, it became quite obvious that aggressive toys were usually preferred over very innocuous ones. That included guns of various types. Luckily most of them are made out of plastic. Tin soldiers were as popular as ever. We also found that if the toy came in a very large box, the children had almost as much fun getting in and out of the box as they had with the expensive toy that the box contained. What does one do? Go back to the toy manufacturers, who paid me, and tell them, "Sell cartons instead of toys and stop making products for children which permit them to express their aggressive instincts?" They would not have accepted my advice and, personally, I'm not really sure whether getting rid of aggressive feelings in a harmless way does not serve as a sort of therapeutic outlet for children, permitting them to behave in a more peaceful manner during the rest of the day.

It has helped me a great deal in my life to realize that in my own decisions and motivations I am not always very rational. I very often play a game which I call an "If" test. If I receive a phone call by a certain time, then something very nice is going to happen. The fact that it usually doesn't has not deterred me from playing the same game. I saved the usual little strip from a Chinese fortune cookie which says, "Something good is going to happen to you." I have it right here on the brass cube holding my pen. Well, some days something good does happen, many other times it doesn't.

Recently I saw a spider enjoying himself in the sink of my bathroom. On top of everything it was raining. Quote obviously a spider was a bad omen. I remember from my Austrian days the proverb that a spider in the mornings brings sorrow and worries. For a while I was waiting for these bad things to happen, and it spoiled at least the beginning of my day. Finally I decided to snap out of it. After all, what about human motivations? This was my specialty, and not only did nothing bad happen, but quite a number of good things which I made happen. I decided to prove the proverb wrong.

Friday the Thirteenth—that's my lucky day. I've never really established any statistics in that respect, but if I were to keep track it might very well be that, because I feel that way about this date, I am much more optimistic and possibly show much more initiative, and therefore something worthwhile and interesting happens. What I've gradually learned, although not 100 percent, is that the facts causing stress and dismay are usually much less important than how we look at them.

I've tried Yoga, Transactional Analysis, Autogenic training, and relaxation. I finally have come to the conclusion that they are all various forms of escapism. My personal way of combatting stress is to do something about it, to face the problem, analyze my own attitudes and patterns. What gets in the way is that quite often without realizing it, we enjoy the negative feelings. An excellent formula which certainly works for me is to decide at the time that I'm brushing my teeth in the morning that I will manipulate events in the day in such a way that I will feel happier and less stressful. I have even gone so far as to suggest this idea to toothpaste manufacturers. Why not put a message on the toothpaste which sends you into the day with the feeling of a fresh start?

In the course of doing research that is based on curiosity and discovering the mechanisms within ourselves, I've tried to analyze various wisdoms anchored in our proverbs, legends and sayings. When people looked out the window and it was raining, they promptly concocted a proverb which seemed to give them power over the weather. "If it rains before seven, the sun will be out at eleven." Nobody has ever taken the trouble to find out if this peculiar meteorological prediction really holds true or not, but it certainly gives you a feeling of being in control of things.

In a sense, what we can do is to make sure to get out of bed with the right foot and use the right approach pretty soon after that. Too often we let our moods take control of us without realizing that we have the power to modify them. It is up to us to exert positive or negative influences over our environment and our feelings. After all, millions of people say their prayers in the morning or in the evening before going to bed without any scientific proof as to whether anybody's listening to them. Those who believe in it do definitely derive a therapeutic value from it. I have developed my own form of influencing the world around me. I reach for a book of poems or philosophical sayings, and read them before going on with my day's work or before going to sleep. I have suggested that television stations have such anti-stress briefings in their morning programs. You can develop such a program for yourself. Why don't you try to dictate some positive thoughts, some of your plans, on a cassette and listen to it sometime during the day or in the evening before going to bed? You might discover that a large number of your fears and anxious predictions never took place, and quite a number of your hopes have come true. Man is irrational in many ways. He can complain about it, or he can be glad about it. I decided to choose the second approach. It makes life much more interesting. If everything were carefully thought out and could be programmed and then put through a "life computer," life would be so boring that it would come close to hell.

When our son went to Russia I was afraid he might come back a Communist. What impressed him most after three weeks' stay there was the degree of security, the uniformity, and indeed the programming that most people had to accept. The Russian students that he talked to admired and envied the insecurity of Western youth. "We don't want to know what is in store for us tomorrow. Marxism tries to teach us that everything has its rational causes and effects." Maybe so. But should they not also have learned to include emotions and human motivations in these explanations? It was a great insight that our son brought back from his visit to the Workers' Paradise.

16 Fear of Embarrassment or Fear of Death

My work continued unabated with the questions and assignments becoming more interesting. Why don't more than 20 to 30 percent of Americans ever use a commercial airline? They are afraid of crashing. That's what they say. Several studies conducted by us demonstrated that what they were really afraid of was dying a frivolous death. I call it the fear of posthumous embarrassment. What they told me, in a more or less clear fashion, was: "Getting killed in a car accident or dying from a heart attack is elegant and legitimate. Getting killed in an airplane crash is kind of ridiculous. How am I going to explain that to my bereaved family? I can hear them making snide remarks such as 'Why didn't he take the train or drive like other sensible people?' " I have learned to recognize subtle emotions. Fear of embarrassment can be, and often is, more powerful than the fear of dying. We solved the airline problem by showing grandmothers and little children riding in a plane, using the fear of embarrassment, but now in the interest of the airline.

Many people don't cut their losses caused by a bad investment because it means they have to admit publicly, at least to themselves and their family, that they had made a mistake. They are afraid of embarrassment.

Patients don't go to a cancer specialist for an examination, not so much because they are afraid of finding out that they have cancer, but because they worry about appearing foolish if the doctor finds nothing wrong. Working for the Cancer Society, we had to tell them that they had better be aware of this fear as much as of the fear of being told really bad news.

Blood doners often faint just when they are about to make their offering. They are afraid of turning out to be cowards. To prevent this they faint. Who can blame them? That happens many more times to men than to women. The reasons are that many women are not as cowardly as men, they are accustomed to blood (menstruation), and they are not as apt to be whining hypochondriacs as men. I am a man, you can believe me.

Revlon's Fire and Ice nail polish was mentioned as one of his great achievements in Mr. Charles Revson's obituary. He invented a long list of beauty products and made millions. Most women will admit that, if they are ugly, even the most mysterious beauty lotion discovered in the Mayan temples won't do a bit of good. But they buy it. The cosmetics industry is only one of many amounting to several billions of dollars based on hopes, on dreams. Women who are not beauties are afraid of looking into a mirror. On a recent talk show a really beautiful woman stated that until she was 17 or 18 she did not like herself, she was afraid that she had never been told the truth about her looks. She was finally convinced.

I am often embarrassed by what I only too frequently discover through motivational research about human nature. Most of it I had never been taught when I studied psychology. The people I encountered in the textbooks were nice, rational, and devoted to the salvation of themselves and mankind. No wonder we are disappointed and depressed when we meet the walking and talking master mold from which the millions of copies populating our literature and our textbooks have been reproduced.

Some day I would like to teach a course entitled "What people are really like." It would concentrate not simply on amusing characteristics, although at the same time, I have to smile about many of our peculiarities. After all, how long has it been since we walked out, erect, into the light from a stooped position and a life not too different from our animal ancestors? Despite everything, I am impressed with the realization that with all our nonsensical behavior, we have actually come a long way. The revolution of our self-discovery has accelerated over the last twenty years at a hurricane speed. Realizing, and understanding, and possibly smiling at our very human frailties may be the necessary beginning of the slow climb to becoming human beings and taking advantage of our hitherto largely unused brain reserves.

What my first boss, Getchell, asked me was to discover the real, innermost force which makes people tick, their basic motivation. This was a difficult task. Is the heart more important than the stomach? Is the kidney or the bladder more vital? We can now transplant some of these organs. That does not make them measurable in their significance. They are interdependent and interrelated. So are our motivations.

Possibly 95 percent of the income of physicians and of a large part of the pharmaceutical industry is due to man's fear of embarrassment. We eat too much—we need Alka Seltzer. We drink too much—we need aspirin. We do not know how to dress properly—we need a cold remedy. Watching television the other day, I counted about a dozen diseases of a minor nature being discussed within a period of an hour. If you were over-active, you needed iron. Geritol was the right product. Pepto-Bismol, Alka Seltzer, Tums, Rolaids, Brioschi should all give sizable commissions to restaurants and to homemakers in their cooking pursuits because, without them, there would be no need for these products. Over three million dollars worth of Valium is sold in a year serving as a tranquilizer because we have not learned how to live properly and how to relax by natural means. Is one of the basic motivations, then, this fear of admitting our irrationality and correcting it?

I have tried, not always with success, to make a list of all my aches and pains. Like a medical doctor, I tried to trace them back the best that I could to their most likely origin. To my shock, a vast percentage of them were brought about by myself. I got myself excited. I worried about something that never took place. When we stayed in a hotel where the bill was picked up by some convention I was addressing, I felt it was my obligation not only to deliver a good speech but also to partake of all the meals and cocktail parties which were offered free of charge. The hidden charge was my bloated and sour stomach and my hangovers. Maybe it would not be such a bad idea if restaurants were to put on their menus the possible side effects. After all, drug companies are obliged to do that when they are describing and advertising ethical drugs. It probably would save the restaurants and the sufferers quite a lot of money. It might cut, however, into the profits of the pharmaceutical industry.

When I call myself a professional cynic, which I often do, I am asked in desperation by other people, "Don't people ever behave rationally? Does everything have to be explained in terms of emotion and irrationality?" The answer is, of course, they do behave rationally. But rational behavior also includes the acceptance of emotions, such as the fear of embarrassment, as a motivator. For thousands of years, ever since the Greek philosopher Plato and even before him, we have been afraid of emotions. Plato compared human beings to passengers in a horse-drawn carriage. The horses, often going wild, were the emotions. The reins on the horses controlled by the driver were his powers of intelligence. Rejecting emotions, however, as irresponsible animals in our make-up is a very irrational type of attitude. If you wanted to live rationally, without emotions, life would be very drab. Many exciting things which we have developed attracted us because of the excitement. Without emotions, they would never have taken place. A formula for rational living which is often propagated by nutritional experts, environmentalists, and other people concerned with human welfare, could go as far as recommending that we all live on a balanced diet consisting, to a large extent, of vitamins and calorie-controlled pills. We would have to live in bunker-like constructions, preferably underground, which more or less adjust themselves to summer and winter temperature, or else live in sub-tropical climates where there is little change in temperature. We should keep away from cigarettes, alcohol and any other kind of excess. We should wear reasonable clothing made out of a combination of natural and synthetic fibers.

When I do work for a company selling detergents, or cosmetics or expensive ties, or am being hired to discover through motivational research what unsatisfied needs people have that could either be brought to the surface or invented, I am entering, whether I like it or not, into this whole controversy. I am going to have to define happiness sooner or later in order to come up with a wise decision. Are people happier when they apply cosmetics or dye their hair or wear wigs or hair pieces? Who knows? If a bald man discovers that by putting on a well-matched hair piece he looks ten or twenty years younger, it may have as beneficial an effect on him as undergoing cell therapy. It is old hat to repeat that you are as young as you feel. It is truer to say, you are as young as you look to yourself and others. All you have to do is tell a person they look quite old and tired, and they quickly will make this observation come true.

The Ford Foundation, in connection with Nova University in Fort Lauderdale, Florida, asked us to conduct a study on the open school. In such a system, pupils are allowed to wander back and forth between at least four schoolrooms. If they are bored by one teacher they can visit another classroom. The majority of the lessons are in the form of either cassette or film, professionally done. The teacher is free now to be a counselor rather than repeating, year after year, the same geography or history lessons. With the help of a modern film called "Animated Computers" it is even possible to develop concepts and to modify these concepts in a way which will make pupils understand intricate mathematical, chemical or physical relationships in a much easier way. Our studies showed the real resistance came from the teachers. Rather than being able to play wise or authoritative men, as their training promised them, they found themselves with an entirely different set of requirements. They had to learn how to take criticism from their pupils, often to give up showing their authority and establish it in an entirely new and different way by developing positive relationships with their pupils. Seldom had they been trained how to teach. All they had learned was the subject of their teaching program, but not the manner in which it should be presented so as to hold the attention of their pupils. The emotion that we were dealing with was their fear of insecurity. The stupidity involved was a complete misunderstanding of what authority meant: Not so much being able to pound the table and to demand respect, but to gain respect and even love voluntarily by earning it. The answers which we got back were centered around these misconceptions. "In the open school they have little respect for me. If I don't barricade myself and surround myself with a certain degree of distance and unapproachability I will lose all of my authority."

We found the same stupidity in doctor-patient relationships. "You mean I should admit to the patient that I really don't know what is wrong with him or that I made a wrong diagnosis?" We suggested to coal mine operators that they admit they had made mistakes in the last forty or fifty years in their treatment of coal miners. It is almost impossible to get over this barrier. How do you get Europe or the African nations to unite? They hopefully have at least stopped fighting wars within the West European Bloc, but they are afraid of losing their identity through unification. "You mean I would have to," asked the French-man, "salute the German flag?" The Germans worried about the same thing. Their identity was associated, apparently to a very large extent, with a language or special dialect spoken, but even more so with the color, shape and size of a piece of cloth. The fact that nationalism had been created artificially and had an emotional basis or even an animal one, of establishing a sort of territorial im-perative, was completely overlooked. The fact that it would be much more logical and intelligent to give up borders and to create a European unity is only very slowly being accepted, against a lot of resistance.

Many of my studies sooner or later became involved in the problem of recommending a change. Even though this change was a very reasonable one, whether it concerned the idea of teaching European children to think of them-selves as European coming from the French region of Europe, or to the tentative creation of a European passport, or to the coloring of a detergent, or to educat-ing women that suds were not needed for cleaning, such a change brought about resistance.

Many of my problems, as well as my pleasures, have come from my role as a provocateur. A recommendation for example to build refrigerators ten feet high instead of wasting the space above them, and using a button to make the shelves within that ten foot refrigerator moveable in both directions—up and down—with the help of a simple motor, aroused a howl of protest. The sheet metal from which refrigerators are made had to be cut down to the average size of six feet for the refrigerator. There was no technical reason why a ten-foot model could not be made; only an emotional one. It required rethinking. I do not have patience to appreciate the hundreds of thousands of man hours or person hours that have to be wasted to invent clever techniques to gradually encourage people to try new approaches. This goes as well for big industry, for the teacher, and for the housewife.

When I decided to throw out our car from the garage and leave it outside so we could use the garage space for an indoor swimming pool, you cannot imagine how much stupid resistance I encountered. No swimming pool manufacturerer in his right mind would even consider the project. Everybody told me it was impossible and I would have problems with the building code. The moisture that would accumulate would ruin the house. I was given a long list of apparently very sound objections. The fact is that the pool has been very successful. We go swimming every morning, 365 days a year. Why are there still garages at all? They do not make sense anymore. With the present price structure reigning over the trade-in value of second-hand cars, the dealer looks up the price in his list and, unless your car is half smashed, gives you the same amount whether your car has been exposed to the weather or not. Most modern cars, when they start at all, start in any type of weather. They don't need the pampering, the protection from the weather or climate that was once necessary. You should see what happens to a car in the average parking lot or garage. You will find stupidity much more frequently than serendipity. You do not even have to strain yourself.

17 How I Turned My Heart Attack Into Hard Cash

On the second or third day after my coronary in 1970, I was more or less fully alert and I started staring at the wall across from my bed. It was grey, white, slightly dirty mauve. It looked like all hospital walls. All kinds of thoughts raced through my mind. None of them had anything to do with the fact that I might not have survived the attack. Instead, I dreamed or imagined how nice it would be if I could look at a beautiful mural across my wall. I asked for some paper so I could jot down the idea. They refused to give it to me. I was supposed to lie absolutely still. I jotted down the idea in my mind. Later on, when I was up and around again, I wrote an article on it and expanded on the whole subject. I called it "The Hospital—The White Prison." It was printed and got good reception and I was well-paid. I suggested that if the wall could be covered with a sheet of plastic, patients might be allowed to express themselves in any way they wanted. The artistic endeavor could range from fingerpainting to abstract modern pieces of art. Maybe they could translate their feelings visually after having partly recovered from their flirtation with death.

Another thought that I developed and put into a tangible form was the following: When the doctor admonished me to take the heart attack as a warning, and told me that I would have to change my way of life, I started thinking. Everybody receives, at birth, a number of chits; 35, 45 or 50. How he uses them is up to him. He may spend five of those chits to make more money or to gain fame or to increase his happiness. At one point, he may have spent all of his chits. There is no bank where he may buy or borrow more. That was the position I was in. What I set up to do for myself first was a kind of game. I entitled it the "Life Style Game." It helped me. I decided it might be of interest to other people. I developed it into a form of quiz and sold it to *Glamour* magazine. This was another way that I counteracted the shock of my coronary. That I got paid for it, too, was an added bonus.

Heart attacks have been described many times. According to what I had read, I should not have been a heart attack victim. My blood pressure was low, I did not smoke nor drink, I was a little bit overweight, but nothing to speak of. Was I type A? Running and rushing? Yes. I kept inquiring why I had a heart attack. Most of the doctors I had talked to told me if I ever found out I would become a real famous scientist. They do not know either. The specific event that led to the attack was a verbal fight that I had with the head of the Malcolm X College from Chicago. We both were on a platform at a conference in Long Island talking about how to bridge the generation gap and related topics. At one point during the discussion, this gentleman called me a racist. He had asked for $150 billion damages to be paid to the blacks for all the harm that had been done to them over 300 years. I tried to point out to him that this was not a practical approach. It was much more important to help black people now and, for that matter, other minorities no matter what color, to help themselves to develop better skills so that they could find employment more readily. Simply asking to be compensated in an unreasonable way would not solve anything. The money would be gone very quickly. This apparently enraged him. The accusation of being a racist ensued. I defended myself. Another gentleman, Dr. Chaim Ginott, who passed away recently, was also on the platform, and reminded the man from Chicago that the first and most successful slavetraders had been his own brothers and the discussion got more heated. I felt a sharp pain. I did not know exactly what it was. The session ended.

It might be interesting to note that there were several doctors present. When I asked them for help—not that I want to curse the medical profession—almost everyone turned away and told me to just lie down and it would go away. I did. The pains did not go away. Finally, we did what we should have done, or they should have at least advised me to do. We cornered a young man and asked him to drive my wife and me to the nearest hospital. Upon arrival at the emergency room, I was told they were not sure what I had, but it was most likely a heart attack. The electrocardiogram did not show anything, but, as I learned very quickly, this was not significant. It takes anywhere from 24 to 36 hours before the damage to the heart muscle can be detected by the EKG. Why no one in the frequent articles advising people on what to do in the case of a heart attack had mentioned that, I do not know.

Finally a delightful, relaxed Italian doctor examined me and made an interesting proposition. His approach was that he too was not very sure, but if I did as I had insisted and drove home with my wife I might die on the way; if I stayed in the hospital overnight, by the next day they could determine whether this was an attack or not and it might save my life. "Should I be wrong in my diagnosis, I will tell you so. Since you have health insurance anyway, the least that will have happened to you is that you will have gotten a good rest overnight." This sounded very reasonable. I agreed. Next day I was informed that I had indeed had a severe heart attack. In all, such a statement seems to make you proud, but I was probably more afraid that I had made a fool of myself and that there was nothing wrong with me.

As I look back, I was honestly relieved that I had had an honest-to-goodness coronary. A heart attack can certainly legitimately be called a "stress situation." Yet, I fought the diagnosis. I did not want to believe it. According to all the things I knew and had read, I was not supposed to have a heart attack. Nor did I feel that I had had one. I had pains for a few hours which were relieved by Demerol and similar drugs and felt rather dizzy and weak. When I felt more comfortable, I wanted to get up. The same Italian physician informed me, when I kept doubting and questioning his diagnosis, that in addition to the A and the B type (the A type being the aggressive, self-motivated, goal-oriented, and the B type being the more relaxed, placid type), there were other distinctions. Those patients who didn't believe they really had a heart attack, and those who became medical and primarily psychological heart neurotics. Those who don't believe the event are the ones who are more likely to survive.

There was another point in my favor. Contrary to some of the literature which many middle-age people read avidly and I read mostly after my attack, I had no particular anxiety, I was not afraid of dying, I didn't feel I was dying, and I did not recall and recount all the events in my life. I'm beginning to believe that many of these stories have been invented to make the heart attack more romantic. Most of these things in actuality are quite different and in a way disappointing.

As far as lessons on how to cope with stress are concerned, I would suggest that you should learn that things usually are quite different than they were described to you. Sometimes a situation of a dramatic nature, such as a coronary, can bring out completely unexpected problems that may concern family relationships, and not at all your own body. My wife sent a telegram to our son, who was in Morocco with the Peace Corps. He arrived a few days later. Unexpectedly, in some consulting session with a psychiatrist, he revealed many months later that when he came to visit me in the hospital he had a secret hope that finally the old man would be, if not out of his way, at least incapacitated. When he saw me, apparently as aggressive and as much in command as ever before, he was caught in a conflict. On the one hand, as he told the psychiatrist, he wanted me to recover. On the other hand, he began to realize that it was not quite as easy as all that to get rid of me.

This reminded me of a very shocking discovery I made at the time of the death of my own father. The stress was of a completely different nature. We found him dead in his bed one morning. As the oldest son, I was entrusted with the task of calling a doctor. Of course everyone in the family was very excited. We tried to awaken him, but I was fairly sure that he probably had died during the night. When running for assistance, one thing I was more afraid of and shocked by than the death of my father was that I might unnecessarily arouse a physician to come to his bedside. He might discover that he was just asleep, or in a coma, and had not died at all. The fear of embarrassment, as I've found in many other studies and events in my life, is often more important that the tragic event. What I worried about indeed was that the physician might become angry with me for having raised an alarm over nothing. As it turned out, an even more shocking thing was that after not having been able to reach one doctor I ran to get another one, and then both arrived. They examined my father, and then talked to each other in Latin, saying, "Mortuus est," not bothering to find out whether I understood Latin. I did, and knew they were saying, "He is dead." Only after they had made the statement did they turn to me, asking, "Is this man related to you in any way, or an acquaintance?" I stated, rather annoyed, "He is my father." They apologized, expressed their regret, and walked off. The lack of sympathy, or the inability or even possibility to take time out for it, may very well be one of the inevitable results of practicing medicine. It is, however, shocking whenever you encounter it.

I have now passed my 71st year and I still have not changed from type A to type B. I have written, in the nine years since my heart attack, about six or seven books; have traveled innumerable times to Europe and around the world; and have been as active as ever, if possible, much more so. Maybe this was an attempt on my part to disprove the predictions of the physicians. I remember distinctly seeing the doctor later. I went for a checkup. The doctor who looked at my EKG turned his back towards me and told me quite brutally, "You are going to die." At first I didn't know if this was meant as a threat or a joke, but apparently he was impressed enough by the changes noticeable in my EKG that he felt he ought to give me a very brutal warning. According to him, I should close my shop and stop working. Obviously, belonging to type A, I did exactly the opposite. I think his advice may have been medically correct, but quite wrong from a psychological viewpoint.

A real problem, which presents itself with more and more urgency, is what to do with the rest of my life? The word rest has, in itself, a frightening sound. I might have another five or ten years to live, statistically. I think I am healthy enough not to think too much about death. Maybe it is only a form of reassurance when I rationalize that no one ever actually dies. A few seconds before, one is still alive and then you become unconscious. It is just as if the electric switch had been turned off. What lies in between is called dying. It probably is not measurable in terms of seconds, nor can one really experience it.

In some of my studies, I was obliged to concern myself with the attitudes of other people towards death. An acquaintance of mine, whose specialty it is to help people organize their time better, poses an interesting question—If you knew that lightning were going to hit you within the next six months, what would you do differently from the way you are doing it now? Most research shows that the best solution, which is the one that I had chosen for myself, is not to retire, but to keep on living as if life were to continue indefinitely. There is always, of course, the secret hope that someday an enzyme will be developed which will retard or eliminate aging and maybe even death altogether.

While conducting some research for a cemetery, I received permission to enter the embalming room. I discovered I was unaffected by the sight of death. There must have been 35 or 40 bodies laid out on slabs. They were being made up so they would look as life-like as possible when the family came to pay their last respects. I am tempted to say "visit them." I thought I would faint or, at least, feel close to it. Instead, there was nothing but a morbid curiosity. My feeling was one of being in a wax museum. The fact that these people had all been alive, had all led full lives with hopes and fears, that it was all over now, they were lying cold, stiff and still, could not be associated by me with these grotesquely made-up and peculiarly dressed mannequins.

One of the frightening aspects of human nature is that even death itself can offer interesting business opportunities. You may not realize it, but there are quite a number of companies selling suits, shirts and dresses that have no backs. They are used for the purpose of showing off the bodies. Since no dead person has ever turned around, it would seem to be utterly logical to save material and money by having them dressed only in a sort of Potemkin fashion. As you may know, there is a story that, in Czarist Russia, the fronts of the houses in the Potemkin village were all dressed up with nothing behind them. This was done in order to impress the Czar and his generals during a visit. This Potemkin approach, of course, is a motivation which is found again and again, and which has often permitted me to discover unsuspected and very human aspects of our behavior.

I learned a few other things while in the hospital which I capitalized upon later. I sold the idea to a cosmetics company that, instead of or in addition to bringing flowers and candy, which the patient is often not allowed to eat, a special cosmetic kit with refreshing toilet water and other tools of make up, whether for a man or a woman, would present a very important help in recovery. Hospital gowns are miserable. They may be practical to a physician, but they only add to the depressive nature of the hospital atmosphere. Studies dealing with what patients most wanted in hospitals showed that, of course they wanted to get out as quickly as possible, not only because of the cost involved but because of the degrading nature of a hospital stay. Most people experience an infantile regression when hospitalized; they feel weak and dependent, and, unfortunately, very often are treated in exactly that way. I've never quite understood why patients cannot be allowed to take their own temperature, or even blood pressure, unless they are really deathly ill. Many of our recommendations were in the direction of helping the patient in a hospital to recover his independence as rapidly as possible. Other improvements could include getting his own food, eating in a cafeteria, and—particularly something that should concern architects designing hospitals—allow a patient to walk out to a courtyard or a garden in the summer when weather permits. Many European sanatoriums have such possibilities. American hospitals are usually hermetically closed and air-conditioned, so that no possibly-contaminating germs could enter or get out. Another innovation which I put in one of my reports, which has not been acted upon, is to have a special room set aside where the family of a non-contagious patient can come and visit him. Even small children should be allowed in this visiting room. This is being done now in prisons. Why not do it in the White Prison—the hospital?

A journalist asked me what new ideas motivational research could develop in the area of gerontology. Well-taken-care-of senior citizens in some cities have special sections in public parks, they get reduced fares on trains, movies, etc. All this is very nice, but what is really much more important is to give older people the feeling that they are still being useful. We are wasting, unnecessarily, their experiences, which could be put to good use. Why not use senior citizens as history teachers? They could record their own memories of wars, revolts, and important political and other events. In the business area, many young people make mistakes which older people could prevent them from making.

We know that the population in most countries is going to age. Some statistics claim that over 30 percent of the people will reach the age of at least 60 years and older. An autobiography, like this one, could also be considered a form of advice which a person, having passed his 70th birthday, could give to younger people: how he solved, or at least tried to solve, problems; what really helped him to become successful; and what he would have better left alone. Personally, I feel that isolating older people in so-called sun cities is psychologically wrong. Instead, they should have more contact with young people, and young people should learn to prepare themselves, not just for death, but how to arrange their own lives, as they inevitably get older.

One of our recommendations in connection with our cemetery studies, which shocked many people, was to arrange school excursions to cemeteries, and to let the students experience what I felt when I visited the embalming room. If you don't want to go that far, young people and children should at least learn to live through the death of pets and other loved things. Many of our superstitions, prejudices, and fears, might be better controlled that way, than by threats of Hell.

We still have so much fear, as far as death is concerned, that we try to deny it in all possible ways. Only in the last few years has the topic of death become legitimate enough to be used on TV shows. There is even the beginning of a new profession—specialists who help lead people to die in a more dignified fashion.

18 Does a Hard Boiled Egg Have a Soul?

My predecessors go as far back as Plato. Zen Buddhists also will understand what I'm talking about. A client comes to me and wants to know something about the real meaning of the product he's selling. A hard boiled egg, yes. But what are eggs really all about? What is the soul of eggs? Of course I must confess that there's a natural process of selectivity among clients. Those who are frightened by such questions simply don't bother coming to me, but thank you, there must be at least over 6,000 multi-national companies in this world who do understand, maybe just out of desperation, what I mean by talking about the soul of an egg. They are not concerned whether it contains cholesterol or not, and how much, but what its symbolic meaning really is. An egg represents a perfect package, an ideal shape, and is full of mysteries. It is the nucleus of life, the seed which has the shape, the color and the thousands of complex intricacies of a living creature.

A study for the American Nurseryman's Association showed us that plants are similarly a symbol of youth and creativity. Probably one of the reasons why quite a number of older people turn to raising orchids or indoor plants may be due to this fact. A plant is something, almost like a baby, that requires care. It responds quite readily. There's a mystery involved in seeing a tiny seed develop into a blossoming plant. The use of such an insight has helped the nursery people to increase their sales considerably. Today the sale of green plants has, despite recession, gone up over 30 percent.

Sometimes the discovery of the soul of products is based on research which goes quite far back into understanding cultural habits. The Carpet Institute wanted us to find out how to benefit by a better understanding of this product. I collected books on Arabian sheiks. It was not difficult to find that we've always had a fear of the bare floor. The type of tent floor is an indication of the wealth of an Arab leader, measured not in how thickly he can cover the floor with petrol dollars, but how many rugs he can put on top of each other, in other words, how many inches he is removed from the mud and dust. Persian carpets had their origin in such a symbolic function. Of course there are elements of safety and security involved. The higher the pile of carpets, the less damp the floor and the more you are protected from insects and animals. The Carpet Institute used this insight, at our recommendation, to show a woman walking with bare feet and feeling the softness and thickness of the rug. They also translated it into other types of marketing and advertising approaches, such as suggesting that a house that had good carpeting, preferably wall-to-wall, would train children to become psychologically softer, be more careful, to be influenced in their behavior by the rich and snug feeling rugs.

How would you sell ceramic stoves? Here again my scientific curiosity helped me. In Mexico I discovered an artist who had shaped a ceramic pot-belly type of stove in such a way that it resembled a human face. The opening where you put the wood or coal was, of course, the mouth, and all he had to do was make a sort of elongated hat out of the pipe and put eyes and ears on the stove.

The fact that most cars either resemble or have names which have something to do with aggression and, if you want to be psychoanalytic, with phallic symbols, is now fairly well known. Whenever a car does not correspond to this concept of penetrating the highway, or moving aggressively forward, it becomes a flop. The failure of the Edsel, as we described before, was due to a misunderstanding of the soul of a car. We don't realize that it is almost impossible to have any contact with the soul of another person or with the idea, in the Platonic sense, behind an object. We are always confronted by a surface, by an outside appearance.

Just think of the whole idea of smoothness. I once concentrated particularly on the psychology of surfaces. A smooth exterior is more moral, it is less dangerous. The reason most likely is that there are no hidden crevices. A rough surface can hide dirt, bacteria or other hidden enemies. In the study on prunes, which has become a classic now, we found that comparing wrinkled prunes to a smooth peach represented, in itself, an interesting marketing problem. As someone put it, our study took the wrinkles out of prunes. I went back to the original

Ceramic "humanface" stove.

meaning of fruit. Fruit is connected with plenty, harvest, ripeness. A young girl is usually referred to as a peach—she's full of life's juice. A prune is like an old spinster. The way we solved the problem was to invent the California wonder fruit, which had been lying in the California sun, and originally was a juicy plum. By reminding people, and giving them at the same time the advice as we mentioned before, to cook the prunes, we indeed almost succeeded in making out of the prune not just nature's laxative, but a symbol of energy. Smoothness also invites caress, it offers no resistance. But you can go too far. We can say about a person, "he's smooth," and mean something negative by it. You can't get ahold of him, he's like an eel, he slips through your fingers.

We associate power with size. Even in the pharmaceutical field, we tend to think the larger the pill, the more powerful it is. It often takes considerable persuasion to get a scientifically trained physician, and even less so a patient, to accept the fact that a very small pill can be as powerful, if not more so, if it is highly concentrated. It took a long while to convince engineers of the feasibility of miniaturization. A one horsepower motor, subconsciously, almost had to represent the size of a horse. The modern motor can be electrically squeezed together or miniaturized in such a way that it is difficult to tell a quarter horsepower motor from a one horsepower one. Here we have these very rational individuals, these engineers, resisting. They do not know quite why. Our studies found that their reasoning was not far removed from that of the cavemen.

We are motivated, more often than we suspect, by factors that are quite ridiculous. Try an experiment. Ask people what they appreciate in coffee. They will tell you the aroma, the flavor, possibly the body. We wanted to check whether there wasn't something we had overlooked. It is possible to distill coffee in such a way that you could come up with a colorless liquid. When we offered this really pure coffee, the majority of people either simply refused to drink it or when they tasted it, they told us it tasted all right but there was something wrong with it. Well, obviously, the brown color was missing.

In a classical experiment, women were asked to select stockings. In the majority of cases, they picked those stockings that had a slight perfume, which had been applied before. When they were asked why they preferred this particular brand of stockings, they gave some very reasonable answers, except they were the wrong ones.

An Italian publisher wanted me to find out what could be done to speed up the unification of Europe. There were many reasons for the delay. The President or the Chancellor of any one of the European countries, without ever admitting it, didn't want to give up his leadership role and become simply a member of a European parliament. But the difficulties had been instilled as early as grammar school. I used as a subtitle for my book, *The Invisible Walls of Europe*. Every European schoolchild imagines a frontier to consist of a deep, dark ditch, or impenetrable walls. Walls give us a feeling of false security. In Mexico, in many European countries, even in England, walls give you a feeling of privacy. In the States we have done away with most of them. We have a more open society.

Knowing a little bit about the physiology of food products has helped me to make suggestions to manufacturers for advertising their foods. When you think of crisp, fresh baked bread, you will notice that your mouth fills with water, but in a very particular way. The juices come down from the top of your palate. Think now about a very tender, barbecued steak and you will notice, if you have ever conducted this little taste test, that now the saliva is produced by different glands, those located in the lower part of your palate and mouth. Describing food in such a way and with such illustrations that Pavlovian reflexes are produced, results from knowing a little about the physiological and psychological associations connected with food. It can help you to overcome boredom and depression and a long list of stresses if you simply get interested in some of these psychological and motivational aspects of the many thousands of products which surround us.

I talked about food. The Romans considered asparagus a phallic symbol because it grows quite rapidly and is erect. There are many parallels in our folklore between giving birth and baking a cake. The oven is compared to a womb, the baked product to the baby. Raisins are a symbol of abundance, their inclusion in wedding cakes originally had the significance of a fertility wish. The very quantity of raisins coming out of a package has dramatic impact. Rice has a similar function. To me it is profitable for various reasons to ask why people throw rice at weddings. It is again an expression of the wish for fertility.

Milk has always been considered the most perfect of foods. Only lately have we discovered that there are quite a number of negative factors associated with it as far as digestion is concerned. It has this high standing, however, because it is the first food we learn to like. It's effortless, and it provides a feeling of security and safety. Probably there are also some associations with mother. Men love breasts, mixing the sucking for nutritional purposes and oral sexuality. Drinking warm milk before going to bed reassures you probably more from its psychological implications than as far as its effect on the digestive system is concerned.

Clothing serves not only to hide our nakedness, it can provide us with a personality. It can even make us change personalities. A few years ago I developed, for Dupont, the so-called Peacock Revolution, persuading men to wear more colorful clothes. But even today a banker who wants to create confidence will not dare to wear an outfit that, in our irrational beliefs, spells frivolity. Thus, if you want to be a crooked banker, and there are some as we have found out over the last few years, be sure to dress very conservatively. In one of my books, I call furniture, wall paper and the interior of our living space the Velvet Lined Cave. One way of finding out whether or not a couple will get along after marriage is whether or not they can agree on the style of furniture that they would like to have. Our studies showed that the kind of couch or table, the choice of modern as against early American, is almost like the choice of a baby. The first visible product of a liaison more easily recognizable and visible than the baby, is the furniture.

If motivational research interests you, one way of getting into it is to look around you and ask what is the deeper meaning of the many products surrounding us. When we think about food, clothing, cosmetics, drugs, toys, the role of liquor, cigarettes and other pleasure products, the meaning why, even today, youngsters are still enamored with electric trains, a point difficult to refute is that we probably could not get along without 95 percent of these products with which and in which we live. They enrich our lives in one way or another. Even the caveman, or cavewoman, decorated the walls as prehistoric discoveries have shown, and used animal skins to cover the bare floor. When she found a feather dropped by a wild bird and playfully put it into her hair, some plants that could be used to paint her cheeks or forehead, the cavewoman probably was the first Charles Revson.

When people today claim they can talk to plants and make them grow better, they are accepting, of not always seriously, their anthropomorphic qualities. I recently heard a horticultural scientist explain, in a rather sobering way, that this belief may be based on chemical facts rather than on a mutual consciousness raising. Plants need nitrogen, we breathe oxygen in and carbon dioxide out when we talk to the plants, he suggested especially after having had a couple of martinis, we are breathing the well-liked carbon dioxide onto the plants. Why do scientists always have to be so clever and destroy our belief in magic?

Adlai Stevenson's hole in his shoes, we found out through subsequent research, probably did more to get him down from his uncomfortable intellectual heights and make an acceptable, normal human being out of him, than any conscious attempts on his part.

Not until the age of 16 or 17, and hardly ever even then, did I wear a brand new suit. My parents could not afford one. If I did get one, my two brothers were the unlucky ones, because I got one that was at least one or two sizes too large. I had to grow into it. Just when it really fit me, it had become shabby, and it was handed down to my younger brother, and then to our still younger brother. My closets are still overcrowded because I had developed in my youth such an overevaluation of clothing, not in the sense of wanting to be dressed always in the latest fashion, but feeling that no suit ever really wore out. Every so often, our son, particularly when I'm away, does a clean-up job. He is quite right when he states that it probably would take me several months before I would miss the suits that he had thrown out. Maybe I'm similar to the Frenchmen who feel that any garment acquires part of their personality, and refuse to have it dry cleaned so as not to lose the flavor expressed in its dirt.

19 Congratulations, You are Now a Public Speaker

I have been able to change quite a long list of apparently permanent character traits through the application of psychological approaches. When I was a student in Vienna, and long before that, I was terrified of speaking in public. I hardly ever participated, even in small clubs, in raising my voice and adding what I often felt would have been a very clever contribution to whatever was being discussed. I read about a course given for students who felt they were poor public speakers. The description of the type of student they had in mind fitted me perfectly. I would rather hide or disappear into the ground than stand psychologically naked and exposed on an elevated platform, a target for anyone who wanted to throw rotten eggs or unusable forms of vegetables at me.

Sigmund Freud's daughter-in-law, Esti Freud, ran this course. Sooner than I expected, she asked the assembled students who was really afraid. I timidly raised my hand. I was called. "Would you please come up to the platform?" I protested. I mumbled that there must have been some misunderstanding since she had asked who was afraid to speak in public. Nothing helped. My knees trembled. There I was. She asked, "What did you do yesterday?" So I told her, with a shy glance at the audience. After a few minutes, she stepped next to me, shook my hand and congratulated me. I didn't know exactly what for, but then she said, "You are now a public speaker." Her explanation was simple. "You told us what you knew about what you did yesterday. That's all there is to it. A good speaker is a person who knows what he is talking about." This was only the beginning. She admitted that, of course, there are many occasions when you have to talk about something you don't know anything about, such as politicians are often forced to do for a living.

Pretty soon we proceeded to the next lesson which I've used very successfully for scores of years. It is based on a simple exercise. Before you start speaking, you take a deep breath and let your voice be carried as you breathe out. In doing so, your voice will automatically become much deeper, if you are a man, and carry much further. If, instead, you are running out of breath, just stop, take a deep breath, and start all over again. Most public speakers, however, are not aware of this little trick. Their voices very quickly become squeezed and tired, thin and flat. Another lesson learned, which helped me overcome my fear of public speaking, and in a way to become an extrovert, was to consider the audience I was addressing. As Esti Freud told me, in most instances you are probably just as smart as they are, if not smarter. I learned to put two little letters on each page of my manuscript, S.W. The meaning? "So What? What can they do to you," or, "Don't be afraid; they're very likely just as afraid or more so of you." To a large extent, what I learned then was that often learning how to breathe may be more important than rhetorical techniques.

In learning how to draw, I have been very strongly influenced by a Greek author who suggested that freeing your wrist was one of the secrets of developing your artistic skill. His specific advice was to take a large sheet of paper and some charcoal, and make big sweeping movements all over the paper. When drawing someone or something, project yourself to the object, as if you were drawing the contours and outlines of an object or person, and just glance every so often at the paper so you won't run it off.

In my book, *The Naked Manager*, I suggest that concentrating somewhat less on the bull's eye of a goal will lead to better results. This is something that I learned from reading Zen Buddhist literature. In training to become a sharpshooter or an archer, the pupils are told to let the trigger do the final aiming.

Changing human nature and overcoming stresses which may make such a change desirable, in our opinion, is very often best achieved by using rather less complicated therapies and techniques. We are so intent upon our becoming omnipotent, solving all our problems, that we overlook the possibility of achieving our goals in an indirect way.

I have been complimented many times for my lack of a Germanic accent. The secret which I used, with the help of a phonetics professor, was based on a discovery that speaking a foreign language properly was due more to learning how to utilize your muscles than to purely grammatical knowledge. I have used

Drawing by E. Dichter of old couple.

this approach in learning other languages. It's a sort of chameleon-like adaptation procedure. Dr. Hans Selye, who is probably the originator of the word stress, developed the concept that most stresses, particularly those that express themselves in physiological disturbances and various bodily symptoms, are due to a lack of ability to adapt ourselves. He calls it the general adaptation syndrome. He compares it to an overloading of our systems with too many demands resulting in a breakdown comparable to a short circuit.

While this is a very excellent medical explanation, in my own experience I have found that whenever I've felt a task was too difficult for me or I had just simply too many things to do, I could succeed just as well by simply changing my motivations and my attitude as I could by reducing my activities. My fear of speaking in public was remedied, not by avoiding such a challenge, but by learning how to get around it. If we want to, by learning a few simple tricks, we can immunize ourselves against stresses. It's almost comparable, at least that's the way I've felt, to taking a deep breath and saying to yourself. "I'm not going to buckle under." Too many people choose copping out, running away, looking for Shangri-la or other forms of escapism. It is, in a way, easier to say "I can take it" than "I can't take it."

I've often thought it would be interesting to set up a sort of stress-watchers clinic where people are taught how to handle their stresses. Some of our stresses we bring about deliberately—we just love them. Others we can do little about. We could call them Weltschmerz stresses. Future shock. We worry about earthquakes or the collapse of the world. A stress clinic, other than life itself, would consist of exposing children from an early age to various types of difficult situations and teaching them how to survive, not only physically, but emotionally. Many natives in remote islands such as New Guinea or Papua, and other so-called primitive cultures, long ago hit upon this stress immunization. They send young men out into the jungle to prove themselves. Eskimos have a similar training period. In order to become a real hunter, you live alone and try to survive the cruel winter. When you come back, you have proven yourself to be a worthwhile member of your tribe.

It is probably impossible to change a person completely. I don't think I ever have become a real extrovert, but at least I have learned to play the role in a fairly comfortable fashion. I can tell jokes, I can get up and address an audience of anywhere from 20 to 1,000 people as I have done so many times. What I learned from Esti Freud, and indirectly from myself, is the ability to discover within the hidden crevices of my personality new resources which I was sure were not there. Being forced to discover such ammunition to face the crises of various types usually helped me to find these tools. Maybe there is a mysterious relationship, comparable indeed to the biological process of development of antibodies, that the more stresses you have learned to face, the more stress immunity you develop.

Motivational research is and can be used to help people overcome their stresses. A company may have a very successful product. One of the applications of motivational research concerns the field of development of new products and the courage or fears of managers. I am thinking of a particular company, there are quite a number of them, which had developed a very interesting new kind of product in the paper field. It replaced linen napkins and towels. It conquered a major share of the market. After a number of years sales started slipping. The person who had developed the product had also developed the inability to look ahead. He was continuously repeating the formula which originally brought him success. In doing so, he overlooked the deeper aspects to his formula, to have been ahead of all the other products on the market by five to ten years. He continued, through advertising and marketing, stating that his particular product had "wet strength" and pop-up features, and similar very glib advertising claims. They were all true, except the housewives who used the product had, by that time, developed a strong feeling of boredom. "What else is new," they kept asking. The manager only repeated the same promise. What he overlooked was that what was really necessary was to be ahead of his time again. This however required a completely different set of personality traits: innovation, abandonment of what is usually referred to as marketing myopia, realization that things had changed all around him. He was holding onto his original success the way a person about to fall into a rapid river holds on to a branch overhanging the river. Our problem was to motivate him to let go, to swim along with the rapid current, and to accept the necessity for change. The real answer was in encouraging him to go back to what he originally was capable of doing, to be innovative and courageous. The way such an attitude usually is explained is "Why rock the boat, why not use a successful formula again and again?"

In many ways, our national and international problems very often suffer from this inability to adapt ourselves. One of the tricks or crutches is to never permit yourself to become frozen in your thinking. I have recommended, and in a sense I have practiced the desirability of changing one's job or occupation every few years. In my own particular field this is done for me since the tasks change not just every few years, but literally every few days or weeks. I might be working one week on a problem of how to sell more hot dogs, and discover their symbolic meaning in order to pull them out of the marketing difficulty of having become uninteresting commodities. A week later the problem I am asked to solve concerns the motivation of members of a community to participate more actively in the affairs of their community.

I helped the manager of the paper company mentioned before by encouraging him to rediscover his belief in himself by psychological limbering-up exercises, by breaking his routine, and by getting him interested in subjects that were not directly related to his occupation. Even in scientific fields such as medicine, there is a slowly growing trend among physicians, Europeans were first, to become interested in areas that have no direct relationship with the label of one's specialty. We used this successfully in this country after having discovered that a surgeon's activity has very great resemblance to the activities of an artist and, in a somewhat undignified comparison, with the activities of a tailor. Interviewing tailors and studying the use of tools by sculptors and painters helped us to better understand the real motivations and ambitions of the surgeon. He was dealing with tissue. It was not made out of the same materials the tailor used, but he did indeed distinguish between linings, texture, thickness, and other special qualities of the materials. The way he handled his tools and the importance of the tools was at least as great as those experienced by a painter. The scalpel was comparable to the chisel and hammer of a sculptor. The result of it was, on the one hand, recommendation to the company selling sutures to encourage surgeons to become interested in these, for them, fringe activities and to talk in more aristic terms about specific products that they tried to sell to surgeons such as sutures and needles. Unfortunately we are often much more inclined to escape a stress by devious means than by trying to mobilize our motivations. The manager confronted with declining sales will fight, based on his supposed but misunderstood convinction and experience, and refuse to drop his passé success formula. Going back to some personal experiences, I wish I had been better informed about the power of self motivation.

When I returned to Vienna from Paris, I continued my studies and my living by becoming a private tutor. My French had become fairly good. I found a family who, as was the custom at that time, needed someone to take care of their two rather unruly boys. They were not doing too well in school. After some preliminary mutual, or rather more one-sided, looking over by the parents, I was found to be acceptable. The deal was simple: I spent the whole afternoon with the boys, helping them with their studies, going ice skating or skiing in the winter, swimming in the summer. One of the very desirable fringe benefits for me was that every evening I earned my dinner, not by singing for it, but by involving the parents of the two boys in French lessons and halting French conversations. This enabled me to complete a couple of years of my studies.

Sometime during this period I got caught in a squeeze between trying to pursue my studies and having only the morning available for them. I also spent several hours during the night doing window decorating. What we now call stress did become too great. The only way, apparently, my subconscious mind knew to get out of it was in a very peculiar fashion. I was on my way to my two o'clock tutoring session. I crossed the practically empty plaza in Vienna as a motorbike was about to cross the plaza. I was neither blind nor deaf nor inattentive. I saw the bike coming from quite a distance away. Secretly, as I found out two or three years later during my psychoanalysis, I wanted to have an accident. This was one possible way out of my squeeze between not having enough time to continue my studies and having to spend all my afternoons and evenings to earn enough money to pursue my studies. Sure enough, the bike ran into me, or rather I ran into the bike. The price I paid was being in a plaster cast for about six weeks, having all my ligaments in my right knee torn (I still suffer from it). Had I known more about motivations, I could probably have discussed with the boys' parents my stress and dilemma. They showed great understanding after the accident. I'm sure they would have shown the same understanding and made my painful escape unnecessary.

Too often in life we choose to run away, hiding behind a conviction that we are not capable of facing our challenges.

20 I Know I Can Afford Cold Cuts, But Still...

A few years ago, when my material success had become obvious, I met one of my schooltime friends from Vienna. I complained to him about my money worries, not knowing exactly how to prepare myself for the future. His very reasonable argument was "How many years do you think you might, statistically, live—10, 15, 20 years? You have enough money by now that you certainly won't starve. You can afford to buy all the cold cuts you desire." It is true—I like cold cuts, particularly Hungarian salami, maybe dating back to my jail experience.

I do remember literally starving when I was a child. This is a difficult experience to pass on to someone else, particularly my children. We were trained by our parents to avoid passing in front of our deli store in Vienna. As far back as I remember, we always owed them money. At times we had nothing to eat for three days in a row. My father simply did not make enough money. It is difficult to realize now that during and right after the First World War the depression was so bad that my father simply did not earn any money. He was a salesman, and lived off his commissions. If he did not sell, no commission, no money, no bread. Going hungry, not just being poor, is a traumatic experience, a stress that is almost impossible to forget. Even now, many decades later, I have nightmares from which I wake up in a cold sweat. I dream I am poor again, I have nothing to eat. During my student days in Paris, there were days too when I simply starved. Sometimes I wish I was forced to do it now, to bring my weight down. It helps me to fall asleep when I add up my assets. During sleep, the childhood dreams come back. They sit on my chest, probably one of the reasons why I keep working although I would be entitled to retire, because of age and income.

I have been concentrating all my life on earning money, ever since the age of 14. I remember the very first cash that I ever felt jingling in my pocket. I had accompanied my uncle into the forests of lower Austria, and learned how to collect edible mushrooms. I sold them to a store. My first purchase was a very manly looking leather belt. I must have been around eight or nine years old.

It probably would be a good idea, in trying to understand people, to go back to the very first money they ever acquired and to find out what they did with it. I became a mushroom expert and, not too far removed from this expertise, is the picking of berries. Blueberries grow wild in the Austrian Alps, particularly in the higher regions. I would bring back baskets and baskets of them and became a regular supplier of the local stores in the small community where my uncle lived. To this day, I enjoy going into my garden and picking berries. I have a number of blueberry bushes which make it unnecessary to bend quite as low as I had to do when going through the dark, heady smelling pine forests in Austria. I'm still dreaming of cultivating the wild mushrooms in this country. Several years ago I saw an ad which advertised the spores of such wild mushrooms. It was a French company that very cautiously in a prospectus said that it might take from two to three years before you could see any results. It has been much longer than that—no results. Anyway I had fun for the $30 I invested. I now begin to realize that I should have studied investment philosophy. I belatedly have concerned myself with it. It has added more stress to my life than the hunger periods. At least I'm more aware of the annoyance of making decisions.

Naturally, I'm trying to learn as much as possible. I listen to everybody I can get hold of, pose questions, read reports, and then, very often, do what my instinct tells me to do. One of my financial advisors told me recently that his task has become much easier because, in order to be honest, all he has to admit is that he doesn't know. I learned a few interesting, logical, and psychological lessons. It would seem to be very rational to rely on success stories. You are being told that a company or a mutual fund has continuously increased its dividends, that the value of the stock has grown. Obviously, you could rely, therefore, on this success story. This is a very dangerous and tricky conclusion, as I experienced myself a few times. Often, it is exactly when these figures look particularly good that the stock is at the pinnacle of the mountain from whence it can only go down. Knowing whether the company you want to invest in has reached the top or not, of course, requires foresight, instinct, or just plain luck. A logical explanation is that when a fund has accumulated enough capital, it has become so big that it is very difficult for it to remain flexible, to change investments.

Because of all of these difficulties, I am interested in Money Therapy. We talk about sex much more openly today than we talk about the role money plays in our lives. An important problem that many people seem to have, at least I do, is to enjoy one's money by spending it. Half seriously, half jokingly, I have decided to create a club, whose purpose it is not just to accumulate money, but to discover new ways of enjoying it. Of course it is difficult to get out of one's skin. I took the Concorde to London. I screamed, because it was my wife's idea, that it was a waste of money. But, then I decided that I should really have the experience of being among the first, although hundreds before have flown the Concorde. Naturally, I used my experience in one of our newsletters, so it shouldn't be a total loss. I also developed ideas from this flight, which we have tried to sell to the public relations department of British Airways. The experience of speed was thrilling, but only symbolized by a small plaque on the dividing wall of the plane, where you saw the figures next to the letter M, signifying Mach (the speed of sound), rapidly increasing. In addition, arriving in London after three hours and twelve minutes, which is a figure that I will remember for quite a while, was something that I could put down in my data book of experiences. On the other hand, while many people asked me, in an attempt to vicariously participate in the flight, "Oh, you are going to take the Concorde, how wonderful!" I had to disappoint them, when they requested an account of all my experiences. Outside of the speed, and the partial lack of jet lag, the airline had failed to provide me with the feeling that should have gone with having been somewhat of a pioneer. I also found the food was quite below standard.

To enjoy expenses that are plain luxury and unnecessary may be recognized as an important experience. It could lead to a liberation from the domination of money. One of the disappointments that I have experienced is that my attempts to find enough financial security, so I could afford cold cuts as my friend put it, have really not brought me very much satisfaction.

A few years ago, shortly after my coronary, I received an offer to sell my company. We agreed on the price. I was supposed to work for three years for a very good salary and, during this three year period, a successor was to be trained. My own contribution to the negotiation was that I was going to receive the same salary for all three years, but would work less every year, and, therefore, have more time for lectures, the writing of books, and possible hobbies. Everything seemed to go very well for almost two years. Immediately after I had signed the sales paper, Hedy hugged me and told me "You are sold now; you are free; you have reached an important goal in your life; you don't have to worry anymore; I hope you finally will calm down." All the plans were perfect. The company which bought me out wanted to put about $1 million into my business and use it, to a large extent, as internal counselors of the conglomerate. One of my greatest stupidities was that I did not concern myself with the internal operations of this company. I was impressed by the fact that they were listed on the New York Stock Exchange, and were, at least on paper, worth over $150 million. Neither my lawyer, nor my accountant, who helped me (for very sizable fees) conclude all the contracts, were smart enough to find out whether this company had any debts.

What then happened, in a pretty rapid sequence, was that they withdrew whatever money I had accumulated in my company, and, instead of using it plus their own promised contribution for the development of the Dichter Company, they decided that it would have a better application plugging the holes in their own net of debts. In addition to the payment for the company, I was also given four notes. Two of those were paid very promptly. When the third one came due, a change in the management of my conglomerate had taken place. From the president's viewpoint, and that of his company, the Dichter Division did not create enough profit. His job then was how to divest himself of our acquired company. The story is one that repeats itself very frequently. However, in my case, there was a particularly poignant note to it. The company thought the way to get rid of me was to sue me. The amount was $20 million and the argument was that they had discovered that I was irreplacable and, therefore, the purchase of my company had been a bad decision. Naturally, they could have simply kept me on as a consultant which would have resolved the problem.

Without understanding all the intricacies of the reasoning on the part of the conglomerate, during the period that the lawsuit was going on Hedy and I had many sleepless nights. Whenever we could bring up enough sense of humor, we felt that we ought to frame the legal document which seemed to prove, at least at that time, that I was worth $20 million.

The usual thing happened. I counter-sued. But eventually the whole problem resolved itself when a second company, consisting of two psychologists, appeared on the scene. They bought my company with their shares which, by then, belonged to the conglomerate. After a few months, they abandoned their new acquisition and simply disappeared.

While this whole story was quite traumatic for me, it also taught me quite a bit about corporate proceedings. In many ways it was comparable to the events that precipitated my leaving Vienna. What appeared to be, in this case, a tragedy, turned out to be, shortly afterwards, a considerable blessing. To my pleasant surprise, I discovered that most of my clients came back to me even though the conglomerate tried to continue their operation without me for a while. I did not end up with all the money that was due me, but did not do too badly either and, in the final analysis, got all my business back.

The Institutes which operated as part of my company abroad were eventually also brought back into the fold since the managers of these divisions stayed, most of the time, faithful to me. I also learned that the size of an organization is not necessarily an indication of its profitability. When this whole interregnum period was over, I had acquired the rather expensive insight that I could do very well with a much smaller staff and, indeed, make more money than before.

My pride makes me think that since I have been successful in conquering other stresses and developing a whole new field of research, I should also be able to discover the secret of smart investment. My wife rejoices when there is a holiday because I cannot check on stocks and, more often than not, become aggravated. One of the problems that I am faced with is that deep down in my blood, or whever such instincts lie or grow, I feel that making money through investments is somehow not quite correct.

A friend of ours is an Italian mason. We have been building houses with him for resale purposes. He once confided in me that he had a similar feeling. Unless he could make money by using his hands, doing masonry and carpentry work, he felt he was doing something immoral. He knew that he would never be a successful builder or contractor because he would have to hire people to work for him and supervise them. I still feel happier when I make a few hundred dollars by writing an article or developing an idea for a company than when I make several thousand dollars through skillful buying and selling of stocks or other mysterious Wall Street products.

We probably have never really analyzed the importance of money in psychological terms. We are fully aware that it is an important measurement of our success, particularly in the United States. Whenever a list of stresses is submitted to people, money stresses come very soon after the stress of death or separation. Yet, in my own experience, having sufficient money does not necessarily reduce the stresses. In my case I would list money worries as one of the problems I never learned to overcome.

I have been approached by many brokers and investment counselors. In most instances I have found that they know very little about selling their customers. What I really hoped they would do for me was to help me crystallize in my own mind how I want to organize the rest of my life. The first problem arises from the fact that financial planning and psychological planning are very closely related. Your life style may be one where you feel that you are happiest if you just more or less drift along. You make enough money so as not to really suffer or starve. Anything beyond that seems like a waste. You usually try to prove something with the accumulation of money but, at times, I and many others feel like saying "What can I really look ahead to?" Maybe another ten percent increase in income, another $25,000 saved, but more or less the same worries.

One of the most distressing discoveries that I have made is that security does not necessarily relate to the amount of money that you have put aside. It sounds like a desirable goal, but when you reach it you begin to worry and spend too much of your time holding on to what you finally have accumulated. In some work for banks, we have suggested that they concentrate not only on helping people learn how to save money, but also how to enjoy their money. I would probably be one of the first candidates for such a course in hard cash psychotherapy. A good training might involve a dramatic attempt to express disdain for money.

During one of the very first jobs I conducted for *Esquire* magazine, I met a very interesting man who was a space salesman, selling pages to advertisers. One way in which he traumatized his potential customers into signing an order was to throw a dime out the window, telling them that if they did not advertise in *Esquire* magazine they were wasting a dime every minute. When that didn't work, he threw a quarter out the window. And he went on, as he told me, usually not much further than a dollar or a dollar-and-a-half. (Of course with inflation today, you might have to use a higher amount.) By that time, the potential space buyer told him to stop and asked him the price for a page. They simply could not see him wasting all that money. When you figure it out, the average sale hardly ever ran more than a dollar.

A similar test that an architect friend of mine tried with me was to ask me to take a $20 bill and tear it apart into small pieces. He said, "Unless you have learned to do this without regret, you will never modernize your office." Well, I'm sorry to report that it didn't work. I bought some new chairs, and a few other things, but did not buy the big remodeling job which he was trying to sell me.

One of the most successful periods in my life, as far as not worrying about money is concerned, was during the period of inflation around 1928 or 1929. Paper money in Austria had lost so much in value that every factory or office of any size issued its own money. A lumber yard printed money on pieces of wood, as did textile factories, using their own material. As school children this was a lot of fun for us. We used to cover our teacher's desk completely with different types of money. It was possibly comparable to the scrip used during the Civil War in the United States. Money had to be spent because it was worthless, it may have lost one hundredth of its value in a day or two. It was a very interesting economic lesson to experience the return to barter trade.

We kept a goat and several chickens in our kitchen. Sure it smelled, but we had real food right under our noses. We could smell it. Bread was rationed. It helped me to understand the descriptions by Solzhenitsyn in *One Day in the Life of Ivan Denisovitch*, where he describes how a prisoner made a crust of bread into a dramatic taste experience. He smelled it, he soaked it in his mouth, he let it slowly dissolve, and made a hide-and-seek game with his tongue and, when he finally was ready to swallow the bread, he had extracted from it more than an hour's worth of pleasure and satisfaction. We used to have little more than crusts. Each one of us children received one edge of the round loaf of European bread, resembling farmer's bread, or pumpernickel which you can get here. We learned to cut off slices almost as thin as those that I later experimented with when I became interested in preparing slides with a microtome for microscopic studies.

You appreciate most things much more when you have been deprived of them. Going hungry is a wonderful way of creating an appetite. These memories have added to my inventory of stresses, but also to my blessings. I know if I really had to starve again I probably would be able to exploit food in a way that those who never did go hungry might never have learned.

These insights have also had a considerable influence on my motivational work. They have helped me, for example, to better understand cross-cultural comparisons. Food, for example, has a completely different significance in different countries. In an analysis conducted for the former French President, Mendes France, who was very much interested in getting Frenchmen, particularly French children, to drink less wine and more milk, we found that to the French wine was not at all the somewhat cynical product which it is for most Americans. It is much closer to bread and to necessary nourishment. To tell a Frenchman, therefore, that too much wine and alcohol was bad for him and his children was about equivalent to telling an American that bread or milk was an immoral food.

In Italy, to eat pasta and to be slightly on the heavy side, particularly as far as the middle-aged population is concerned, is still considered as an important protection against starvation. The joke, "Eat, eat," attributed to Italian mamas, is pretty close to the anthropological truth.

In Germany, right after the Second World War, an analyst of their culture discovered what they themselves referred to as a 'Fresswelle,' a wave of overeating. They had starved so long during the war that they had to make sure that they now had enough to eat. What always surprises and shocks me is how close we are to animals. Animals always, or usually, overstuff themselves in order to prepare for a period of potential lack of food. To the American, a two-inch thick steak has a similar significance.

Wealth and deprivation can express themselves in many different ways. To quote Italy again, it is still possible to find women on beaches on the Italian Rivera who do not shave their legs or their armpits. They also reject, very decidedly, the use of deodorants. Hair, perspiration, and almost all products of the human body, even excrement, are considered to be a sign of abundance. Deodorizing oneself is almost equivalent to partially removing one's soul.

I once spent several days in Brazzaville, in the former French Congo, and I discovered the well-known fact that taking somebody's picture, a very innocuous and flattering idea for us, is interpreted as a threat of taking away the soul of the person. They violently object to this psychological robbery. Even dirt can mean wealth and some cultures are quite adamant about not letting themselves be deprived of it too readily. This is very important when you are trying to sell Frenchmen, Frenchwomen, or even Germans detergents. I got myself into considerable trouble once when I published official statistics that the majority of Germans changed their shirts only once a week, that they changed their bed-sheets only every four weeks, that French families resisted dry cleaning—they felt not unlike the African natives. Sending their clothes to such an establishment would get them back cleaner but their personality would have been removed.

Once you understand these paradoxical aspects of human nature, you can then think about how to correct or change the situation. One could argue, of course, whether the French people are not just as happy by cleaning their clothes considerably less than Americans do; or whether it really makes that much difference, as far as the German is concerned, whether he changes his shirt every day or only once a week. But I have often been called in, and still am, to find out about such attitudes. A detergent company, quite understandably, is not happy with the situation. They want to understand it first, and then they want to change it. They simply want Germans to buy more detergents.

Findings of this type are particularly interesting, at least they always have been to me, because they point out that many of the stereotypes we have and that various nationalities have about themselves are not necessarily true. I got myself in trouble with my statement in Germany, because the Germans look upon themselves as extremely clean. By most standards, they are. The Americans, however, have possibly been brainwashed, to be convinced that the world would almost collapse if they did not control their body odor or did not take a shower or a bath at least once a day. Maybe motivational research, or certainly advertising, has contributed quite a lot to it, and produced a sort of guilt feeling on the part of Americans. No one has examined it. It has some relationship with the puritanical heritage of the first settlers and, later on, with the enforced attempts to spread civilization among the frontiersmen and women. What has always surprised me is that practically no university in the world, even anthropology departments, have really bothered analyzing the structural differences and indeed the meaning of very many of our daily activities. It simply seems to be more legitimate, or sounds more impressive in a scientific paper, if the taboos of the Samoans or Papuans are studied, than if the bizarre doings of a cosmopolitan Chicagoan are put under the anthropological magnifying glass.

In motivational research we concern ourselves with sampling. I've aroused the ire of many of my colleagues by stressing the fact that most of us are not capable of diagnosing our own actions. Our very human motivations are comparable to an iceberg; only the tip is showing. We quite frequently rationalize the reasons for our behavior. I have also created controversies by stating that classifying people according to their actual income is completely misleading. It still seems to me that it is just common sense not to simply inquire, in a questionnaire, how much money a person or a family earns, but to find out whether they have increased their earnings over the last five years, taking inflation into consideration, or whether they have been standing still or moving down. The real motivating factor is the dynamic change in their income, rather than the absolute figure.

The fact that I starved in my childhood is a very important aspect of my personal motivations. If someone tried to classify me according to my actual income, he probably would have to put me into the class of millionaires (which still makes me uncomfortable). I cannot quite identify myself with this group, because basically my motivations are those of a relatively poor man. My anxieties have not changed too much. My fear of starvation simply has much less basis; it is to a very large extent subconscious, but unfortunately still bothers me in my dreams. Therefore, if someone wants to use me as a subject in a market research study, he certainly would have to know all these facts about me in order to arrive at fairly reasonable conclusions about my behavior.

My anxieties have not changed very much. I have not become any happier or more self assured through the fact that I can consider myself almost wealthy. As I look back, I realize that I had less anxiety when I had no money. Now I have to worry about losing whatever I have put aside. Now I have to spend considerable amounts of time with lawyers and accountants in figuring out how to reduce my income tax.

During my last trip to Europe, I discovered, with great shock, that even the Swiss are beginning to worry about finances. This was partly due to scandals in one of the large Swiss banks. This was almost as shattering as hearing that there is absolute scientific proof that God does not exist and that there is no life after death. On the other hand, we are also living in a sort of waterbed world where things are continually undulating and changing. To discover anxiety among people who have reason to feel insecure is acceptable, but to find this also among the supposedly safe Swiss can only result in two reactions: either you laugh about it in a sick humor sort of way or you look around for another country which might offer more complete safety. I, for one, haven't found it yet. Who knows? Maybe it is really behind the Iron Curtain. But, as far as I know, even there the problem of safety and security has not been solved.

I can remind myself continuously that, in all the years that I may have left, I probably will have enough to eat and a roof over my head. Still, it does not reduce my nightmares. Silly? Naturally, because when I think about it, most of the things which I really have fun with don't cost very much. I like to grow vegetables, to read and to watch television. I own a greenhouse. O.K., that might be a sort of luxury.

I continuously try to learn new things: how a computer really functions, but even more importantly, how to fix a television set myself. Most of my dreams and wishes have very little to do with material things. I'm not a car buff. For me, most cars just have four wheels. As far as clothing, I feel most comfortable during weekends when I can wear my old clothes. I probably am a miser if you want to use this expression in the customary sense.

I met a client of mine in Paris who also stayed at the Hilton. I walked down to the next corner to get a taxi. To my amusement, my client had done the same thing. We joined together in a cab and we started laughing. What he was doing was exactly what I had in mind. We were trying to avoid having to tip the bellhop who, to my viewpoint (and I still feel that way) stood in front of the hotel entrance in a completely unnecessary way. He expected a tip for opening and closing the car door. A waste, we agreed. We also seemed to be of the same opinion that while this could be considered a miserly action, we both enjoyed good things and did not mind spending money on them. But to simply waste it was considered almost stupid, if not immoral.

I tip just as much as I feel is necessary unless I am using the tip as a sort of bribe to influence my destiny. Whenever I am visiting a potential client and am hoping to get a job, I feel that by earning a particularly enthusiastic "thank you" from a waiter or cab driver, I can put pressure on the eventual outcome of the succeeding interview. However, if the aspirant for the tip thanks me too profusely, I really begin to feel badly. I must have overtipped him. I admit that then I often take revenge, without making distinction as to who it might be, by undertipping the next victim.

21 Suppose I Were as Devilish as Some Think I Am

Is not what you are doing extremely dangerous? Could you not be induced through large sums of money or pride to lend your thinking and your manipulative skill to get the wrong president elected or to drive this country into what is called euphemistically a 'preventive' war? More than once have I been asked these questions.

I don't know the answers. I trust my own decency. I consider working for a detergent company almost like an interesting game. I make no secret of the fact that I obviously don't care whether Lever Brothers has a larger share of the market than Proctor and Gamble. While I am engaged in such motivational study, I am a professional. I want to impress my client with how clever I am, but it goes deeper than that. Maybe I am a psychological Peter Falk. I observe the hidden clues; I listen with the third ear; I interpret. I see where others are too blind because they are too close to the trees. I find the solution and produce sales increases. I have acted as a discoverer, as a general on the battlefield of free enterprise. If my candidate gets elected, I have a feeling of power. It is not that different from the pride of a scientist, an archaeologist, except that my "dig" is the stone-pile of human motivations.

In the course of such an aggressive discussion, challenging my diabolic potentials, I sat down and developed a believable scenario as to what a person like myself, with the help of some powerful organizations, could achieve. The purpose was to make people aware of how power manipulation really takes place. Maybe I was also thinking that such plots ought to be studied and even developed as exercises by college students. It would be a valuable experiment in real political science.

We wonder how Watergate was possible. Had we had a training in playing political "who done it," we might have been more suspicious much earlier. I shall try to present in this chapter, such a political "Mission Possible" plot.

If I repeat again that I would not accept such an assignment, I might be protesting too much. Somebody else may, however, seriously consider such a plot and here is where the danger lies.

Laughing it off is easy. I remember when se saw the first harmlessly young, immature Brownshirts walking the streets of Vienna and Germany. We laughed, too, and took comfort that they were beardless rowdies. Austrians in particular kept reassuring themselves, "It Can't Happen Here." In America we still feel absolutely and categorically that it never can.

We came close to it, though, during the Joe McCarthy period, and during the reign of "Emperor Nixon." I was planning to leave the United States. Half forced and half planned, I guessed twice right, when leaving Vienna early enough and then again when abandoning Europe to its destiny.

This scenario could help you to be a little less naive about what is going on around you and to think about the possibility of some of these unlikely things really happening. Rather than leaving the country, you may consider fighting such a possibility. It may relieve your frustrations. This was my decision and it has helped me. I have gradually learned to read between the lines of news reports, particularly to read foreign sources and listen to shortwave broadcasts. Seeing your country through the eyes of an outsider can be very revealing.

Here is the "secret" correspondence which *could* take place between a "motivational devil" and his clients.

HOW TO MOTIVATE VETERANS TO VOLUNTEER FOR ANOTHER WAR AND TO PREPARE AND MANIPULATE THE AMERICAN PUBLIC TO ACCEPT INVOLVEMENT IN ANOTHER REAL WAR

TOP SECRET
Memo to Dr. Dichter From Pentagon:
We are requesting you to prepare a secret plan for the following purpose:
American troops may have to be sent to the Near East or to the Philippines. Many of these troops may have returned only a few months or a year ago from fighting in Vietnam. We want to motivate the public and the veterans to join in

the fighting although they at first may be absolutely opposed to it.

You are to develop a detailed plan, setting forth the rationale and also indicating the tactical methods to be used to implement the plan.

Memo to Pentagon from Dr. Ernest Dichter:

We acknowledge your assignment. Here are first the basic principles developed as a result of our research:

The Vietnam veterans and large sections of the population are frustrated. This frustration will be turned into aggression. The vets will be utilized to become the spearheads of a pseudo-revolutionary group. The purpose of this group, tentatively called "Reveille," will be described as being designed to literally turn America around, to help in rediscovering the original purpose of the foundation of the U.S.A. In short, we are suggesting, on the surface, a second American Revolution as the basic rationale.

In order to make this "about face" succeed, real and imaginary enemies have to be developed as targets. While the assignment is to entice or manipulate veterans and the public to volunteer or support another war, the publicized rationale for such a war will be to prepare the country for the alternative of peace.

Several studies indicate that we have never seriously contemplated the consequences of a permanent peace; such a change in attitudes will require a militant force, as peculiar as that may sound.

Here are the steps which we are proposing:

• Most people are confused. They are looking for a meaningful explanation of world events and the facts swirling around their heads. We are proposing that such an explanation be provided to Vietnam vets and the public.

• Even an at first unbelievable and gigantic "World Conspiracy" is more comfortable to live with than a continuously changing world scenario, that does not seem to have a comprehensible plot.

• We are using our psychological knowledge of attraction of crime stories. They are neat, if complex, and everything falls into place at the end.

• We want to place the vet and the citizen in the role of the super-sleuth, an especially rewarding and psychologically admired role. It puts the passive victim into a "manipulative" and supposedly powerful role.

Here is our scenario:

1. Nixon's downfall should be portrayed as the result, and he the victim, of a leftist conspiracy. He was being utilized by Kissinger, a devious, clever, modern Machiavelli. Kissinger really works for our enemies. He talked the weakened President into a 'detente' with Russia, China, and probably Cuba. Kissinger was utilizing Nixon's vanity and, later, Ford's weakness and psychological lack of leadership. The Vietnam war had, as its primary purpose, to

weaken the American people and its economy and to possibly bleed them white. The military have already become suspicious of Kissinger and have had his offices bugged. The liberals screamed and denounced it as another step in the direction of Watergate and of "friendly fascism." Vesco stated that, long before Watergate, the liberals were out to get Nixon impeached.

We have to present Kissinger's role as not new. Machiavelli, Richelieu, Bismark, and others have played similar games in history. The fact that Kissinger is Jewish should be used, but with caution. It will only make his cleverness and devious ways more plausible. As many believable press stories as possible should be assembled and put together in book or pamphlet form, entitled: "Whose Side Is Kissinger Really On?".

2. Inflation, unemployment, and the energy crisis could believably be portrayed as part of the gigantic plot engineered by the "enemies" in the East. They are now using much subtler methods than simply military threat. They are wearing their enemies out, weakening them with promises of peace, as Hitler did. Solzhenitsyn mentions this as a common tactic in much of his writing.

3. The Vietnam war was not only a military failure, but a psychological and political one as well. It served the enemies within the U.S. well by weakening our belief in ourselves. To many veterans, we seemed to be on the wrong side of the battle front. The North Vietnamese and Vietcong were fighting against corruption for a better life for their people. We were perpetuating a semidictatorial and rotten regime. The real goal, however, was never to defeat anybody but ourselves.

Our basic rationale will be, therefore, to give veterans and the public a chance to make it all right again. In a sense, the killer becomes the giver of life. The warriors who did not have a chance to be heroes nor treated as such have a chance to become antiwar warriors.

War offers many elements of attaining immorality. The Vietnam veterans, for various reasons, were robbed of this chance. Having to use technically perfected weapons which made personal contact unnecessary made them even more alienated, and gave them a feeling that all had been useless.

There is a lot of pent-up violence which can erupt dangerously if there is no outlet. It can be channeled into another war if the proper methods, mostly covert, are used, and thus prevent violence at home.

The American male, like most other warriors, uses fighting to impress his women. There is a close relationship between sex and violence, as rapes at My Lai and other areas showed. The reactions to the Mayaguez incident proves my point.

In our plan, the veteran will be given a chance to demonstrate his virility again, to disprove his castration and impotence often experienced by an evasive enemy, robbing him of the clear-cut elation of winning a battle.

The vet's frustrations shall first be heightened by reminding him how he had been victimized. For example, in trying to control drug abuse, he was searched, including his body cavities. He was not allowed to close the door of his barracks. All his personal possessions could be examined at any time.

A campaign entitled: "Do you still remember?" will be started.

We shall further ask groups of citizens to live a day as a Vietnam veteran, using pseudo-officers to enact similar brutalizing experiences. The purpose of this step is to bring back all the memories in a vivid fashion and to create a deeper understanding among the public of what it was really like.

We shall at first, however, only build up frustrations and tensions without offering release.

In my work for CBS during World War II, I discovered that the Nazis never killed the enemy in their propaganda films. They elevated hatred to a crescendo and then released the audience into the street, looking for 'enemies'. American films usually killed the spy, the Nazi or Jap, in the film and produced a happy ending. Thus the audience had nothing further to do, and their frustration was dissolved.

4. Our plan on how to entice Vietnam veterans and hundreds of thousands of malcontents to enlist in another war and to create a positive attitude in the public will have all the appearances of a "better," "just" war. We shall call it an awakening to America's real values. We shall discard moral considerations. Our plan is based instead on concepts of effectiveness and value for the individual. Another important psychological aspect that should be exploited is that war often has the effect of demonstrating to an otherwise quite uncomplicated person that he is capable of change. We shall remind the vet that there are many deeper layers of his personality that he was not aware of, but that he discovered, particularly in a situation of danger, unsuspected levels of consciousness ranging from deep visceral animal-like fear to a god-like elation of his power over life and death, including his own.

Many veterans have become addicts to this raised consciousness which they cannot maintain unless they use drugs or become alcoholics, or go back into battle.

Every meeting and every action that we shall ask them to perform will be presented in terms of an almost religious or voodoo experience; or in different terms, as a form of transcendentalism, promising enormous new discoveries of the self, in reality completely unrelated to the goal of defending one's country or anybody else's cause.

The average person usually, unless he is a hard drug user, hardly ever has had experiences of this sort. We can and will offer it to him.

5. Appeals to patriotism and containment of communism will not work any more. They will not be used. Instead, a fight for peace and change of the

whole system, which can substitute for all the hidden advantages of a war, will be the main theme, without mentioning a new war as the real goal.

6. The Vietnam veteran came back frustrated and bitter. We shall motivate him to channel his militancy into a feeling that his job is now to become the leader of an elite, designed to bring America back to meaningful goals and to mobilize the disgruntled majority. He was the underdog before; he can now be on top.

7. We shall offer the veteran the chance to bring meaning into his war experience and to assume a leadership role, compensating for his loss of dignity during and after the war. In a continuous flow of information, through newsletters and confidential reports, he shall be told about the rottenness of the U.S.

8. The American public has become cynical and disillusioned. It clamors for leadership. The veteran can mobilize others—the unemployed, (increased through the energy crisis), and disillusioned groups—to join in bringing about a reawakening of America.

9. Respectable authority figures will be used as the sources of this information, such as Nader, Jack Anderson, and various Senators.

10. Action will gradually be suggested. Here are the facts, this is what you can do about it. Join "Reveille." Get others informed. Wear a secret sign in your button-hole. Organize calls, expose corruption.

11. We are using our invisible, therefore doubly dangerous, enemy as a target. This enemy can be portrayed as having infiltrated from the outside and being centered abroad and inside the United States, engineering outbreaks in various parts of the world, such as labor unrest in Britain; or indirectly utilizing the conspiracy of large corporations, such as the petroleum industry.

12. In reality, we are utilizing the desires of the veterans to become dominant after their brutalization and humiliation.

13. Of course, we shall need real leaders to mobilize these enraged vets and channel their emotions, giving them a purpose, a feeling of belonging and strength which they had experienced temporarily during their war experience.

14. Vets often suffer from various guilts; having had to submit blindly to authorities, having enjoyed killing indirectly, not having had any responsibilities. Our job is to help them to get rid of these guilts, through various media and through compensating actions.

15. Resistance against being forced out of the role of the professional veteran who refuses to become active again in any form has to be removed. Many vets enjoy negative and passive roles.

16. Fear of being manipulated could be removed by open admission to vets that we are asking him to help influence, motivate, arouse (that is, manipulate) the rest of the nation and that he is best qualified to do this.

17. We have to offer psychological promises: become a real revolutionary,

change rotten America, become a savior, a hero, a member of a new aristocracy, bring back old-fashioned American virtues.

18. Pragmatic promises will also be offered: wear a dashing, modern uniform, get training in the use of the latest weapons, possibly money rewards, pay lower taxes, have women admire them and be available to them.

In order to reach all these goals, the veteran has to first fight a formidable enemy, who is smart and shrewd. He has to learn to take him on and recognize him whether he is in the United States or in some other country with tentacles right here.

Each of these rationales will be translated into a series of specific programs, using all available media and channels and employing techniques ranging from films to comic books, the establishment of political cells, the participation in any issue that can be exploited for the overall purpose of this war (peace) battle plan.

Our techniques are borrowed from psychiatry and modern clinical psychology. Brainwashing in reality is more than simple pressure or torture. It is the mobilization of group pressure, guilt feelings, and building up of frustrations and outlets to relieve tension.

19. The role of women will be given particular attention. This new war for peace is being fought to give virile men back to American women and to mothers, sons who proved themselves as heroes and subconsciously as substitutes for their aging fathers.

20. The possibility of including women in this new army will be considered. Utilization of women's liberation may play a role. Possibly women should accompany their men into battle in foreign countries, or take over jobs of fighting the invisible enemy at home, to protect their families. They should be encouraged to participate in this war (peace) campaign against exploitation. Comparable to the Israeli army, women will wear uniforms, parade, and show their influence and militancy in as many different ways as possible.

Translating our rationale into specific strategy and tactical procedures, the following recommendations are being made:

1. A mystery leader, sort of Big Brother, will be created. We have always been opposed to dictators. Thus, keeping this person (who may not really exist) mysterious will remove the fear of the imperial president. In reality, Big Brother will be groups of people, consisting of behavioral psychologists, propaganda experts, and military leaders. This mystery man will ask through posters and possibly commercials that Americans wake up.

2. A film is suggested tracing back how America has been sliding into a morass of corruption and dangerous attempts to be governed in a semi-fascist fashion.

This same film will show what America could be like if it begins to take its own destiny into its own hands again. The first part of the film will create frustration, anger mixed with guilt feelings. The viewer will become convinced that he has been duped and played for a sucker by his present leaders, especially Kissinger, and indirectly by a weak president. They used the Viet Nam war only as a testing ground and a means of subduing the more militant members of the young population and of weakening the nation.

The demonstration of what America could be again—the hope of the world, the cleaning up of the smeared image of America, the re-establishment in the American creed—would be the topics of the second part of this film.

3. A magazine will be created, entitled: "The Voice of the People." Through continuous exposures to the conspiracy of the petroleum industry the automotive industry, and other forms of big business which cooperate with the "enemy," and their tie-up with the present government, they can be portrayed as the real enemy.

This conspiracy could be shown to have been partially inspired by outside forces who have the final destruction of the American system as their goal. The concept of the American betrayal will be broadcast in as many different forms as possible.

For a while, no immediate answer will be given, in order to build up the anger. The only way the vets and the public can release their pent-up fury will be by joining a group of people bent upon the same goal of saving America.

The mysterious person, the invisible leader, should have the aura and the charisma of a saviour, a modest person who does not seek any personal advantages and is willing to give up his whole life to the cause of bringing about a return of America to its former virtues.

Comic books, not unlike underground literature, will be printed and distributed in colleges and be available at newsstands. They will make use of the newest trend of interest in magic and mystery.

We shall approach meetings of the National Guard, the Veterans of Foreign Wars, and the American Legion.

The concept of a post-industrial imperialism which has taken over with the connivance of the government will be told through various media.

A very effective means used by communists and Nazis is to stage political cabarets where people can be aroused through hostile caricatures. Material could be sent to public personalities, even comedians or people like James Buckley, Jr. or Merv Griffin.

Public debate under the title "America's Doom" or "Is America sliding into a morass that it can't get out of anymore?" will be initiated.

Bumper stickers, which are becoming popular, should be distributed. They could be tied in with the energy crisis, saying something like "Let's stop being suckers" or "Yes, we can do something about it: call 'Reveille'."

Another theme might be: "Are you willing to fight the real war?" or "We are mobilizing for the war that will really count—Join Us!"

Uniforms should be issued to the new revolutionary army, so that greater visibility is achieved. Of course they should look semi-military, but not enough to arouse the present government to prohibiting the wearing of these outfits.

The concept of American betrayal should be constantly used. People will be made to feel guilty. Every day some news item about corruption will be published. "What have you done about it?"

A questionnaire will be sent out or broadcast asking: What have you done about changing the situation:

a)   got mad inside

b)   resigned yourself

c)   tried to get to another country

d)   looked for a group to join which will take action

Newscasts will be developed with the title: "What is the real news behind the news?" Reveal once a week another piece of secret information. Create a feeling of accumulation of frustration and anger.

Distribute stickers for windows, flags on long rods for cars, indicating through a symbol the need for change.

Another form of protest might be to refuse to pay a part of income taxes until corruption has been stopped. If possible, those who have declared their readiness to participate in Operation Reveille' could be promised a tax reduction.

Organizations like Common Cause or American Civil Liberties Union will be portrayed as softies, who act only as safety valves, draining off the anger of the people who are ready to fight.

The topic "They trained you to fight, but sent you to the wrong country; use your training to fight the real war (for the honest, strong America)" should penetrate all approaches.

"Unless you do, you will have become the real draft dodgers and betray your family and your children."

"You, the vet, and the unemployed, are expressing what millions of Americans really feel."

Did this "secret" document frighten you? It should have. It is simply an exercise, but I think a very valuable one. Wars and dictatorships have been started with the use of less finesse. Modern behavioral techniques and mass media make sophisticated manipulation even more likely, rather than having diminished it.

The answer to such possibilities is to educate people to use methods of persuasion for intelligent political education. While I worked for CBS, we tried such an approach. We asked people to listen to a news program as it came off the wires and to stay in the studio for a discussion afterwards. We used this discussion as a lesson in political education, training people to become aware of apparently innocuous news which, if properly understood, was a warning signal.

The scenario which I presented to you may help you to recognize such dangers in the future, even though the specific details may be quite different.

End of scenario. I have not quoted you all the details of this assignment. It was a real one, and I was even being paid for it. The reaction to this imaginary drama of a devilish motivational researcher was, luckily, negative. Primarily, the reaction was because too many people who read the manuscript felt it was too dangerous, and it seemed to have too many resemblances to real possibilities.

Although the original task was given to me by a magazine, it was not an entirely new one. The movie producer, Stanley Kubrick wanted me to work with him on his anti-atomic war film, "Dr. Strangelove." We met in his apartment in London and had dinner together. What he wanted to know was whether it was too dangerous to use humor in order to expose the danger of an atomic war. Unfortunately, because of financial differences, I did not continue with the assignment. My opinion, in any case, was that humor is an excellent way of exaggerating dangerous issues to such an extent that people become aware of the consequences.

Quite a number of people believe, even now, that the characters that appeared in this film were copied from life. Kubrick's purpose, as he explained to me, was similar to my own scenario for the magazine: to get a number of people to start believing that such conspiracies and impossible events can actually take place. When you think of the Reichstag fire which was obviously a scenario, and other situations such as the still unfounded rumors connected with the assassination of John F. Kennedy and other American politicians, we had better start thinking seriously about such supposed science fiction.

In order to come back to the question of whether a motivational researcher could be used for dangerous purposes, naturally he could. This can be avoided, however, not through legislation, but more through the fact that all parties and all groups would have access to these so-called experts. At least, while the danger would not be completely avoided, it would have been minimized. Maybe it is poor comfort, but all things connected with progress can, under certain circumstances, be used for devilish purposes. Splitting the atom can be, and was, used for the bomb, but it can also be used for purposes of development of nuclear power plants. Almost everyone who has better technological knowledge than the average person must decide for himself for which purpose he wants to use this knowledge. The surgeon who has a sharper scalpel or a better tool in his hands can use it to control life or death. This does not apply just to magic scientists.

An engineer building bridges has a similar problem. Almost everyone who buys a pistol, supposedly for self defense, even with the official authorization which, fortunately, is necessary in most states, can use it either to kill or to actually combat criminality.

Just because motivational research represents a somewhat further developed method of influencing people, in my opinion, does not mean that you should stop progress altogether. The solution can only lie in the personal moral and ethical make-up of the scientist. In some areas we may have already gone too far when, for example, we are suspecting in almost every kind of food, the possibility of its contributing to cancer. It can go as far as forbidding glass to be used in windows because it is potentially dangerous. The answer really lies in better education and not in increased control and more legal restrictions. Just as in the education of children, only those admonitions which are accepted by the individual deep down within himself are really effective. Only then do they no longer need any threats or words of punishment. Only when man has learned to fight the devil within himself can we honestly claim that we have made a further step in our very slow maturing process of human intelligence.

22 Column A or Column B?

After our son had succeeded in growing his beard, at age 16 or thereabouts, he decided to get to work on me, not in the sense that he wanted me to also grow a beard. That is one of the goals that I have never been successful with. He grew one beard after another, put it into an envelope, and numbered it. I haven't inquired lately about what ever happened to these envelopes. Anyway, he, like so many other thousands of students, was involved in demonstrations and in various attempts to make his voice heard as part of the youth revolution.

It was inevitable that he would question motivational research. We decided amicably that we were going to make a differentiation between Project A and Project B. In one column, Column A, we would put all those tasks which would, in both our opinions, contribute to the betterment of mankind. They did not necessarily have to be particularly profitable. In Column B would be all those projects done for large corporations for which I charge a very profitable honorarium. We even went as far as to prepare a separate list of folders which dealt with A projects. Some of them were completed.

Going over the various studies and assignments which I have worked on over the past 35 years or so, I discovered, to my son's pleasant surprise, that I hadn't been as mercenary as I had thought. The main point is not to cite my good deeds but to make it clear to the reader that we need more persuasion techniques rather than fewer. Manipulation may be a dirty word, yet this is what it really comes down to.

I have been asked to give lectures many times—I even prepared a cassette program on the psychology of effective fund raising. The obvious approach would be to rely on the generosity of people, their so-called altruism, and present them with various requests. Hospitals need money, the Cancer Society does, school boards do. The list of organizations that we've worked for is quite long: the Christian Children's Fund, the Epilepsy Foundation, Care, United Way, United Jewish Appeal are just a few examples. What I'm proud of is not only that the motivational approach works, but that I could overcome some of the resistances based on conventional kinds of thinking. You ask someone to give money. You are asking them really to give up something that means a lot to them in one form or another. They could have used the money to have fun with. The correct psychological approach then is to promise them fun for their contribution. To convince them, which is not as difficult as it may sound, that indeed they will feel better about themselves. Fun, after all, has exactly the same purpose. We translated this, describing to the giver the wonderful feelings of having made a contribution. The only difference is that we stressed the fact that it was primarily a contribution to himself, rather than to the cause. I recently was interviewed on a national television network, on the subject of charity and giving. Betty Furness, who did the interviewing, tried very hard to get me to admit that the millions, or billions, of dollars that America has contributed to the rest of the world must, after all, be a sign of altruism. I hope she finally accepted my somewhat less beautiful explanation, that Americans, like many others, like to be loved, have a strong inferiority feeling, and have so far only learned that the simplest way to get love, in a way the cheapest, is to buy it. Cheap because it does not require any deep down personal involvement.

When I'm confronted with a task, I try to apply some upside-down thinking. I shove aside the obvious answers people give, and ask whether, if we go deep enough into their unconscious, we might not discover other equally important motivations. I feel like a psychological archaeologist. Most of our personalities have several layers. The upper layer may not reveal very much, or may mislead us. Another technique which is very helpful is to identify yourself with the person or the groups of people you are trying to understand. Giving does not just involve money. It also is a tangible expression of how you feel about a particular cause, it is a demonstration of your own emotions. Margaret Mead, the well-known anthropologist, discussed with me quite some time ago what she felt was a typical American characteristic, the fear of demonstrating one's feelings openly. Maybe this applies not only to Americans but to Anglo-Saxons in general. When you make out a check or give cash, you are confronted with what

I've discussed in a previous chapter, the fear of embarrassment. The embarrassment consists of a number of aspects, one of which is standing there with my naked emotions, worrying about giving too much or giving too little. The practical application of this principle was to help the potential giver to determine the correct amount: a percentage of his income, or measuring the dollars on the basis of the worthiness of the cause.

However, the cause seemed to be much less important than we originally thought. If you don't suffer from any kidney problems or have no one in your family afflicted that way, being asked to give to the Kidney Foundation is very uninteresting. When we contribute we also understand this to mean that we are becoming members of a group. Being told, therefore, that the group we are joining is an interesting one, as selfish as this may sound, is a very concrete and practical motivation.

Why don't more Europeans come to the United States? Another A Project: it brings money, it helps our balance of trade. The obvious answer for a long time was that the U.S. was too expensive. After two devaluations of the dollar, this no longer holds true. Even when the dollar was high, my professional cynical attitude, which is another way of describing a motivational approach, made me disbelieve this all-too-ready answer given by Europeans in previous surveys. Again, applying my archaeological shovel, being half European and talking to Europeans helped me to find a deeper reason.

Europeans, although the gap has narrowed since, felt that we in this country were living in a post-industrial society. Coming here was comparable to reading a newspaper of 2, 3 or 4 years from now. While this is an extremely thrilling experience, it is also quite frightening. Are there many people who would know the exact date when they would die? Coming to this country meant, to the average European, seeing his own world with all its good and bad possibilities three or four years ahead of time. Even the good possibilities we found to be frightening. I understood it after our discussion with several German social scientists who had come here, expenses paid, courtesy of the State Department. After a couple of drinks I posed the inevitable question, "Well, how did you like this country?" They retorted, "Do you want the official answer or our real impressions?" When I nodded to the second alternative, they pulled out a series of photographs, newspaper clippings, and various other proofs of their impressions. Most of them dealt with slums, race riots, poverty, and other Americana. For a moment I was enraged. What ingratitude! Even before my face got red they calmed me down and gave me this very intelligent explanation. "Yes, we found all these things. But we also found many good things. But we have to keep on living in Germany. In order to restore our equilibrium, we had to convince ourselves that America was not perfect. We really liked it here, but we wanted to balance our impression, not because of our scientific objectivity, but because of our need to be more or less at peace with ourselves."

Another finding of the study was that not only do we export ugly Americans, but a lot of them live right here. The complaints, superficially, were quite valid, but again aroused a deeper resentment. Just try, in the average American hotel, to order breakfast in any other language than English. Maybe, if some of the waiters are Puerto Ricans you can order in Spanish; if not you'd be lost. Stop someone in the street and ask him for directions in Italian, or French, or German. He'll laugh at you, he will make you feel inferior. "If they come here, why don't they learn our language?" Americans have not learned to understand how to behave as hosts. In relaxed circumstances, they do invite foreigners to their homes, and are extremely courteous. This is also reported by visitors. This A Project again led to some interesting practical applications. One was the necessity of persuading Europeans that when a cab driver asked them where they came from and, possibly five minutes later, how much money they were making, he did not really mean to pry, it was a form of democratic behavior, difficult to understand for Europeans who often take years before they will permit their friends to call them by their first names.

When we took our children to the old country for the first time, we went to a fairly good restaurant in Vienna. There were at least six or seven waiters serving us, an experience that our American-born children had never had. It made them nervous and irritable. "Why don't they go away? What do they want?" What they were accustomed to was the American restaurant, where the waiter, if you do not know exactly at the moment what you want, abandons you with a mumbled remark, "I'll be back later folks, when you've made up your mind."

Another project our son approves of concerned an educational approach called the University without Walls. For a few years now, some colleges and universities have made it possible for a person in public administration, or in a community college, to get a Ph.D. without having to abandon his job, and carry through studies which are very much job-related. I was asked by Nova University, in Fort Lauderdale, to find out what really motivates these people to go through the expense and time investment to become participants in such a program. The obvious answer was to get a degree and, possibly earn more money or get more recognition.

Let's go down again to layers 2, 3, 4 or 5 of our psycho-archaeological mound. Many of these people felt that would soon be over the hill. They needed encouragement. They were tempted to become bureaucrats, to follow their daily routine, and bit by bit to move up at the pace of a very tired snail. This opportunity, offered by the Nova Program, became a continuous challenge, as they told me. They met other people in similar age groups, mostly 35, 40 or older. The main value that they derived was mutual support. Whenever they were about to give up or drop out, they had a chance to discuss this temporary weakness with their colleagues. Knowing that others struggled similarly helped them literally make the grade. Having found this more human motivation, our suggestion was that part of the curriculum should be devoted to help in self-analysis, that the participants be instructed not only in the subject matters that interested them and which they needed for their degrees, but also in how to overcome such self doubts. In a way it was an application of Adlerian psychology—to offer them more frequently little red flags, which would be, psychologically speaking, proof of their progress.

This idea extends to experiments in the field of agriculture, where it was found that when someone was asked to thin out the beets, the rows which were interspersed with little red flags (which, of course, could be any other color) were more rapidly finished than rows which seemed endless: a very simple device that you may want to use when a task seems too big for you. When I practiced psychoanalysis, one of my clients was a Ph.D. student, who was an actor at the same time, and just never could seem to make it. I finally came up with the idea of asking him to permit me to visit him in his apartment. There he was, sitting at his desk. Right in front of him were at least 50 books, all needed to acquire his degree. Instead of being encouraging, these books were like a multi-colored dragon staring him in the face, on a day-by-day basis. Every time he sat down, he was reminded of all the work that was ahead of him. Even the most courageous person would have been flattened by the sheer psychological weight of the task. My therapy was relatively simple. I took all the books home and left him just one. At each subsequent visit we analyzed his difficulties and I gave him one more book, thus limiting his task. Within a couple of years, the visits became less and less frequent. They were no longer necessary, and the pile of books became smaller and smaller. Eventually, much sooner than he had anticipated, he got his Ph.D.

There was a parallel in my own life to the University without Walls project. At the age of 14, I was forced to quit school for a very simple reason: I had no money to continue and I had to support myself. For about four or five years I worked as a salesman in a department store, I became a window decorator and did secretarial work. At one point it became clear that while I was now making enough money to help out my family and to keep myself afloat, this might very well be the level at which I would stay for quite a number of years. I inquired, therefore, what other opportunities existed. Vienna had always been a social democratic regime. Just about that time a new law had been passed permitting students who were intelligent enough to continue their studies in the evening and during weekends. The term used was not University without Walls, we were called Externists, in contrast to the Internists. All my friends who had wealthy parents went through the full eight years of Gymnasium, the equivalent of a high school with some college training.

It took me two years to cover the eight year curriculum. I failed the exams in Latin and math. I was not going to take this defeat after all my effort. I decided I was going to lick the problem. Something exciting and interesting happened. I suddenly saw the light. Latin was more or less a routine learning process, but math was different. I immersed myself until, in a lightning moment, some of the basic philosophy of math became clear to me. I'm talking about fairly advanced mathematical techniques, which usually, in this country, are only taught in colleges of engineering. I presented myself three months later having resolved that I wasn't going to yield, another very simple way of combatting stress. I passed with the highest praise possible. I remember even now how the Director of the College held me up as a shining example of real determination.

Thus I knew all about the psychological temptations, weaknesses, and psychological indications to simply drop out and give it all up when I interviewed the participants in the University without Walls project.

Fighting drug addiction was acceptable to my son and to other well meaning people as another A project. The deeper I dug below the surface of the drug problem, the more I discovered that it was much less related to the influences of a poor family background, lack of discipline, a breakdown of morality, and other similarly easy excuses. Some of the answers are contained in the kind of language the drug addicts use. They go on a trip, they get high. One of the explanations was that the regular school curriculum does not offer enough excitement. I know this goes against all our accepted standards. We go to school to learn, to develop discipline. My recommendations to the organization concerned with drug problems was to institute, in as many schools as possible, surprise parties, creative exercises, theatrical performances, and other means to keep the pupils busy and to offer them a trip without having to take drugs.

The main lesson to be learned from these A Projects is that the same methods used to sell toothpaste or cars can be applied to socially more interesting problems. The principle which is involved is to abandon your naive approach and to concern yourself much more with the not necessarily equally "nice" real explanation.

If you want to help, as I tried to do with the unification of Europe, another A task, you have to familiarize yourself with the frequently not so idealistic competitive psychologies of your subjects, in this case European politicians.

The list of A Projects that we have worked on is quite impressive. One of the negative points to mention is that I have found that it is generally much easier to work with B clients, not just because of the money involved, but because they are more capable of thinking along new channels and accepting new ideas. You would assume the opposite to be true.

Herman Kahn, the well known futurologist, accused me of having too much of a positive conviction as far as mankind is concerned. Despite his own often

Column A conference in the Castle.

very provocative optimism as far as the next two hundred years are concerned, he himself frequently has doubts that it is really possible to change humans. The tasks which his Hudson Institute undertakes are far more theoretical than mine. In a seminar which we conducted jointly, we attempted to combine our views to develop for businesses and various industrial enterprises the various principles which both of us feel will govern the development of the next 10 or 20 years.

The population growth, of which we've been so much afraid, will slow down. In many countries it has already reached a zero point. We are going to have less fear as far as technological developments are concerned, and will learn to use technology to conquer our own environment instead. We are going to become more and more individualistic instead of remaining dependent on large organizations. Kahn, in an area where I am no expert, is convinced that we are also going to have sufficient sources of energy and that we are probably not going to expand the real energy crisis. We are going to learn to develop new forms of energy from differences in temperature in different layers of ocean water (geothermal energy). Our nuclear energy, despite all the protests from environmental groups, will move ahead.

In an indirect way, I have tried to establish a closer cooperation between our two institutes and have begun to achieve it. Our son Tom now works for Herman Kahn and, as both told me, he might possibly be the bridge between their approach and my more pragmatic one. One of the problems which we are dealing with is that so many of the well-meaning people trying to defend endangered species think of themselves in such a self-assured fashion. They consider almost everyone who has not identified with them and is not of their opinion to be representative of devilish multi-national companies governed only by selfish motives. Many of the organizations dealing with the defensive consumers feel that almost any large company is not too far removed from criminality.

I had some discussion about this with Ralph Nader with whom I have appeared a few times on speaker platforms. My opinion was that again the answer must lie in educating the consumer and, at the same time, to give the large manufacturers the benefit of the doubt. True, they are not all angels. But how can you explain the fact that the tires for cars last about ten times as long as they did 20 or 30 years ago? Is it only due to better roads or better cars or better drivers or has there been a competitive motivation which made tire manufacturers interested in making longer lasting tires?

To take another example, electricity today is much, much cheaper than it was 20 or 30 years ago. The same is true for the telephone and for individual calls. Interestingly enough, right now fares for flights are being continuously reduced. Many of the so-called mass produced products can compete in quality very easily with hand-made products and, quite often, are just as good. What is lacking is the snob appeal, the feeling of being hand-made. Those people who want to pay for all this luxury are welcome to it. Why, however, prevent millions of people from buying products made on a mass basis that they can afford?

I once had a very heated discussion with a Belgian during a conference in Brussels about motivational research. He very seriously defended the view that art and everything connected with it should be reserved for those people who are appreciative of it. I found this to be a sort of aristocratic envy. This kind of feeling is more frequent than we normally assume. We have books, museums, classical music, and many other forms of culture which are today available to people who, 30 or 40 years ago, could never even dream about such possibilities. The thing that is necessary is to educate people and to encourage them to make use of these possibilities, again a task which can be achieved through proper motivation. Very often the so-called lack of interest is not a genuine one but is brought about by those culture snobs who say: "Art is really too good for proletarians. It should be reserved for people like myself."

A police officer who came to see me in a half official, half private matter wanted to know what he should do to defend himself vis a vis his colleagues who laughed at him because he went, quite regularly, to ballets and was genuinely interested. We discussed the problem later on with a ballet group which accepted the problem and adopted it into their publicity. We showed a man with muscles and hair on his chest and stated that even he could enjoy ballets without having to worry about loss of virility. This idea was suggested by us and used in order to reach other, more manual occupations. We showed, in a few TV commercials, how a ballet dancer, because of his athletic ability, very often could defeat heavily muscled, athletically built opponents.

One of the first jobs which we always have to accomplish is to convince the people and ourselves that the experience which we have had with industrial and commercial products, even when they produce profits, can be just as interesting and human as our work with A Projects.

We have found that many of the "vicious," large companies can be convinced to combine social interests and goals with their commercial ones. Many of the do-gooders, the environmentalists, members of the "new class" are so worried about the preservation of certain species or about preventing the building of a nuclear power plant because they suffer from their own guilt feelings. They either benefit, and usually do, from the technological advances that they are supposedly fighting against, or they subconsciously feel that they should have done something about involving themselves in social issues a long time ago. They now try to overcompensate. They even predict the end of the world if certain things are not done. Too often, such behavior is based on the lack of other goals. A Canadian advertiser asked me what these professional protesters would do once all their goals had been reached. They may have to look for new issues, hopefully of a more constructive type.

Too often the people in charge of projects concerned with more humanitarian goals have been raised in an academic atmosphere. They have not learned how to approach a problem pragmatically. I try to ask, "What kind of answers could be utilized if you had them?" rather than conducting a two million dollar project starting with Adam and Eve. Another factor which makes it more difficult to get involved with well-meaning organizations is that they are so darned convinced of their righteousness that they are inclined to consider everybody not involved in their particular goal to be automatically vicious and devilish.

23 Stop the Mama Business

Whenever I feel that things are getting too much for me, that I cannot go on like this, or when I feel overtired, I make a universal appeal to "mama." I'm not quite sure to whom this one-word prayer is addressed: my mother, who has been dead for many years, my wife? If I were a religious man, I could easily substitute the word God. I've always wondered whether the Greeks were not more impartial by having goddesses. It is probably a form of male chauvinism to look upon God as a father. The Catholics have, to some extent, remedied this one-sidedness by making it possible to appeal to Holy Mary.

I use this 'Mama' expression as a verbalized sigh, a sigh of content. Apparently I have developed this habit to such an extent that my grandchildren quote me, and have invented a counteraction by admonishing me to "Stop the mama business." It is very comforting to have an omnipotent force ready to help you, if only you appeal to it in the appropriate way. There are millions of people who do it through prayer. This cry for help whenever we realize our human weakness, and how many easily breakable strings hold our anatomical puppet together, is very understandable. In a novel by Solshenitsyn describing the siege of Stalingrad by the Germans, the author most likely quite correctly describes how many of the soldiers, in their bottomless misery, cried out for "mama."

Marco Vassi, who teaches relaxation and is the head of the Penthouse Press, came to visit us the other day. In one of his books, he describes how he invented new approaches to make people aware of their own bodies, and to get them to let go. An ingenious idea it was, although somewhat cruel, to ask them to imagine that an ax, a guillotine, was chopping off their limbs, one after another, and finally their heads. All these separate parts, however, were still connected to the body by strings, and could be operated by a puppeteer: themselves. He discovered the ability, based on the intense horror of his people, to become a godlike creature.

Our political decisions are strongly influenced by this deep desire to find someone on whom we can lean. Erich Fromm, in his book, *Escape From Freedom*, describes this eternal dilemma. Despite many years of democracy, we still have never learned to really act democratically. In a study conducted for an insurance company, I analyzed to what extent our schools really help in indoctrinating our children with democratic beliefs—not just the ability to recite the Declaration of Independence or to know American history but, much more important, what I call behavioral and motivational aspects of democracy. Decision making, being able to accept criticism, and more than anything else, the willingness to take action as a citizen to remedy ills should be taught our children at an early age. Only lately has the youth movement in many countries discovered this necessity. At first they started out by raising hell and smashing windows. Bit by bit, they are recognizing now that a more effective method is to work within existing laws.

In my own life, I have been forced to accept the role of father because, although he was a nice man, I never really had a psychological father. When I was nine or ten years old. I remember being ashamed of my father. One of the most depressing experiences that I can remember is, when I walked home from school and was standing with a friend and he suddenly pointed to a middle-aged man who was reprimanding me. I don't remember exactly what it was about, either I had missed synagogue or I had not done something else I was supposed to have done. This friend, quite innocently and without realizing what damage he was doing to me, asked, "Who is this crazy man?" I remember this incident even now. When I was 14 years old, I had to start making a living. My father became ill and died a few years later. I had to support the family. I was the oldest. Whether I liked it or not, I had to assume a role of provider and father which had never been completely fulfilled by my father. My two brothers very readily accepted, with relief, that I had assumed this burden.

I remember a patient, when I practiced psychoanalysis, who was a tall girl. She came to me with a complaint that, because of her statuesque qualities, she was being forced, by whatever group she belonged, to assume a leadership role. She tried to reject it. She came to me for help, complaining that she simply was not cut out to play that role, and people would not believe her. Talking to young interns in the course of a motivational analysis of the doctor-patient relationship, I found a similar kind of phenomenon. The young doctors would tell me that they were being asked questions of all types, to which the only honest answer would have been, "I don't know. I did not even finish my studies, nor do I have enough experience." The temptation, however, to accept the adoration that comes with being looked upon as a saint, magician and medicine man was too great, and to the detriment of many disturbed and resentful attitudes between doctor and patient, they frequently could never quite give up this too easily acquired role. Where does a father run, what does he do, if he feels that he is not qualified to play the role forcefully assigned to him? With my young patient, the therapy consisted in asking her to play act. By chance she was also interested in acting and was apparently quite good at it. I helped her solve her conflict by advising her to act as if she were a leader, but to keep it a secret between herself and me that it was all a farce. It was not long before she reported back to me that she was enjoying playing a role, as long as it did not have to be real. There are a number of therapies now which use, as their approach, similar concepts.

It is much easier to be a follower than to be a leader. If one is lucky enough to believe in himself to such an extent that it becomes strength, wonderful.

We spent two delightful weeks on a little island called Bequia, about an hour's boat ride from St. Vincent in the Caribbean. While in the hotel, which was delightful and small, we were told about a peculiar colony called Moon Hole. We had to take a cab and then walk on a small path more or less through the jungle to reach it. I was warned that it was very exclusive and few people were allowed to visit. The hotel manager called up anyway and it turned out that Mr. Johnston, the owner, builder and president of the Moon Hole Association, knew about me. He invited us to lunch, with the consequence that we spent a few days in one of his houses. These houses are worthy of mention because they are built out of native rock, without any particular design. As he explained to us, you just start with some native workers, study the terrain, look at the view, decide it might be nice to have a window there, and maybe the door could go on the other side, and maybe a few steps up and a few steps down again. The result is a strangely fascinating, primitive and disorganized and, at the same time, very natural type of house and colony. He attracted a number of people who were looking for a mama, who were trying to escape. It was an odd mixture of advertising executives, managerial types, artists, and younger and middle-aged copouts. They were finally fulfilling what they had sighed many times when the load had gotten too heavy. The sobering aspect of this experience was that we discovered, when talking to some of the people there, that more than the normal percentage had sold their houses. What they could take even less than the rat race was being away from civilization. It was a flight to the extreme—no telephones, no electricity. The bathrooms were without ceilings. I think the weather was warm all year round. None of these facts really meant anything. It was actually quite comfortable. Many aspects of bourgeois convenience did exist. Mrs. Johnston had trained a number of the young girls from the island to become maids and cooks. She did the shopping for you, assigned a girl to your house, and took care of everything. We never knew exactly what we were going to get for breakfast, except the one thing we were sure of, because we could smell it, delicious homemade, freshly baked bread.

Many communes and Walden I and II's fail because dreaming about escaping is easier than actually doing it. In my experience, crying out for mama may be about the right amount of relief that one should expect as long as it is done half in jest and not too often. The only really more effective solution is to control your motivations. I, for one, believe that it is better to have done and experienced 20 different things in one year than to have fictitiously produced mental fatigue and cut short one's life by doing one and the same thing over a period of 20 years. I realize that there are many millions of people who belong to the latter category. I think they are shortchanging themselves. Motivational research has provided me with continuous change. Almost every few days I am "forced" to approach a different problem. When I say "forced" to, I deliberately put it in quotes, because I am not. I am intrigued by each new challenge the same way the mountaineers give us their explanation for why they climb Mt. Everest: "Because it is there."

24 Things that Puzzle Me

Despite over more than 45 years of hunting for motivations and insights, I still have quite a list of unanswered questions. One of my fantasies is to meet with a really intelligent priest, bishop or cardinal. He must be open-minded, however, Maybe my approach would be, "Convert me. Do it skillfully. And don't manipulate my emotions and fears." Someone once said that few people remain agnostics or atheists on their death bed. I doubt that this will apply to me. I consider God with a long, white beard, an omnipotent father, to be simply a projection of narrow-minded human thinking. Goethe once said, "If lions had a god, he would look like a lion." Ours, therefore, looks like a human being. In the Old Testament he gets angry, he punishes, is benevolent, can even be bribed—is a prayer anything else?

Another thing that has puzzled me is how a priest of whatever rank can bless soldiers who are going into battle and pray for victory. My limited intelligence makes me think that what he's asking for is to make more efficient killers out of the beneficiaries of his benediction. Throughout my life I've been on various sides of enemy armies—as a youngster, the English and the French and the Americans were portrayed to me, in school, through all public propaganda, as villains. Eating small babies was one of the milder brutalities attributed to them. During the Second World War, when we arrived in the States, the Germans, including the Kaiser, who I had been told as an Austrian kid were wonderful, brave people, now were incredibly horrible, and indeed they were. The people I was supposed to consider on my side now had changed. And though, in each war, both were deadly enemies, they had their respective clergies pray for their country's victory—the German ministers pray for the victory of the German Army, the French priests, the French Army. It must be tough, being God, and even tougher to appeal to Jesus Christ. The Son of God preached universal love. Yet it is still being done. In the recent film about the war in Algeria, Catholic French priests blessed French soldiers, who brutally tried to suppress the striving for independence of the Muslim Algerians.

How could Jesus combine his world-shaking sermon of love with this complete detachment and almost rejection of his mother, his brethren, and almost hardly ever any mention of his father? Maybe, not being a theologian, I don't understand that his earthly father was being replaced by God and therefore, in a way, was non-existent for him.

The Bible puzzles me. I've read it many times, on lonely nights in hotel rooms, and on other occasions. Certainly the Old Testament is full of deceit and begats, incests, and struggles for power. It's a fascinating history of human frailty. And it is trite to state that you can defend almost any kind of human or inhuman action with an appropriate quote from the Bible. The Dutch Reformed Church has been skillful in demonstrating that Bantus in South Africa, being black, certainly have no right to be treated as equals.

Having lived in several countries—Austria, a short while in Germany, and a couple of years in France, and many, many years in the United States—nationalism is another strange and puzzling phenomenon to me. I can understand it, as a psychologist, as a way of reaping a feeling of security by living within political, by and large imaginary, boundaries. I wrote a book, at the request of an Italian publisher, on the unification of Europe, and called it *The Disease of Nationalism*. Several hundred people were interviewed. They had a completely erroneous concept of identity. They were dressing the same way to a very large extent, they were drinking the same martinis and dancing the same dances. What horrified them more than anything else was the thought that they would not be Frenchmen any longer but Europeans. The fact that their real identity would not only be preserved and strengthened, once the outward, mostly superficial frills had been removed, was never accepted by them.

My father-in-law was mildly religious. When he returned from a few months in a concentration camp from which he mysteriously escaped because of his age, he decided (and many other religious people will feel that he was wrong) that if God could permit this to happen, He either was blind, deaf and unconcerned, or He did not exist. I share this belief. Over six million murders for no reason that any logical mind could understand are difficult to combine with belief in a loving God. Religious Jews may have felt that this was a sublime test of their faith. The majority of them who survived also survived this test and kept their faith. I can only humbly admire them. I don't think I will ever understand them.

Why did God (or the all-penetrating universal power in which I'm more ready to believe) not organize our lives better? Do we have to experience as we get old, bit by bit, the failing of successive functions of our bodies? Would it not be more humane if most of us died suddenly, maintaining our health until the last moment? Some primitive tribes simply kill off old people, and make it an almost joyful occasion. The Cretes did this with their kings. We're not quite as civilized, at least not yet. Maybe the assassination of presidents is one way, without anyone daring to admit it, of serving a similar purpose. Some courageous people commit suicide.

Having to discover, over thousands of years, bit by bit, the secrets of the world we live in, I can accept. It provides excitement and the thrill of discovery. Whoever put all the cogwheels together could, however, have made it a little easier for us to find out how the whole machine really works. Why must it take thousands of years before we find out what causes cancer?

Many of these puzzlements could be classified as stresses which are unnecessary and would be best buried under layers of unconcern. People often spend wasted hours telling each other about the irrationality of life. Not only ordinary people, but playwrights, philosophers, and novelists portray it for us, supposedly for our entertainment. The assassination of Edward the Second by his courtiers and barons because he was a homosexual is an example of such entertainment. Christopher Marlow put these tragic events into language which sparkles like a well-polished diamond. It is a gripping and violent drama, as the announcer gently admonished possibly timid television viewers. But it is also another document of human brutality and stupidity. Edward is murdered to save the realm and Christendom. How many wars have been fought to save supposedly valuable treasures for mankind, and squashed them in doing so?

Why are so many people still attracted by communism, when a visit to Russia or any other Eastern communist bloc country would permit them to find out that the system does not work? Is it a form of escapism? Walk through the streets of Moscow or any other large city in the U.S.S.R., and you will see long lines of people waiting to buy fresh apples or meat. Communism has ruled for over 65 years. Why do they have to buy wheat from the capitalist countries? The real puzzlement is that the new communists, as in Portugal, seem to be inflicted with blindness.

My skill is motivating people. Facts apparently are the poorest way of doing it. I.B.M. asked me how they can make their sales training more effective. They teach the salesman precise data on the superiority of their products. When they meet a client, the problem is how to understand the motivations of the customer who may have subconscious objections. Our answer was to suggest that the salesmen learn to analyze their own objections first, to develop within themselves an "Aha" experience, the discovery of possible hidden objections to their occupation. It is this sense of insight and revelation which cannot be taught verbally. You can tell people about lovemaking, but somehow it is not the same as experiencing it.

People may persist in trying to solve conflicts, whether in Northern Ireland or in the Middle East, by warlike means because they have never learned to settle differences through negotiations. Can we have courses in elementary schools teaching children the art of settling conflicts by peaceful means?

Crime stories or television programs are not bad because they show violence, but because they teach the art of solving problems through force. Once in a while it is the more clever cowboy who carries off the victory and gets the girl; too often it is the one who has the faster draw. How can an occasional repetition of the Ten Commandments, particularly the one telling us "Thou shalt not kill," have a chance if the competition, in daily hour-long doses, gives millions of viewers (too often including children) the slow infusion treatment of the excitement of crimes and their efficacy, even if in the end the bad guys are killed? The lesson is still, "Got a problem? Kill!"

The list of injustices and irrationalities in human history is a depressingly long one. You can shrug your shoulders. Often that is the only way out. You can shake your fist in fury and despair at mankind's chances to survive its own stupidity. I have tried a pragmatic approach whenever possible.

A cause of stress and hangups is often the feeling of helplessness about the irrationalities of our behavior. Motivational methods can be of help. I use a descriptive gesture to help my clients to better understand the difference between ordering someone to do something and convincing or persuading him with effective approaches. When you raise a warning finger or shake your fist, you are using a very useless approach. Throwing people in jail, even threatening them with execution, has not lowered the crime rate appreciably. My gesture is one where you reach with your right arm around your head and then try to establish contact with your object of persuasion. What I intend to indicate is the need often to go around your intended behavior change. You must ask yourself, what can I do in order to bring about the change? Too often we simply put an exclamation point behind our wish or threat. Another parallel would be to think of railroad switches. Telling the train to move in a different direction and to use other tracks does not help much. When you throw the appropriate switches, you "motivate" the train to go where you feel it ought to go. The motivational approach works with children, with grownups, and with nations. We are too infantile, too impatient, and lack the skill to think through what methods to use.

I learned to play behavioral chess. So can you. Visualizing the consequences of your actions or those of your partner can be of great use. Offering alternatives can help. A hijacker may want notoriety more than money, or be intent on revenge. We have clinics for sick people. Why not have similar clinics for latently sick people? There are suicide prevention departments. Apply the same methods to potential criminals whether they are individuals, or violently opposed groups of people in conflict.

I have been called in to find answers or suggest approaches to such apparently unsolvable problems as birth control in India. Other projects concerned themselves with improving or changing the image of a professional or ethnic group—Italians, Jews or even Anglo-Saxons. The answer is not easy, but it does lie in finding a proper level, a correct motivation. Even when the results are impossible to achieve, having tried relieves a good deal of your frustrations and stresses.

Persuasion techniques are more complex than violence. They require more thought and more deviousness. Problems of nationalist pride, of religious conflicts as in Northern Ireland, changes in cultural concepts as with birth control, are also complex and often the result is devious distortions and convulsions due to the animal brain within us which still has more power than we assume.

25 How Not to Be Afraid When Chopping Down a Tree

I was swinging my axe (I was younger then) full of vigor. I was breathing hard. Lambie, an occasional handyman, appeared behind me and watched. "You're afraid of this tree," he stated. "You're fighting it. Yes, it is big and strong, but you have a sharp axe." He took it out of my hands, and told me gently, "Let me show you." He taught me some very valuable tricks. "Let the axe fall, put all your weight behind it, don't push it. Before you swing the axe as far back as you can, like a golf club, take a deep breath and, as you let it fall down, breathe out. If you feel like shouting to dramatize your exhalation do so." He told me, further, to hit the same spot on the tree. Slow down, take a breather as he had told me in the beginning, and above all, don't be afraid of it. It will come down sooner or later.

It was a very valuable lesson. Everybody's life is full of real or psychological trees, obstacles and tasks that have to be tackled and chopped down. Lambie would have been an excellent psychotherapist. Despite the fact that he lived about one hour from New York City, he had only been in the city twice, in his youth. He also had other habits which were fascinating. We raised cows. He talked to them. They seemed to understand. Even when we had to slaughter a calf, he talked to the carcass. "You're going to make wonderful eating," he would say. He probably understood better than many anthropologists that cannibalism was nothing very bad, that by eating an animal that you love (although he did not include humans), you are incorporating it into yourself and perpetuating it, giving it eternal life.

In my motivational work, I'm often asked how to increase productivity, how to get an employee to accept a new job. At first he balks, grunts, shows all the signs of a slow motion acrobat. I applied what I learned from Lambie in order to turn on the power for drive, accomplishment, and results. As Lambie had correctly diagnosed, in most instances the explanation for inaction or lack of initiative, the inability to get off the mark, even if in the wrong direction, is fear. The employee, the individual, the worker, doesn't trust his own ability. He will never admit it. He'll admit instead one more ingenious excuse after another. Just as Lambie had suggested, I have often broken down the task for myself into small, comfortable challenges, and tried to apply the same technique with others. I once had hired a bulldozer operator to level part of my property to make a road on an incline. He told me, at first, that it would be impossible. There was no way that it could be done. He said, "If I tried that, I'd be a goner. My machine would turn over, and I'm out of business for good." Remembering my handyman, I took a different approach, and asked him whether he could cut a small parking space for his bulldozer into the hillside so it wouldn't be on my path over the weekend. "No problem," he said. After a few minutes, there was the bulldozer standing on an even platform instead of precariously leaning downhill. Here was my chance. "Could you make this parking space a little longer?" I asked, "I may want to store some timber here." "Sure," the operator said. "All I have to do is continue cutting through the hillside without moving off this approach." A few minutes and several yards of parking space later, I took a look at his progress and he gave me a wink and a smile. "You dirty so-and-so," he said, "you tricked me. But I guess I've got to admit, you were right. I know what *we* can do."

Another approach which I have learned is to visualize improvement. Just as companies have sales curves, I tried to establish curves for my gradual growth. How many new languages have I learned? Can I now repair electronic equipment by myself? Even, to some extent, television sets. In most instances I've found that with more or less normal intelligence and proper books and instruction sheets, a much larger number of supposedly complex everyday machinery can be tackled. The first resistance and difficulty to overcome is fear. Too often, we have relinquished our rights and turned them over to a monopoly group, ranging from physicians to mechanics, dentists, and repairmen of various backgrounds.

When I lived in Paris as a student, I was starving. On the same floor where I lived, in a small hotel, there was a tailor. He approached me, timidly, asking me whether I could bring him work from fellow students. A few minutes later, I was sitting at one of his sewing machines, learning how to operate it. Our discussion had revealed that we were both from Vienna and that he needed work which he expected to get from my colleagues. I, in turn, also needed a way to keep from starving. Comparable to Lambie, he asked me whether I had any status objections or any other fears of becoming a tailor. It looked like a perfect way out—57 broken needles later, I had learned to use the machine efficiently enough to be of real help to my newly-acquired tailor friend. I got as far as learning how to put sleeves together and fit them into jackets, fix frayed cuffs of slacks, sew on buttons, and even make buttonholes neatly, surrounding them with a beautiful frame of complexly intertwining threads.

Professor Dr. Moritz Schlick was another person, at the other extreme of my learning process, who had a deep influence on my life. In a way, his approach was not too different from that of my handyman, although he was my philosophy and logic teacher. He convinced me that in most instances there was no reason to be afraid of big names. He used to have foreign visitors come to our seminars, including Bertrand Russell and other famous philosophers. Schlick would say, without blushing, "I'm sorry, I'm not bright enough. I don't understand what you're saying. Could you please repeat it?" By the same token, he taught us as students (at least that's what I learned) to utilize the same approach. When one of us would give a very erudite sounding explanation of what ethics was all about, he would stop the fledgling philosopher and tell him, "I don't understand you. Are you trying to tell me something, or are you just using words which sound good? If the second is true, you should be in an acting class," thus forcing us to think.

I have used this same approach many times with clients. I ask them to repeat, in clear and simple language, what their problem really is. I've often earned my fee without needing very much analysis afterwards. Professor Schlick taught me how to distinguish between scientific questions such as "When did life on earth most likely start?" and theological questions—"Is there a God or not?" Other questions were put into a separate category: those dealing with actual human behavior, and not on how people ought to behave. What he taught us was how to think, and not to simply remember facts. If this was our goal, we had the choice of selecting another professor who would let us pass, based on our good memory.

Motivational research is much less based on psychology, much more on logical and clear thinking. Many solutions to stress problems, I've found, can also be approached by logical therapy. Schlick taught us that the categorical imperative by Kant, an awe-inspiring name among philosophers, is just so much nonsense. It consists of the statement that the moment we ask about the reasons for our actions—what good will come of it for us or others, for example—they cease being purely ethical in the purest sense. There are certain laws in human nature, proclaimed Kant, that represent categorical imperatives, admonitions and demands, which are valid without having to ask for ulterior motives. Schlick told us that this was a completely meaningless postulate. Are people capable of acting in such a categorical fashion, or are they not was the real problem. Once posed as such a question, the answer becomes quite obvious. They are not. Even in attempting suicide, those of us who survive it usually are aware of our intent upon creating an effect, a punishment, a demonstration.

There is no absolute good. It is determined by culture and historical period. The Watergate conspirators, as they stated, felt that what they were doing was good. The rest of the country and the prosecutors did not agree with them. The definition of what is good or bad, therefore, is man-made. It is relative. It changes—we can bend it to suit our particular purposes. We can be dogmatic about it, and define as good those actions which would be approved by most people, if they knew about them, in a given historical period. Or good could be defined as that which has the most beneficial effect on the rest of the population.

Switching back to our underlying theme, stress can be good or bad depending on how it is digested and used. Without stresses at various periods of our lives, we probably would be suffering from an incurable stress: boredom, a feeling of worthlesness and lack of goals. I learned from Professor Schlick also that this relativity of what is good or bad has a strong pragmatic element. We can use a failure as the lesson from which to learn to acquire success, or we can permit it to be the beginning of a series of failures. We are all influenced not only by people, but also by events. The fact that I changed my allegiance, as it were, several times throughout my life, probably has made me much more principled. It has permitted me to get fresh starts without the traumatic effect from which most people suffer. This experience has helped me to understand competitive views in the commercial field. Over a period of several years I have often been called in to help motivate customers to buy a particular product. Within a few months or a year, the competitive organization might approach me and ask me how they can fight back. Thus one way which I've discovered of solving my own difficulties, problems, and confusions among corporations is to act more like a chess player. Putting yourself into the shoes of the other person is a well-established and effective formula but not often exercised.

Facts which I have learned or have been presented with have had little influence on changing my approach to life, to stresses, to fears, and to hopes. Insights, however, have been very important. I have used the term of an "Aha" experience several times throughout this book. What I meant to describe by it is a realignment, a sudden clicking, of your emotional or thinking apparatus. After this snapping in or turning on of a switch has taken place, things usually are never quite the same again. My psychoanalytic training, of course, has helped me quite a bit, not so much the particular aspects of my childhood that have been brought back into consciousness, but the experience of seeing the very same phenomenon in an entirely different light. It was almost like saying, "Aha, this is really why I'm doing it," and not at all what I had considered all along to be the real reason.

All of us have prejudices. Before I went to France, I looked upon their workers and the inhabitants in general as somewhat degenerate. Having been brought up in a Germanic culture, hard work and what is called in this country the Protestant Work Ethic pervaded a good part of my daily life. When I saw French workers drinking wine several times during the day and taking long lunch hours, I was appalled. Living in France for a while, it dawned on me that there apparently was nothing very wrong, that this was just a kind of life style. Wonderful cultural achievements, even reaching into the technological sphere, had been accomplished by Frenchmen, despite their wine drinking and other more leisurely types of attitudes towards life.

When I studied biology, I had to dissect various animals. I even got a little experience with human bodies. Having looked at the anatomy books, I expected everything to be beautifully colored, almost as in a child's coloring book. Not only was everything a bloody mess, but the heart was not where the book said it was supposed to be, nor was anything else. Here was another important lesson: If you expect perfection and accuracy in everything, you are bound to end up with hangups. Whenever I have to see a physician and he tells me honestly that medicine is not a science and he simply does not know what my mysterious pains mean or where they come from, I am torn between two attitudes—should I admire his honesty, or be angry about his lack of infallibility?

Accepting imperfection and even programming it into your plans will make life easier. Most things take longer, cost more and are less perfect than we paint them in our fantasy. If stress is tension, then relaxing is its cure, or one of them.

Despite all his wisdom, Lambie resisted my idea of placing our cows on a platform so I would not have to bend down to milk them. It seemed to be lazy and almost frivolous to him. When we had sold our cows, he would still appear at five o'clock in the morning to start work. While we had them, he would milk at this inhuman hour. I could never convince him that the cows would be just as happy to be relieved of their milk at seven or eight o'clock in the morning.

Trash farming has never taken hold. Straight furrows and clean fields, whether biologically good or not seem to satisfy our sense of neatness and perfection. Whenever I go on a trip I like to leave my desk as clean as possible. It is almost a feeling of not wanting to leave disorder behind in case I do not come back.

We discovered a long lost relative through a newspaper story about his hobby of raising wild strawberries. He told us about his ordeal. His mother was in Monte Carlo when Hitler marched into Austria. She insisted on going back so that she could vote in the elections which took place at that time. It was unfinished business which almost cost her her life. How could she leave her country without this feeling of having closed the book behind her in an orderly fashion? He has since passed away, leaving us some of his plants as a beautiful memento.

26 It Ain't Necessarily So

You can reach an orgasm the customary way, or by enjoying suffering. We are all fascinated by astrologers although close to 200 scientists declared them to be charlatans in the majority if not all cases. The desire to look into the future is a very understandable one. It gives us a feeling of omnipotence; we feel godlike. Economists are particularly skillful in using complex formulas which supposedly permit us to know whether the inflation is going to increase or decrease, whether we have bottomed out and whether the recession is about over.

The ability to combine the past with the present and to make plans for the future is a uniquely human one. Semanticists, those people concerned with the meaning of words and their effect on human behavior, call it time-binding. We can tie periods in our lives together. The normal expectation would be that we can learn that way. We usually don't. When the Germans were to the east of France, the French generals decided the best protection against another invasion would be the Maginot Line. As we all know by now, the Germans simply went around it. The French guns, as incredible as it may sound, could not be turned around. What happened was that the lesson learned from previous wars had not been applied to the new one.

We may now be talking about a nuclear holocaust. In the meantime, the

Communists may defeat us by very quiet financial and political manipulations. Important for our personal planning we want to know whether, within the next 5, 10, or 20 years, we might be experiencing an energy shortage, a food shortage, whether the world will be overpopulated, and, in general, what life might be like. I consulted a rather pessimistic economic adviser and, quite unexpectedly, he asked me how many guns I had at home. I told him I had a very simple 22 rifle. He seemed appalled. "You need at least three guns for every floor of your building." What does that have to do with your economic forecasting? His answer was frightening. "We are facing a super-inflation. Unemployment is not going to be reduced appreciably. Sooner or later, you can expect food rioting. You have to think of all the worst possible things and protect yourself against them." The fact that even three rifles would not hold off any rioting crowds very long added to my belief that if things come to that point, whether one survives two or three weeks longer really doesn't make that much difference but I did not seem able to convince him.

I became interested in analyzing the psychology of the doomsayers as part of some of our recent assignments. Many companies came to us with problems which indicated a desire to reverse negative predictions of the future. You can use computers, such as the Club of Rome did, and come up with some forecasts which may influence you to use the guns—not to fight off possible rioters but to shoot yourself. Motivational research helped me to answer not only some of these questions but also those raised by our clients, such as how to increase productivity, how to improve relationships between banks and municipalities, how to motivate people to move back to the inner city, and what the future of cars might be. In most of these assignments, the first conclusion was that "It ain't necessarily so."

Public opinion polls and standard market research are not of great help because if you ask people in what way reduced income and inflation will influence their buying behavior, they obviously are going to give you a logical answer. They are going to do some belt-tightening, they say. They will buy cheaper merchandise. they are going to have to cut out luxury items. No matter how many percentage points simulating accuracy you put behind these answers, they are still wrong. In reality, people are buying many more luxury items than before. Mercedes car sales have increased by over 23 percent. The cosmetic and jewelry industries are doing very well. People are gambling more. Minority groups, probably even harder hit than the average by recession, spent more money on individual homes and are less willing to give up symbols of status and influence. Instead of a straight doom psychology, we find a peculiar over-compensation expressed in statements like the following: "I might as well enjoy myself; who knows what's going to happen next?"

Thinking about your own life and its future, you may well want to use this motivational research approach yourself. If we could program it, the modern computer would have to include the possibility that most of us have the ability to counteract and change futurological predictions. To a very large extent, many of the developments that we are afraid of can be stopped. The population explosion has petered out to such an extent in the United States that we are now talking about zero population growth. This change dates back only a few years.

A builder's organization asked us how they could defend themselves against antigrowth people. We found that a number of these people were much less against growth than they pretended. What they were more afraid of was of losing face with their friends. Think of someone who has been talking at cocktail parties and in public meetings about the rape of the land and what has to be done to protect the environment. When you present such a person or such a group with facts which indicate the new zoning regulations, low density programs, and many other new laws have slowed down growth to such an extent that we are faced with almost the opposite problem, they have trouble, not so much with changing their minds, but with admitting to their friends that they have changed their minds. It takes a certain degree of courage to overcome this basic fear of losing face.

Guilt feelings are another interesting motivation. When defending the character of a neighborhood, fighting the big, bad builders, the real reason behind it is often that such an opinion molder feels that, for years, he really didn't bother very much with the particular section of the community that he lived in. He now overreacts to prove to himself, and to his friends, that indeed he does care.

In some work which we did in analyzing the reaction of war widows during the Second World War, we found that many women who had lost their husbands overreacted because, subconsciously, they discovered within themselves a feeling of relief that the uncertainty was over. Very often they had known their husbands only for a week or two before he went off to war, and now he was dead. They were, in a sense, free again. This caused considerable guilt feelings among them. Through hysterical behavior, they demonstrated to themselves and to other people that they had indeed loved their husbands despite the short marriage.

In thinking about the future and conducting motivational research, one of the difficulties is that people inadvertantly use the psychological framework of the past or the present. Many of the stresses or problems that I'm suffering from now, I could have avoided had I been smart enough to foresee what my life would be like ten years later. Our house is much too big; we bought too many gadgets; and we have become slaves to very many unnecessary frills of our daily lives.

Correct research design has to be of such a nature that it first transposes the consumer to the changes of environment which he will experience. A very smart piece of advice, which I do not always follow, is that when you buy a house you should think about what selling it will be like. Although we all shy away from thinking about it, a mother should start as early as possible thinking about a life without her children, since sooner or later they will leave her. Spouses should think about what life might be like if they were alone. A German advertising agency used a very clever approach showing in a crowded ad a television set, a washing machine, ski boots, radio sets, tape recorders, vacuum cleaners, and a long list of other appliances and gadgets. The headline they used was: "This is what advertising has persuaded us to buy. Things that our grandparents never missed." I myself have written a scenario for a film entitled "The City without Advertising." At the stroke of midnight all neon lights, all lighted store windows, all posters disappear. A literal-minded policeman decides that all insignias on cars which make them recognizable as a particular make represent advertising also. He proceeds forthwith to remove all these means of identification. As you can imagine, fairly soon the city has to introduce police state methods. People aren't allowed to recommend products to each other, for this is also advertising.

Many consumerists and apparently liberally disposed economists wanted to convince us that by reducing our buying, wastefulness would be avoided, and our economy would revive. This was only two or three years ago. Now they are somewhat confused. More and more studies show that the only way to get the economy going again is to get the consumer interested in spending money. If he spends money, more products have to be produced. This requires more workers. Workers have to be paid. They will not work any harder unless they have products that they can buy with the money. We are dealing, therefore, with a cycle which, by the way, is one that the communist countries are trying to introduce. I have been asked, during visits to some of these places, what can be done to increase the productivity of the workers living in this socialist paradise. Their productivity (a well-known fact despite all kinds of Lenin medals offered to them) is much, much lower than that of the capitalist worker. The only answer I and the communist economists could come up with was one of common sense: why should a worker work more if, by earning more, he still cannot buy any more products? Why should he produce a better product if he's paid a standardized salary, regardless of how good or bad the product is which he produces?

In looking ahead, we should be very careful not to let masochistic pleasure creep into our oracles. There is undoubtedly a feeling in most of us that, if things have been too good for a while, we have been tempting the gods and we deserve punishment. We all suffer from the 'seven fat and seven lean years' legend of the Old Testament. Many very wealthy people contribute to charity and try to be useful members of society, in order to overcome this guilt feeling.

David Rockefeller, Jr. once stated that he never felt comfortable about being rich. A Pillsbury heir has sworn that, by the time he reaches the age of 30, he will have given away his total fortune in order to free himself from the misery of wealth. I'm convinced that the rhythm of our life, even the economic fortunes of the whole country, particularly those of the United States and possibly of the whole Western world, are dominated by this masochism.

I have confidence in the future. I'm not a naive, positive thinker but, by first destroying the present frame of reference and convincing myself that it ain't necessarily so, I can foresee at least two to three times as many new concepts and innovations. They concern our working conditions, the nutritional field, and the discovery of new sources of solar energy, which will make us laugh at the predictions of collapse which, under various titles, help sell books that, most of the time, have very little basis in reality. It is not that I feel that this is the best of all worlds but rather I am convinced that human needs and human desires are insatiable. It is not enough any more for the philosopher to simply analyze the present society. By delving down and bringing to the surface, through proper research techniques and more correct thinking, the real changes in our behavior, he has the power if not the obligation to make some of his predictions come true.

I am, if I want to be (and I do), in charge of my own destiny. I don't have to stand idly by with amused curiosity trying to find out whether and which ones of the predictions will come true. I have advised many of my friends and clients that it will become more and more necessary in making recommendations for their own lives, for the introduction of new services and products, that they become aware of their own power. The awakening and introduction of social responsibility is probably one of the most important new trends which can make us look hopefully towards avoidance of wars and the solution of many of the problems that we are supposedly locked in with right now. Maybe what we are confronted with are, in reality, the hunger pains of a society which is awakening to its individual and social responsibility and power. Many of the stresses that thinking about the future can produce can also be remedied if we reject fatalism.

27 Which Way to Happiness, Please?

I have often asked myself which moments of my life were really happy and which ones full of misery. I have even suggested and tried myself to set up a happiness diary. Reading it at the end of a week or a month or even a year later can be very enlightening. It is a way of becoming aware of yourself and then arranging your life accordingly.

As I look over my partially real and partially imaginary happiness book-keeping system, I discover such highlights as having fixed a minitape recorder myself after the electronics expert told me it could not be done or was too expensive; speaking for three hours with an Italian after I had told him that I really did not know any Italian. (I did know at least more than I thought I did.) What made me happy was the discovery of a new skill, slumbering within me, when he reminded me, "You spoke Italian for at least three hours."

Getting my first book in a solid hard cover form for me to hold and to fondle the way one does with one's first baby was another highlight, as was discovering a plant which I thought was dead come alive again. Even seeing my first radish reaching a large enough size to be eaten with cannibalistic love must be listed among my happy moments.

I am not counting the conventional scenes of bliss, the birth of a son, the marriage of your children, the birth of your grandchildren, not to forget my own wedding which preceded these "happenings." They are among the blessings most of us take for granted.

When I feel unhappy, I have tried to set up a stressogram and a blessogram. It can be as simple as a list used for comparisons. By deducting the stresses from the blessings, if your blessings are more numerous, you can arrive at a visible shrinking of your number of stresses. A lot depends, of course, on what you include in your blessings and your "stressings."

One of my proudest moments and a clear feeling of blessing was experienced when I became, quite accidentally, a writer of children's stories. I knew it was going to happen sooner or later. Sasha, our oldest grandson, reaching the age of six, posed a very embarrassing question. "What are you really doing, Grandpa?" "Well, I am sitting down." "No, I don't mean that. What *are* you?" Well, after a few feeble jokes, I had to admit that I understood what he wanted to know. How do you explain motivational research to a six-year-old? I had to start with psychology. I didn't want to tell him that part of my work consisted in making people buy things, whether they needed them or not. Psychology was a much nicer way and, in many respects a more accurate way, of referring to my activities.

I remember that Sasha had been very cranky before, but when he was asking me these deep questions he was feeling happy. That was my chance. I reminded him of how he had changed, and that he really consisted of two Sashas. Within a few minutes, he participated in the game and reminded me that he also at times was very impatient, he couldn't wait for things. He also became angry with his little sister, Megan. Therefore, we were really dealing with four Sashas, and the longer we talked, the more Sashas we discovered. Next step—well, Daddy too changes. Do I have ten Daddies? Being a very moral grandfather, I didn't feel I should answer his questions in such a way as to put doubts in his mind. I hit upon a lucky parallel. "You're really like an onion." We went into the kitchen to get one. "You see the outer skin? Let's look for the real onion." "Good," said Sasha. So we peeled off the first layer. "That's it." I said, "Now wait a moment. There's something underneath." We peeled off the second layer, and the third one and the fourth one and the fifth one, and pretty soon there was nothing left of the onion. This was my attempt at explaining to Sasha what the human personality was really like: an onion. "Where is the real me?" asked Sasha, frantically. How was I going to answer that? I told him patiently that a lot of people had been trying to find a nice, simple explanation to this question, including me. We went on to talk about emotions. Frankly I had never thought about the word itself, but obviously it had something to do with movement, with motion, just like automobiles. I remembered such phrases as "feeling like being on top of the mountain" and being "down in the dumps," and our next analogy developed very quickly. "Grandpa, you are funny. First you tell me I'm like an onion, now you tell me that I have mountains and valleys inside of me."

This little exercise led to a very exciting success story. I jotted down not only the onion story, but another, and another, and yet another one. A whole series of them, each dealing with attempts at explaining normal psychological phenomena to six-, seven-, and eight-year-olds. Fairly soon after these story-telling sessions, we went on a trip to Frankfurt. In the hotel where we stayed, there were quite a number of cocktail parties in connection with the International Book Fair. Here was a chance to get some free drinks and some nice hors d'ouevres. So we went to one of the parties thrown by Hachette. Between drinks I told Monsieur Schuwer, whom I discovered among the people milling around, about my Sasha series. "Send it to me. "We'll buy it." They did. It was beautifully illustrated, and it was my first attempt to become a child psychologist or to write psychological books for children.

I have always held the opinion that fairy tales and certainly most comic strips and the so-called typical children's stories are filled with more violence than the most bloody crime stories on T.V. If you have a chance, try to reread some of the supposedly wonderful and charming stories by Grimm. If we complain about materialism, how come we tell a three-year-old about princes and princesses, about gold and diamonds, about discovering treasures instead of more important values such as wisdom, discovery, learning. We often talk about human nature and the difficulty of changing it, without realizing that a good portion of this so-called human nature has been unwittingly created by us through the type of education, symbols and fairy tales that we start feeding our next generation. The wrong search for happiness is often started that way. Becoming a prince or a princess seems to be the universal goal.

There are probably as many theories and philosophies about happiness as there are people. A coal miner may be happiest when he has shown the owners his strength by another wildcat strike. An artist finds it by receiving recognition in the art world or by knowing that he has done a good job. Literature on the dozens of possible avenues, all supposedly leading to happiness, exists in abundance. I have studied most of it from progressive realization to transcendental meditation and everything in between. All these methods work sometimes and none of them do at other times. The secret is whether you believe in them or not. As a psychologist, I am convinced that the mind either dominates, or is certainly closely related to even the most physical aspects of the body. You can develop a cold if you feel that this is the only way out of your unhappiness with your job. You can hypnotize people into developing fever blisters and even arthritic pains. It is logical, therefore, that if you believe in any of the messages by various gurus, that they indeed will help you.

We are at times not affirmative enough, cannot say no, and don't always do what we really want. Affirmative training thus does its job. We are tense, take things too seriously; relaxation and meditation will be good for us. Prayer is a very old form of transcendental meditation. Maybe what is most significant is that we are discovering that the many scenes painted in beautiful irridescent lights do not guarantee happiness. I have always felt that the long list of paradises which advertisers have been using have no real foundation. The South Pacific islands turn out to be quite a disappointment, as I found during my stay in Samoa. The beaches are black and smell from human "nightsoil" since the ocean does not always do its job properly. Talking about the unsoiled virginity of these places, New York City smells heavenly and can be called clean without much exaggeration when compared to such a dream island. Tahiti is possibly even worse.

What about some of the other accepted standards and images of utter bliss. Enormous wealth, either through hard work and luck or winning it in the lottery, is one. Analysis of such dreams tells us clearly that the objective facts are not necessarily proof of having reached happiness.

Happiness is much more independent of concrete goals reached than we normally assume. I inquire often of other people to find out what makes them happy, assuming they are. To a large extent, I have been showered with trivialities. "Don't worry about anything, let life take its course, roll with the punches." Unhappiness is similarly defined as lack of money, losing money, feeling lonely, being sick. I did find, however, many people who had little money, had not lived on a South Pacific island, were even sick, but could still register a feeling of happiness.

Life is continuously changing and developing. It is a moving target. I have found in my own life happiness is continuously developing and changing. It always seemed to me that there are two types of security: a static one and a dynamic one. The static one is an illusion. You are dreaming of having solved a problem, of having made enough money, reached a high enough position, and being ready to take it easy. Most people become restless when they have reached that kind of goal. Taking it easy is a peculiar and dangerous false definition of happiness. I believe in the type of security which comes from one's ability to adapt oneself, to accept new responsibilities, and to build up a skill bank into which you pay deposits and receive dividends.

I call this security 'dynamic security.' It has helped me personally because I am convinced that I can always scale down my living standards if the need should arise. Some of my personal habits probably have their psychological explanation in my not too conscious excursions into psychological "slumming." The owner of a men's store in our neighborhood kids me about the old clothes which I like to wear since he knows that I have lectured about and researched the question on how to get men to buy new clothes more frequently. In my peculiar way, I feel happy about my ability to put an old suit to use by at least wearing the slacks.

In our study on fund raising, we found that most people, even when they are charitable, really give because it makes them feel good about themselves. They can play God and feel powerful. They can save somebody's life, they can buy love. Being able to give money alone does not make them happy; they are even more thrilled if they are allowed to contribute ideas, and to feel they are participating in epilepsy or kidney research. Happiness, then, to them is a feeling of being part of what I call constructive discontent. I arrived at this definition when I asked myself whether, having arrived once and for all at a goal and having solved all my problems, and the world's as well, I would be happy. You can try this experiment yourself. Imagine there is nothing whatsoever for you to worry about. You have all the things you want, all the money, all the power. All danger of wars or crises are gone. Hunger has been eliminated from this world. We have abundant resources of energy and food. In short, we have arrived at the millenium. What will you do now?

Possibly one of the real reasons why so many people are doom-sayers and prophets of the end of the world is because they are afraid that they have lost all their reasons for pursuing a goal, getting excited, enraged or militant. Being discontented means you have something to fight for, you have a goal to look forward to.

In order to accept this new, admittedly so far personal, avenue towards happiness, we have to rethink many of our religious and philosophical ideas. Everything we have been taught and promised consists of holding in front of us carrots of various shapes, colors, and brilliance: wealth, peace, or at least peace of mind. Even our school system with its degrees and grades has established reachable red flags; they motivate us temporarily but invariably must end in disappointment because there are always mountains behind mountains.

On a more philosophical level, I try as often as possible in my motivational work to use what I call my secret subversion. When a manufacturer of chewing gum asks us to find the real motivations for using his product, I do a professional job for him. I tell him that chewing increases salivation but it also is a form of protest against the establishment. Since I feel that such an attitude should be developed under certain circumstances, the modern youth should learn to ask questions and to challenge blind obedience to authority, I advise my client to defend and explain this attitude in his advertising. I am using his millions of dollars of publicity budget to sell "independence" via chewing gum. Far-fetched? Maybe.

Telling Procter and Gamble to utilize their detergent commercials to influence family relations by showing the husband or the sons taking care of the laundry can achieve more than a well-planned president's committee resolution on equal rights or even a pronouncement from Gloria Steinem.

Which way to happiness then? The road you choose is most likely not marked with any clear cut directional sign. In a way, you have to set the direction. The more new scenery it leads through, the more you are capable of seeing the rich, colorful landscape within you, the more assured you will be of being on the right road. Happiness is not a permanent state. It is closer to an organic change between tension, excitement, and relaxation. Nature follows the same rhythm, even love does. Maybe this is a secret we can learn from our animal past. Is a cat happy when she relaxes completely? Probably as close to it as cats can be. Most animals have an advantage over us; they stay active and run after the mouse or the rabbit, even when they are old. They sneak off into the woods or any other corner to die without much complaint. While they are alive they live, live, live.

We have something called willpower and even if, at times, I have expressed doubts about it, it usually has a working brain and controllable emotions. Using them is simpler than we think. I remember the many instances when I felt depressed. When I asked myself what it really was that got me down and decided to snap out of it, it was like a miracle. What appeared black and hopeless turned into an endless horizon. Discontent as a definition of happiness sounds very downbeat. Goalless satisfaction is all right for a cow.

I, for one, would like to destroy all mantras, the Nirvana images gurus recommend, whatever their particular school may be. Presidents have talked to us about the Great Society, religious leaders about paradise and the seventh heaven, advertisers about playing golf, lolling on the beach, as great way stations after having traversed hundreds or thousands of miles of hard work. I prefer to knock down or rewrite the road signs by putting a big symbol for continuous challenge on each one of our maps for happiness.

No one can give an answer to the global question of what happiness really is. Everyone has to find the right way for himself. For me, personally, happiness consists of a symbol which does not describe a goal but, instead, continuous challenges and striving. If you can say, as your life seems to come closer to its physical halt, "I have found the right way for me and I have lived accordingly," then your life has made sense. You can look back at it in your autobiographical case history with satisfaction.

I am happy to be able to say that my deepest satisfaction has been my creative discontent.

Hedy and E. Dichter today.

Index

About the Author

Dr. Ernest Dichter is recognized internationally as the father of motivational research, a method which permits us to unearth the real reasons why people act the way they do. He has applied his methods to every conceivable problem in over 6500 studies conducted for political leaders, civil organizations and commercial companies. His autobiography is a lesson in living. an unusual success story achieved with one basic but powerful idea. Dr. Dichter was born in Vienna, earned psychology degrees from the University of Vienna, and is a professor at Nova University, Ft. Lauderdale, Florida, and Mercy College, Dobbs Ferry, N.Y. He worked for CBS, for scores of advertising agencies, and maintains several offices abroad. In 1946 he founded the Institute for Motivational Research. This is his twelfth book. Others include *The Disease of Nationalism*, *The Naked Manager*, and *Total Self Knowledge*.